"*Without Warning* is a vivid testimony to why modern-day weather forecasting deeply matters, especially to those so often in the path of these dangerous storms. But it is also a story of resiliency—a portrait of people and a town that lost almost everything but somehow found the strength to go on. It's only through the stories of survivors that we can try to comprehend the precarious nature of tornadoes and prepare as much as one can for a phenomenon that is still so violently unpredictable."
—HOLLY BAILEY, author of *The Mercy of the Sky*

"Jim Minick turns anecdote into story, and story into the personal history of an American town, a town that represents a blueprint for responding to other natural crises. The images are often haunting—the *ding-ding, ding-ding* of a railway crossing bell, lost photos found in a pasture ten miles away, a "mountainous grave" of debris. Twelve years of interviews and research accompany this work, allowing the author the time it takes to become familiar with people—in some sense, a neighbor. Minick wants us to witness the resilience, generosity, kindness, and capacity for change that the storm broke loose that day, amid all its terrible destruction. His hopeful voice is one worth listening to—from the book's beginning to the wonderful epilogue that concludes it."
—JOYCE DYER, author of *Pursuing John Brown: On the Trail of a Radical Abolitionist*

"This is vivid, compelling narrative history with the detail, tension, and pacing of fiction, meaning it's hard to put down. Though I've never been to Udall, Kansas, I feel as if I visited in 1955 and met the residents. Their stories are ones we're all going to need more than ever. If catastrophe strikes us like it did Udall, the big question is going to be, how well will we survive as a community?"
—DAVID L. BRISTOW, author of *Nebraska History Moments*

WITHOUT

WARNING

The Tornado of Udall, Kansas

JIM MINICK

UNIVERSITY OF NEBRASKA PRESS   LINCOLN

The University of Nebraska Press is part of a land-grant institution with campuses and programs on the past, present, and future homelands of the Pawnee, Ponca, Otoe-Missouria, Omaha, Dakota, Lakota, Kaw, Cheyenne, and Arapaho Peoples, as well as those of the relocated Ho-Chunk, Sac and Fox, and Iowa Peoples.

Library of Congress Control Number: 2022045653

Set and designed in Questa by N. Putens.

For the people of Udall—

gone, here now, and yet to come.

We are going to go where our stories go—the ones we dig up and the ones we invent. If we don't make better stories, the worst of stories will make us.

—WENDY S. WALTERS

CONTENTS

ILLUSTRATIONS

AUTHOR'S NOTE

THIS BOOK IS A WORK OF CREATIVE NONFICTION BASED PRIMARILY on hundreds of hours of interviews with survivors of the 1955 Udall tornado. I also interviewed weather experts and drew heavily on library files and museum archives. As much as possible, I've tried to make sure that what you read here is based on facts.

But good storytelling, whether fiction or nonfiction, requires imagination, and certain scenes in this story only had a few known details. These moments I chose to imagine and develop. When possible, which was the vast majority of the time, I shared a survivor's section with that person or a family member, and when possible, I also shared these imagined scenes. To these many patient people, I'm extremely grateful. Any errors are all my own.

A word about dialogue: I use quotation marks around any dialogue gathered directly from an oral or written source. Dialogue not in quotation marks is what I imagined based on these oral and written sources.

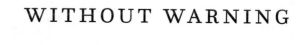

WITHOUT WARNING

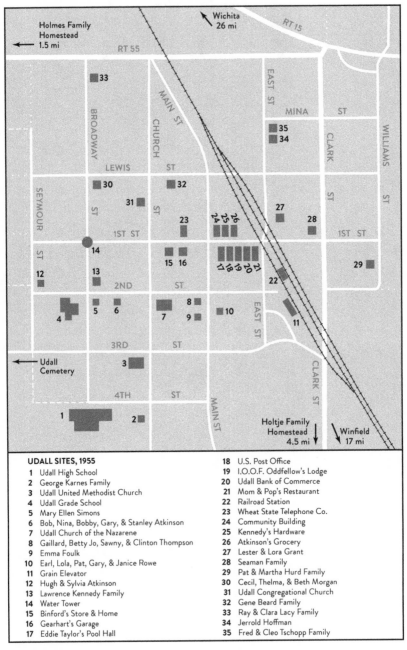

UDALL SITES, 1955

1 Udall High School
2 George Karnes Family
3 Udall United Methodist Church
4 Udall Grade School
5 Mary Ellen Simons
6 Bob, Nina, Bobby, Gary, & Stanley Atkinson
7 Udall Church of the Nazarene
8 Gaillard, Betty Jo, Sawny, & Clinton Thompson
9 Emma Foulk
10 Earl, Lola, Pat, Gary, & Janice Rowe
11 Grain Elevator
12 Hugh & Sylvia Atkinson
13 Lawrence Kennedy Family
14 Water Tower
15 Binford's Store & Home
16 Gearhart's Garage
17 Eddie Taylor's Pool Hall

18 U.S. Post Office
19 I.O.O.F. Oddfellow's Lodge
20 Udall Bank of Commerce
21 Mom & Pop's Restaurant
22 Railroad Station
23 Wheat State Telephone Co.
24 Community Building
25 Kennedy's Hardware
26 Atkinson's Grocery
27 Lester & Lora Grant
28 Seaman Family
29 Pat & Martha Hurd Family
30 Cecil, Thelma, & Beth Morgan
31 Udall Congregational Church
32 Gene Beard Family
33 Ray & Clara Lacy Family
34 Jerrold Hoffman
35 Fred & Cleo Tschopp Family

Map 1. Udall map before May 25, 1955. The tornado traveled from southwest to northeast, perpendicular to the railroad tracks. Erin Greb Cartography.

1 What Used to Be

ON MAY 25, 1955, AROUND FOUR FIFTEEN IN THE AFTERNOON—
roughly six and a half hours before the tornado—Gary Atkinson headed
to the football field. School was out, but he had papers to deliver, and
his empty canvas bag bumped against his knee as he walked the three
blocks. The *Winfield Daily Courier* came from the county seat via airplane,
dropped from the sky to the fifty-yard line, if he was lucky. Sometimes
the pilot overshot, and the bundle ended up in the weeds or even the
nearby cornfield. Or worse, sometimes the bundle busted when it hit the
ground. If Gary got there before the plane, he'd at least be able to watch the
papers land or could pick up the loose papers before they all blew away.

Gary was a crew cut twelve-year-old, the middle child of three boys.
Like his mother, he had dark hair, pale skin, and wide-spaced brown
eyes, and like his father, he leaned forward a little, with curiosity and a
broad smile. Most people called him ornery. The first time, he didn't know
what that meant; later he just shrugged and grinned. His parents had
their own business downtown, Atkinson's Grocery, which also included a
butcher shop, and to Gary, delivering papers was far better than stocking
shelves. Outside he could whistle, put down his papers and walk on his
hands, and at the end of his route, stop in to bug his best friend, Dickie
Braddy. In a few months, Gary hoped to have enough paper route money
saved to buy a new fishing rod to go along with the .410 shotgun he got
for his birthday.

The winds blew out of the west, hard and hot, so the plane came in a little higher than normal. A young man pushed out the bundle, which fell and bounced a few times on the twenty-yard line. It didn't bust. The pilot and helper waved and turned north toward the town of Rock to make the next drop.

Gary walked the first section of his route, so he could fold individual newspapers. And he started throwing these papers onto front porches—first to the Karnes's, where the father, George, with his wife and two kids, had just moved to town to manage the grain elevator. Then next door, the Woods family. Gary double-checked the accuracy of his throw to the Woods's front porch. They were teachers at the high school. Mr. Woods was the principal and PE teacher who coached all the sports. Gary hoped to play catcher for him in a few years.

A block east was old man Clodfelter's, the custodian for the Methodist church. He was a retired farmer with a metal hook for a right hand, his right arm amputated after an accident in his orchard. He once told Gary he had come to Kansas in a covered wagon. Mr. Clodfelter nudged his glasses and nodded as he pushed his lawnmower. It was the first gas-powered lawnmower in Udall, a homemade contraption with bicycle wheels and a Maytag engine that sputtered blue smoke. Gary nodded back and kept moving and folding. By the time he reached his own house—which his grandfather had built just a year ago—Gary had folded all 115 newspapers, one for almost every house in Udall. Now he could ride his bike for the rest of his route.

Gary had inherited the paper route from his brother Bobby, who was fifteen, three years older and thus stronger and taller and a better thrower of newspapers. This also made Bobby a better pitcher when they played baseball in the backyard. Gary didn't mind so much—he liked playing catcher, crouching to create a target, yelling directions to the outfield, which usually consisted of little brother Stanley, who was only five and too young to catch many balls. Sometimes Stanley played ball wearing his cowboy boots, hat, and cap gun six-shooter slung from his belt.

Along with the paper route, Gary inherited from his brother the family's old one-speed bike, the same one Bobby had used to deliver papers until he bought a new ten-speed. This was also the same bicycle Bobby and Gary used to pedal around town with their pet raccoon riding on a shoulder. Bobby had raised the coon from infancy, and it would hold onto his collar and chirp and cackle every time they leaned into a turn.

And this was also the same bicycle the two brothers were riding together years earlier, when Gary was five, riding on the seat and holding on while Bobby, who was eight, pedaled and steered. They were close to home when Gary stuck his big toe in the back sprocket. The moving gear fascinated him, and he just wanted to touch it. That gear cut the toe clean off.

For a moment Bobby didn't know what was wrong, until he saw the blood coming out of the stub. He sat his screaming little brother down on the sidewalk and went back to retrieve the big toe from the middle of the street. He thought maybe they could save it, sew it back on. Instead, it ended in a quart jar of alcohol that also held their dad's finger, cut off in a big rig when he worked in the oil fields. And still later, that jar held Bobby's tonsils and adenoids, the adenoids looking clean compared to the greasy toe and greasier finger. The jar stood on the mantel, a testament to the family's toughness and humor.

Growing up in his brother's shadow, Gary also learned how to sometimes cast his own tall shadow. When Gary was nine, Bobby told him he had climbed the water tower for the first time. Gary immediately wanted to do it too. Bobby tried to dissuade him, but Gary declared he'd do it anyway, without him. So one evening, while his parents were at the store, Gary snuck out to meet Dickie Braddy, and the two boys took to the alleys to avoid being seen, especially by the city marshal, Wayne Keely, who everyone knew feared heights and wouldn't climb after them.

The water tower was 150 feet tall, and the tank looked like the head of the Tin Man in *The Wizard of Oz*, but instead of a face, huge black letters spelled out U-D-A-L-L. The tower stood in the middle of the intersection of First and Broadway so that the streets made a circle around it. All the older boys with their cars and dates cruised this circle on weekends, showing off, hooting and hollering. Sometimes on Halloween, outhouses suddenly appeared in that circle. Pranksters hauled them in from backyards and lined them up for display. This was in a town that also sometimes woke up to find a donkey—or a car—on the high school roof, the pranksters having worked all night. So the Udall water tower was like a magnet. Old folks said that once you lived under it, you could never leave for good.

The two boys grabbed hold of an I beam leg and started up. Heavy cables ran from the top of one leg to the bottom of another to make X's on all four sides. Halfway up, I beams ran horizontally from leg to leg, all the way around, and here the boys paused to catch their breath.

Gary craned his neck—the silver tank still looked like it was far above, but below, the houses looked equally small. After a moment he climbed the next fifty feet to the platform that circled the tank.

At the walk-around, Gary and Dickie slowly skirted the tank. Its silver surface radiated the day's heat. To the east, just three blocks away, they spotted the Atkinson family store, the light still on, and a block and a half south was Gary's home. To the west the sun settled on the long fields of corn and wheat, and they saw Dickie's home a half-mile away.

Farther to the west, they found their friend and classmate Ray Holmes's homestead. Once, before Gary inherited the bike, Ray had helped him play a prank on all the town kids. The two boys rode Ray's horse to town, a paint named Queenie. They offered rides on Queenie and charged a candy bar or ice cream. The unsuspecting kid parked his bike, bought the candy, handed it over to Ray and Gary, and hopped on the horse. Instead of taking the kid for a ride around the village, though, Queenie lurched to the west and galloped the mile and a half to her home, every time. Ray and Gary waited a bit as they enjoyed the sweets, then they hopped onto the now-gone kid's bike and rode it home, where they found Queenie drinking from her trough and the kid fuming. The boys did this a couple times—free ice cream and free rides on bikes—before everyone caught on.

For a while up on the water tower, Gary and Dickie stayed on the west side of the tank, away from the view of most of the townsfolk, in case anyone looked up, but they doubted they'd be seen—people rarely looked up at the tank. It was a permanent fixture of this place, there to hold water, welcome visitors and tell them where they were. There, too, as a reference for directions. (Oh, I just live two blocks north of the water tower, someone might say.) And the water tower was always there as a landmark for when Udall residents were coming home from trips; they could see it from miles away, like a permanent upside-down anchor, holding the town to the sky.

Let's go all the way up, Gary said, pointing to the roof, another fifty feet higher.

Dickie nodded and, behind Gary, grabbed the ladder that took them to the very tip, where the red light circled and glowed at night.

At the top the roof sloped, a sheet of riveted tin with little to hold onto except for the ladder. It went all the way to the light, so the town water man could change out the bulb when needed. Gary scooted over to make room for Dickie, and the two sat gazing at the small world below. The elementary and high schools lay before them in the southwest corner of town, and to their left, in the southeast corner, beside the tracks, stood the grain elevator, the only other tall structure around. The evening train rolled through, the conductor laying on the horn, and the steady *ding-ding* of the crossing bell sounded clear from half a mile away.

Udall called itself a city, but Gary had been to Wichita often enough to know that his little hometown was not much more than a village. The whole town ran eight blocks east-west and seven blocks north-south, with the railroad cutting across the northeast section on a diagonal, all of it not even a whole square mile (see figure 1).

As the train left town, a man stood on the caboose and threw up his hat in a wave. The boys couldn't tell if it was at them, but they hoped so and waved back.

Gary climbed the ladder to the light at the very top tip. A red glass ball rotated around the light, part of it shaded, so that the whole thing "blinked" its warning at night. Gary pushed the ball, and it swirled its giant circle, the bearings rolling metal on metal. Soon he hooked his hands around that ball and started running sideways, gaining speed so that he spun all the way around the top. Gary wanted to holler—it felt so good to spin so high, to fly in a circle—but he didn't in case anyone might hear. Dickie took his turn at spinning the ball, then they headed back down.

At the walk-around, Gary stopped. He had been thinking about this for a long time. If he really wanted to outdo his brother and go down in the history of Udall as the coolest kid around, he had to do what no one else of his generation had done. He'd been told of his great-uncle Dick, of how he was the only one crazy enough to do this. Gary had been practicing. He knew he could do it. With Dickie standing on the top rung of the ladder, Gary said, Watch this. He put his hands on the hot metal walkway and jumped up into a handstand, right there, one hundred feet off the ground, the world suddenly upside-down.

You're crazy! Dickie shouted.

Gary lowered his feet, grabbed the handrail, and laughed, and this time he whooped, just once, before following Dickie. From the tower's leg, they climbed onto the bracing rod and glided from one rod to the next all the way down. In the glow of dusk, the two boys stood on the ground, quietly saying, See you tomorrow, as they headed home for the night.

With his paper bag still full and most of the route in front of him, Gary headed east on his bike toward Mrs. Foulk's old folks' home, where he delivered two copies to the front porch. Gary liked how the town's three old folks' homes seemed to empty his bag quickly, each resident in each private rest home demanding their own paper. He also liked how two of the owners—Mrs. Foulk, with her giant, round glasses, and Mrs. LeForce, with her easy laugh—often had cookies for him. Mr. Selbe, the other care home owner, never seemed to smile, but he always had his money ready. Some residents spoke with an accent, as if they were from somewhere far away, and sometimes one of them would forget to pay and Gary would have to ask for help from one of the owners. That or they'd complain about not getting their paper during the coming week.

Next on Gary's route was tall, thin Gaillard Thompson, just getting home from work in the oil fields, and across the street Earl Rowe, the mayor, whom everyone called Toots. At a street corner, Wayne Keely waved from his police car and shouted, You behaving? Gary yelled back, Of course.

Up and down the streets Gary pedaled, tossing papers, making sure they reached front porches. Most of the houses were two-stories with fancy gingerbread decoration at the gables, and many of them had wraparound porches, like the doctor's widow's house, Mrs. Simons, who still gave lessons on her grand piano. She moved with small, quick steps, and the first time he delivered to her, she asked, So you're the new courier for the *Courier*? He just shrugged.

Like usual, Ben Rudd waited on his front porch. A retired farmer, Mr. Rudd lived alone, and every Saturday morning he had his nickel and dime ready along with a glass of water for Gary. Looks like a storm coming, Mr. Rudd said and pointed to the growing clouds to the west. All day the wind had been blowing hard, and Gary felt it as he pedaled.

If he read the paper, which he never did, Gary would have found this weather forecast on the front page, pretty much the same forecast as the day before:

"WINFIELD AND VICINITY: Mostly cloudy through Thursday; occasional thunderstorms this afternoon and tonight and Thursday afternoon and night. Little change in temperature. Low tonight near 60; high Thursday near 80. (U.S. Weather Bureau, Wichita.)"

The forecast made no mention of tornadoes. Instead, at the top center of the May 25 *Courier* was a photograph that might've caught Gary's eye: a cow and her four newborn calves from Pearl City, Illinois, with the caption: "THIS HOLSTEIN'S A REAL PRODUCER." "Such births," the caption continued, "are said to occur only once in about 18 million times."

The weather *was* on the editor's radar, however. One headline read "Winfield Lashed by Wind," and reported gusts of sixty miles per hour damaging windows and TV antennas. Another headline, this one front and center underneath the cow, read, "Five Persons Killed in Storms," and the article covered a series of "damaging storms which struck . . . the Midwest and South . . . during the night." Three of the deaths—two boys and a man—had occurred in Augusta, Georgia, where a storm interrupted a ball game the three were watching from a tree. When rains came, they tried to take shelter by a concrete wall at the city's ballpark. Heavy winds blew down the wall and crushed them. "Tornadic winds whipped many areas," according to the Weather Bureau, including the "Great Lakes region and the Lower Mississippi Valley." In addition to heavy rains, many places had significant temperature drops, like Chicago, which experienced a plunge of twenty degrees in one hour. All of this pointed to huge, unstable air masses over much of the nation.

After Mr. Rudd's, Gary pedaled to downtown Udall, where he delivered papers to all the business owners, including the banker, Mr. Tracy Hilderbrand, a grim-faced man who didn't seem to like him. The *Courier* cost fifteen cents a week, which Gary collected on Saturday mornings. The bank only stayed open until noon on Saturdays, and Gary usually arrived five minutes before twelve with a whole raft of nickels and dimes. Mr. Hilderbrand about bit off his pipe every time.

The town of roughly six hundred people had a barbershop, two pool halls, its own phone company, the oil company, a drugstore, two hardware stores, the Community Building, and three restaurants. At Mom and Pop's Restaurant, Mr. Whitehead, one of the owners, had a glass eye. Often he took it out, wiped it on his dirty apron, then put it back in, just to scare the kids.

Some of the townspeople were retirees, mainly farmers, while many commuted to Wichita to work at Boeing or Coleman or one of several other industries there. But they still did their shopping in Udall's five stores, including Gary's folks' grocery. At Marquette's General Merchandise, Gary's mother always bought their school supplies, and at Binford's, a small grocery with a clock and shoe repair shop in the back, she always warned the boys to buy only packaged goods, nothing by the pound from the loose bins. She knew he tried to sell an apple or banana to kids who came in for a candy, but she didn't like how Mr. Binford fixed a farmer's shoes and then came up front—without washing—to sell bulk candy or crackers. Plus, he usually had a dog in the store as well.

Grant Gearhart, with his thick-lens glasses, liked his paper left near the front of his auto repair shop, so no cars at the gas station could run over it. Gearhart was famous with the boys in town, who called him "Greasy" behind his back. He started out as a blacksmith—he still had his forge—and could pick up blistering hot horseshoes with his bare hands. If the boy was smart, he said no thanks when offered one of these shoes. Gary's granddad worked part-time for Gearhart, so Gary often stopped to say hello.

From downtown Gary pedaled across the Santa Fe Railroad tracks to the station, where he delivered a paper to the stationmaster, who made knives while he waited for trains. Just down the track, within sight, a crew had stopped for the day—their task: building a new rail siding in town. They rested in the shade of their living quarters, an old, converted passenger car.

Sometimes Gary and his family rode the train to Wichita to the north or Winfield to the south. They took what everyone called the Doodlebug, a short train that made the daily mail run with just an engine-passenger car and usually a caboose. Every morning it delivered a bag of mail to the platform, and if the engineer saw passengers waiting, he stopped and gave them a ride. Then they all doodled on down the tracks.

Gary looped through the eastern side of Udall, delivering papers to families living in big two-story houses like Gary's third grade teacher and the Hurds, who operated the local telephone company. Then Gary rode his bike back across the tracks.

On the north side of town, Gary waved to Clara Lacey, who was very pregnant. On the same street, Broadway, lived Mary Taylor and her son, Eddie. Crippled during the war, Eddie ran one of the pool halls downtown, walking there every day with his cane. Mrs. Taylor was one of the town's two telephone operators; she also had a small baking business, making wedding cakes and the best pecan pies in the area.

Then there was mean Mrs. Willis and her son, Earl. Gary didn't fear Earl so much, but he did his mother. Earl always wore overalls and had a scary laugh. He walked fast, swinging his arms, and he didn't talk much. Instead, he just grunted. He was older than most of the town kids, but he liked to play kickball and baseball with them. And usually, he wanted to play by Earl's rules, so if he struck out, he might run to first base anyway and refuse to leave. Then the kids would start saying, Earl, your mother's calling. You better go home because your mother is calling. He'd do his funny, forward-leaning run and head home, only to find his mother hadn't called, so back he came, demanding again to play.

To Gary, though, the hardest fifteen cents to collect every week was from Mrs. Willis. She had white hair and long yellow fingernails that seemed to stick out three inches, like claws ready to scratch. She never spoke much either, and both Gary and his older brother, Bobby, thought she was a witch. They especially avoided her house at Halloween, but sometimes they couldn't, like when Halloween and collection day both fell on a Saturday.

Once a week Mrs. Willis and her son came into the Atkinson family's grocery store, and every time, Earl ran to the candy aisle and started filling his pockets—Root Beer Barrels and Bubble Gum Cigarettes, Red Hots and Atomic Fireballs. His overall pockets bulged with the loot. His mother went about her own needs, filling her basket. She never reprimanded nor stopped Earl; she just ignored him. Finally, after Mrs. Willis paid for her goods at the register, Gary's dad walked them to the door, where he stood blocking it. Now Earl, Mr. Atkinson would say. You're either going to pay for that candy or you're going to put it back. Earl looked to his mother, who shook her head, then he trudged back to the candy aisle and emptied his pockets. Sometimes it took Gary a half-hour to wipe clean Earl's pile of candy and sort it into the appropriate boxes.

On his bike Gary was hungry, ready for supper, and his paper bag was almost empty. He curved around the water tower, and with his home in sight, he tossed his last paper onto the Lawrence Kennedy family's porch. Then he coasted the half-block into the driveway, where he dismounted, leaned the bike against the elm tree, and went in to eat.

It would be the last time he ever rode his bike, the final paper he ever delivered, the last meal he ever ate.

Severe Weather Warning #1

"Teletype" posted from the National Weather Service, Wichita, KS

Date: May 25, 1955

Time: Noon, 12:00 p.m.

SEVERE WARNING

SEVERE THUNDERSTORM WARNINGS HAVE BEEN ISSUED
FOR EXTREME EASTERN KANSAS ALONG LINE FROM TOPEKA
SOUTHWZRD TO COFFEYVILLE AND WXX EASTWARD
INTO MISSOURI FRO PERIOD NOW UNTIL 1–2 P.M.

THUNDERSTORMS HAVE BEEN OCCURRING IN THAT ARE
THIS MORNING WITH THESE AMTS RAIN REPORTED

CHANUTE .90 TO 10.30 A.M.

INDEPENDENCE .60

PARSONS .50

IN ADDITION TO SEVERE ADD AREA BLACKWELL
TO WINFIELD AND EASTWARD.

ADDITIONAL RIVER INFORMATION

AT 11.15 AM THIS MORNING THE BIG ARKANSAS
RIVER WAS 3.8 FT AND RISING

EARL ROWE YELLED TO GARY ATKINSON AS THE BOY THREW A COPY
of the daily newspaper onto the front porch, right at Earl's feet. Watch
your aim, buddy! Rowe liked to tease, and Gary knew it, so he grinned
as he pedaled away. The boy was the age of Rowe's eldest daughter, Pat,
both of them in the same class at Udall, seventh going into eighth. Earl
knew Gary and his family, knew the boy liked a good prank, and thus
reminded him of himself.

As mayor of Udall, Earl tried to keep up with the news, so before supper, he usually sat on the front porch reading the newspaper and smoking
a cigarette, while Lola, his wife of seventeen years, fixed the meal. She

often hummed while she worked, usually hymns she was practicing for church. She didn't like his smoking or allow it inside, which he understood. He had tried to quit but with no luck, so the porch became his smoking room. Before he went in for supper, Toots drove his new Chevy into the garage, just in case the brewing storm brought hail.

Earl and Lola had three children: Pat, age thirteen; Gary, nine; and Janice, just five. Usually, after they finished the evening meal, the kids headed out to play so Earl could get a few hours of sleep before heading to work for his midnight shift on the drilling rig.

Almost everyone called Earl by his nickname, Toots, a childhood moniker given by a younger brother who couldn't pronounce *Earl*. Now, at thirty-eight years old, Toots was over six feet tall, with thick, black hair and heavy whiskers that seemed to sprout immediately after he shaved. He had been mayor for just two months, on the city council for six years before that, and he was chief of the Udall Volunteer Fire Department as well. He was a well-liked leader, quick to laugh. He was also a hard worker, having quit high school in the middle of his senior year to earn money by following his father into the oil fields to work as a roughneck. Eventually, Toots landed a job with Stelbar; over the years he had worked his way up to the head driller on an oil rig. He liked working the "morning tour," the graveyard shift, because he could come home, get some sleep, and then work some more on the family farm.

Early in their marriage, Toots and Lola bought the farm just outside of Udall, 190 acres that they still owned and tilled in 1955. But back in 1942, he was drafted into the army, so the couple sold all their cows, chickens, and pigs and bought a house in town—they figured it would be easier for Lola and the young kids when Toots was away. He passed his physical and was ready to go to basic training, but two days before he was scheduled to head out, he got a deferment. Uncle Sam decided he needed Toots in the oil field more than Toots in the battlefield. Throughout World War II, Toots would get ready to ship out only to get deferred again. He was sorry he never did go to war but also, like Lola, relieved.

When Earl's cousin Gaillard Thompson got home from the war, Toots helped him get hired on at Stelbar. The two were like brothers, and their families lived catty-corner from each other. They also shared the storm cave or cellar that sat behind Toots and Lola's home. The families, however, did not share Betty Jo Thompson's great concern about tornadoes. Gaillard and his wife and children had spent several nights in the cave; the Rowes never had.

After supper Earl went to bed, and Lola sent their daughter Pat to the Holtje wedding shower at the Community Building, a block and a half away. The two had been invited, but because of the ominous clouds, Lola decided to stay home. She was superstitious, always knocking on wood and avoiding black cats. So she told Pat to run their gift up to the party before it started and to apologize to Ms. Holtje. Pat did as she was told.

On her way back home, Pat said hello to Mrs. Simons, her piano teacher, who was out picking up her newspaper. Mrs. Simons, the doctor's widow, lived in a huge, yellow Victorian house with a beautiful wraparound porch and inside, in its own music room, a piano on shiny wood floors. Over the years it seemed like everyone had taken piano lessons from Mrs. Simons, including Pat's mother. Pat had just had a lesson earlier that morning. She didn't really like playing the piano, not nearly as much as riding her bike or skating on the sidewalks, but her mother made her take lessons, and they both loved Mrs. Simons—how she stretched the lessons with stories and gave a Snickers if you did your lesson well. Pat always got that candy bar.

Looks like a storm coming, Mrs. Simons said. Pat nodded and hurried home, but the clouds to the west didn't bother her. In the kitchen she asked her mother if she could play softball with the other kids in the vacant lot nearby. They did this every evening, swinging the bat, yelling and laughing and running hard. Wilmer Butcher would be there, a cute boy a few years older than Pat. Her mother debated and finally said okay, so Pat ran out the door.

Dusk came, and soon it was too dark to see the ball, let alone hit it with the bat, so the teenagers dispersed, yelling, See you tomorrow. Pat called for Corky, the family dog, who liked to follow her and chase the softball. He was a large, reddish colored stray her father had found along a country road a few years earlier and brought home for the kids. The dog ran and nudged Pat with his nose, happy for the attention. As she walked home, Pat noticed red lightning filling the western sky; it looked like a huge fire.

She found her mother on the porch visiting with her aunt Emma Foulk, or Aunt Emmie, as the family called her. Emmie lived across the street and took care of a wheelchair-bound woman. Every evening in the summer, Lola and Emmie liked to relax on the porch and talk about their day or the neighbors, the weather or politics. They could listen to the kids playing nearby. They could watch the sky turn slowly into a glow. Darkness soon called Emmie back to her own home, and the street became quiet, except for the gathering wind.

Severe Weather Warning #2

"Teletype" posted from the National Weather Service, Wichita, KS

Date: May 25, 1955
Time: 4:36 p.m.

SEVERE WEATHER FORECAST MAY 25TH AT 4.36 MXXX PM
SCATTERED SEVERE THUNDERSTORMS WITH THE POSSIBILITE
OF TORNADOES ARE EXPECTED FROM 4.30 PM TO 10 PM TONIGHT
IN THE AREA OF DODGE CITY TO AMARILLO TEXAS TO WICHITA
FALLS TEXAS TO ARDMORE OKLA TO WICHITA KANSAS TO DODGE
CITY KANSAS ... TXXXXXXX WICHITA IS ON THE EXTREME
NORTHEAST EDGE OF THIS AREA AND IS LESS VUNERABLE TO
THESE STORMS THAN THE AREA SOUTHWEST OF HERE... ...

IMMEDIATE BROADCAST IS DESIRABLE.....
. PLEASE AND THANK YOU ...

EARLY IN THE DAY OF MAY 25, 1955—ROUGHLY TWELVE HOURS BEFORE
the storm—Aileen Holtje (soon to be Wittenborn) helped her mother in
the garden. As she weeded the long rows of beans, she thought about
the evening ahead, when most of the women of Udall would gather to
celebrate her upcoming wedding with a bridal shower.

Aileen, a small woman with pale blue eyes, was twenty-seven, an elementary school teacher living at home with her parents and two younger
sisters. School had just let out, and her wedding date was less than two
weeks away. She wondered what her fiancé, Roy, was doing. He worked at
the newspaper in Arkansas City, almost thirty miles to the south. Since it
was a Wednesday, he would have to work until midnight to get the grocery
ads out on time. He liked his job but hated working late.

The Holtje farm lay four and a half miles southeast of Udall, and as
Aileen and her mother hoed the garden, they commented on the weather.
It had started out cloudy, with temperatures in the fifties, but it quickly
turned hot and humid. The air felt muggy, and the wind blew hard out of
the south. As the day wore on, clouds grew taller and taller through the
afternoon. By the time they headed to town, the women felt as unsettled
as the weather.

The Community Building, where they gathered for the wedding shower,
was the pride of the town—a newly constructed cinder block structure
that had a stage and large room along with a kitchen and bathrooms. In
1952 the citizens had raised over $8,000 to buy materials and build it,
with much of the labor donated. They acquired this money in all kinds of
ways—by holding minstrel shows and parades, festivals and box suppers,
where men bid on picnic boxes, hoping to sit with a particular woman
who made the supper, the particular woman pointing to her particular
box to help. On most Saturday nights, Udall filled with people crowding
the streets, and the Community Building filled with them dancing to
country music. So this building was the ideal place for the wedding shower.

By seven o'clock, when the Holtjes arrived, the weather had only gotten worse—no rain but distant lightning, gusty winds, and dark clouds,
some greenish, a sign of hail. To Aileen it all felt strange as she watched
the large room fill with women.

Aileen had graduated from Udall High in 1948, gone to college that summer to earn enough credits, and then, as a seventeen year old, returned that fall to teach first grade, which she had done for seven years. This meant that practically every woman in town knew her as a friend, classmate, relative, or their child's teacher, or all of these. And this meant one hundred women came to the shower bringing one hundred lovely gifts. Aileen couldn't believe how many gifts. The whole front of the stage overflowed with boxes and good wishes.

First, the women gathered for a skit and song. Thelma Morgan and Cleo Tschopp, Aileen's fellow teachers and the two cohosts, had chosen "An Apple for the Teacher" as the shower theme, and so the two of them performed a faux ceremony that included saying some silly vows. Cleo took the male part, so she hid her diamond ring in an old shirt pocket. For the skit's finale, they sang a duet of "Don't Sit under the Apple Tree."

Then it was time for the gifts. The women watched Aileen open each one, then they passed the gift around to admire—a waffle iron and tablecloths, cookbooks and a mixer, sheets and towels. Earlier Aileen had selected crystal with a tulip pattern at a jewelry store in Winfield, and the shower hostesses had gone together and bought several place settings. Aileen was overwhelmed by the kindness and kept saying Oh my and Thank you, over and over.

Even inside the block walls, the women heard the thunder intensify. Thelma Morgan's daughter, Beth, and her friend Allene Holmes, along with Aileen's sisters, Normajean and LaRue, kept bringing more gifts to Aileen for her to open. The women worked quickly, as the guests waited and admired. The Holtjes knew no one would leave until all the gifts had been opened.

Finally, around 9:00 p.m., Aileen opened the last box, and a few guests started to leave, even before the refreshments. First out the door was Betty Jo Thompson. She feared storms acutely and knew her husband, Gaillard, would be looking for her. A couple others followed, but most stayed to eat. Cleo and Thelma rushed into the kitchen to start serving. They had made cupcakes topped with apple-shaped frosting to go along with the cider punch and other snacks. Beth Morgan and Allene Holmes poured drinks, served the cupcakes, and helped as needed.

As the room cleared, Aileen Holtje and her mother debated. Should they carry the gifts to the car, risking a cracked plate in the rush, or should they leave them and come back the next day? They decided to leave them, so they moved the tables of gifts to the center of the big room in case a window broke and rain poured in.

In the great room, while the other women worked, Aileen kept touching those gifts.

Around the same time that Gary Atkinson started riding his bike to deliver newspapers, his mother, Nina, left the family grocery store to walk home and fix supper. Bob Atkinson Sr., her husband, would follow after he closed the store at 6:00 p.m.

Nina had pale skin, arched eyebrows, and round cheeks with slight dimples. Her dark hair grew even curlier in the humid May weather. The three-block trek took her past the Community Building, Gaillard and Betty Jo Thompson's house, and the house of her father, Clyde C. W. Clarke, a widower. Here she stopped briefly to say hello and pick up her youngest son, Stanley, age five. While Nina walked the last block home, Stanley ran from tree to tree in his cowboy boots, shooting at birds and cats and imaginary outlaws with his six-shooter cap pistol.

When Nina opened the door to their home on Second Street, she smiled at the newness of it all, especially the kitchen cabinets and counters her father-in-law and a friend had fashioned out of oak flooring salvaged from a nearby house. Both of her older boys, Bobby and Gary, had spent many summer days pulling nails out of that old lumber, and now the wood gleamed shiny and bright like glass.

Still, though, Nina wished they had had money for a cellar.

About an hour later, her oldest son, Bobby, came home. He was tall for his age and handsome, with big brown eyes and a high forehead. He had just finished his freshman year in high school, where he had earned straight A's and been elected class president. Udall High was small, with only eight people in Bobby's class, which meant he played three sports: football, basketball, and baseball—and he also played trombone in the band. With school out and the paper route no longer his, Bobby worked odd jobs on surrounding farms. Sometimes, though, he liked to ride his bike into the country to go skinny-dipping with his friends.

Gary soon followed his older brother into the house. He hung his paper bag on a peg by the door and tried to filch a cookie, but Nina said no, supper was almost ready.

Then, lastly, Nina's husband appeared in the door. Tall and a slim two hundred pounds, Bob had spent six years in the army, including fighting in Okinawa during the Second World War. When he was discharged, he worked for a while in the oil fields around Udall, before he and Nina bought the grocery store in 1947. He was good with his hands, even with the missing finger, which had been smashed off in an oil rig. The same hands knew how to butcher as well as write in clear, cursive strokes. He had used his excellent penmanship often during the war to send letters home to Nina.

Bob usually brought home old produce from the store—wilted cabbage leaves or wrinkly apples—and after supper he and Bobby took them out to the rabbit hutches in the backyard. Bobby had his own little business— rabbits ate leftovers and begat more rabbits, which his father butchered and sold in the store. At fifteen Bobby already knew how to drive. In a year, once he earned his license, he wanted to buy a car. So he worked odd jobs and raised a lot of rabbits.

Nina stepped out on the back porch to check the weather. On the western horizon, the sun cast an odd light that seemed to be pressed close to the earth, while the overburden of clouds rolled higher and higher into the sky. Those clouds moved as if they wanted to beat back the night and replace it with a different dark.

Storm Report from the National Weather Service
Tonkawa, Oklahoma, 64 miles south of Udall, Kansas

Date: May 25, 1955
Time: 2055 CST (8:55 p.m.)

MRS. ROBERT C. WALKER REPORTED SEEING THE FUNNEL OF
A TORNADO LOCATED ABOUT ONE MILE EAST OF TONKAWA.
MRS. WALKER HAD A MICRO-BAROGRAPH IN OPERATION AT
THE TIME. WHEN THE TORNADO WAS SIGHTED EAST OF TOWN,
THE BAROGRAM SHOWED A SHARP FALL OF ABOUT .08 INCH
Hg. (MERCURY) FOLLOWED IMMEDIATELY BY A SHARP RISE OF
ABOUT .10 INCH Hg. . . . SHORTLY AFTER 2100 CST (9:00 PM) THE
"WORST HAIL IN THE HISTORY OF OUR CITY" FELL BUT WITH
ONLY LIGHT WIND. HAIL WAS HEAVIER TO THE WEST. SOME
OF THE HAIL . . . MEASURED ALMOST 3 INCHES IN DIAMETER.

A BLOCK FROM THE COMMUNITY BUILDING, AT THE THOMPSON'S house, Betty Jo ran onto the back porch shortly after 9:00 p.m. and right before the rain began. A small, sharp woman, she also sometimes had a sharp tongue, especially when she was nervous, especially before a storm. As a child, she had lived through a terrific hailstorm while visiting family. Her aunt had pulled her close as they took shelter in a closet. Wind rocked the house, and hailstones pounded the roof and blasted all the windows to litter the floor with glass and ice. Through it all, Betty Jo held onto her handkerchief, and when the storm was over, she had torn the cloth to shreds.

In 1955 Betty Jo was thirty, and she and Gaillard, age thirty-one, had two kids, a girl and a boy, Sawny and Clinton, ages eight and seven. Gaillard liked to tell people he and Betty Jo had met on a blanket. Usually that stirred up a look and then a laugh. The couple had grown up in Udall, their families living across the alley from each other. Their mothers were friends, so when Gaillard met Betty Jo on that blanket, they were only a few months old.

They didn't get along as kids, and Gaillard never much thought about Betty Jo until after high school. In 1943, while still a senior, he received his draft notice. He walked across the high school stage one last time to graduate. Then, two days later, he was in the navy.

Gaillard served on a tanker ship, the USS *Escambia*, whose job was to refuel the larger ships of the fleet. During the Pacific conflict, he woke up one morning to find another nearby tanker had been torpedoed by a Japanese submarine. All ten thousand barrels of 100 octane exploded, killing one hundred men. Gaillard also experienced two typhoons with 125-mile-an-hour winds and one hundred–foot waves. His ship popped and twisted in those waves. He knew the power of wind.

Betty Jo and Gaillard wrote to each other through the war, letters that became filled with love. When he returned home to Udall in 1945, he married Betty Jo.

In the intervening years, Gaillard worked for the same company as his cousin Toots Rowe in the oil fields around Udall, but while Toots worked the nightshift, Gaillard mostly worked during the day. On May 25 Gaillard's crew set up a pump six miles out on the Walnut River. The wind blew hard all day, first cold and then hot. It coated the men in dust as they built the foundation and then set the pump in place.

Gaillard liked his job driving the twelve-ton truck; he liked seeing the big machines work, and he liked the other fellows on the crew. They were rough, but they got along, often "messing" with each other. Once, when Toots and Gaillard worked the same shift, someone set a hot wire to a metal bench to shock the others at lunchtime. Another time Gaillard dozed off only to wake to little fires burning just a few inches on either side of him. Gaillard always suspected his cousin had masterminded these pranks.

The evening of May 25, Gaillard came home from work to their house on South Main, and after supper and after Betty Jo headed to the wedding shower, he sat down to watch *Gunsmoke*. Over the TV gunfire, Gaillard heard the wind picking up. He expected Betty Jo to come home at any moment, and when she finally did, the two of them put their kids to bed.

Gaillard wanted to go to bed as well. He was tired and had to get up early for work. But Betty Jo kept looking out the window. He knew what was on her mind—that storm from her childhood and the storm bearing down on them now with her children asleep nearby and the storm cellar too far away. They called it the cave, a twelve-by-twelve cement block hole in the ground, and it belonged to Toots, who lived across the street. If a tornado threatened, Betty Jo and Gaillard crossed the 150 feet, taking their children to spend the night on bunk beds Gaillard had built in his cousin's cave.

So, instead of going to bed, Gaillard and Betty Jo stared out the window. By the brilliant flash of lightning, the couple tried to cipher the strength of this storm and what they should do.

Like her parents, Beth Morgan had grown up in Udall, with her father, Cecil, on the city council and her mother, Thelma, one of her teachers. In fact, her mother taught her four out of her eight years in elementary school, where she and her friend Allene often had to stand in opposite corners because they talked too much. Even then they traded chalkboard messages until Mrs. Morgan caught them.

So now, at sixteen, Beth was ready for some independence that a summer job would bring. The telephone company had hired her to work as a switchboard operator. On the evening of May 25, Beth was supposed to sit beside Mary Taylor, the main operator, who would teach her what to say and where to plug in the lines. Beth Morgan didn't want to go to the wedding shower, but her mother, who was one of the cohosts, had different plans.

All day the weather had shifted and blown in a troubling way. Beth ignored it for the most part. But the weather had made her mother uneasy, and that evening Thelma wanted to keep her daughter close, despite Beth's wishes. At supper they argued, both of them strong-willed. Years earlier, before Beth was born, Thelma Morgan had been one of the first women in the region elected to a school board. She and her husband also had owned a small grocery in town, and when Thelma became pregnant, she continued to work, which at the time was considered "outlandish." She just ignored the comments and did as she pleased.

So Beth came by her determination and stubbornness naturally. She argued that it was her first day of work, she couldn't possibly miss it. Her mother insisted she needed Beth to help her with the wedding shower. Beth tried once more, but her mother said no. The two walked to the shower right past the phone office. Light filled the window where Mary Taylor worked, where Beth wanted to be.

At the wedding shower, Beth and her best friend, Allene Holmes, did what the others asked, but mostly Beth pouted. Allene tried to cheer her up, saying they could drive around after the shower. Allene had taken driver's ed the previous year, and tonight she had driven from her family's farm to Udall alone. I'll work the pedals, Allene said, and you can steer. They had played that game before, the devious danger thrilling.

Beth didn't really care about driving. Instead, she admired the gifts and wondered what Mrs. Taylor was doing. As the storm thundered louder, most of the women dispersed. The dozen remaining women washed dishes, put away leftovers, and swept floors. When they finished, they waited for the storm to pass so they could head home.

Then the electricity went off. The Community Building and all of Udall slipped into darkness.

Storm Report from the National Weather Service (excerpt)

Blackwell, Oklahoma, 55 miles south of Udall, Kansas

Date: May 25, 1955
Time: 2127 CST (9:27 p.m.)

THE TORNADO STRUCK BLACKWELL, OKLAHOMA ABOUT 2127 CST. IT TRAVELED FROM SOUTH TO NORTH WITH ALMOST COMPLETE DESTRUCTION OVER A PATH ABOUT TWO BLOCKS WIDE, AND CONSIDERABLE DESTRUCTION EXTENDED 3 OR 4 BLOCKS FARTHER ON EITHER SIDE. MR. NAVE, WHO LIVES JUST SOUTH OF THE SOUTH CITY LIMITS OF BLACKWELL, REPORTED A SHORT PERIOD OF WIND AND HAIL (ABOUT TWO INCHES IN DIAMETER). THE HAIL WAS FOLLOWED BY A LULL DURING WHICH HE WENT OUTSIDE. INSTEAD OF THE AIR BEING COOL FOLLOWING THE SQUALL, IT WAS "HOT." THEN THE TORNADO FUNNEL WAS SIGHTED APPROACHING FROM THE SOUTH. IT CAME WITH "THE ROAR OF FORTY FREIGHT TRAINS." THERE WAS LIGHTNING ALL AROUND BUT NOT IN THE IMMEDIATE VICINITY OF THE FUNNEL. MR. B. H. JONES LIVING ON THE NORTH SIDE OF BLACKWELL, ABOUT 4 BLOCKS FROM THE DAMAGE AREA, REPORTED SQUALLY WEATHER WITH WIND, RAIN AND HAIL FOLLOWED BY A SHORT PERIOD OF QUIET. HE WENT OUTSIDE, HEARD THE "ROAR," AND IMMEDIATELY SOUGHT SHELTER. UPON EMERGING, HE SAW THE TORNADO FUNNEL LEAVING TOWN IN A NORTH-NORTHEAST DIRECTION, STILL IN CONTACT WITH THE GROUND.

PAT ROWE HELPED HER MOTHER GET HER TWO SIBLINGS INTO BED,
then she watched TV with her dad, Toots, before he headed off to work.
The family had just bought their first black-and-white TV a few months
earlier, and now, every evening, they checked the 10:15 p.m. weather out
of Wichita. The weatherman announced storm warnings for Oklahoma
but none for Kansas.

"Aren't you glad we don't live in Oklahoma?" Pat asked her father.

He yawned and nodded. Toots listened to the rain hitting the roof
and was glad he had pulled the car into the garage. He put on his boots
and gathered up his lunch pail. He usually met his men at Eddie's Pool
Hall around ten thirty, and from there they carpooled the seven miles
to the oil rig.

Lola stood at the front door, watching the storm and her neighbors.
Betty Jo Thompson came running through all that rain carrying her child;
they disappeared into the cellar. Gaillard soon followed in the car. Then
the wind came on even stronger, and Lola yelled to Toots: The chairs are
flying off the porch. And the big tree is falling! She ran to one bedroom
and grabbed their youngest sleeping child, Jan, while Pat ran to the other
for her brother, Gary. He, too, had been asleep and didn't want to get up,
so Pat threw him over her shoulder and carried him to her mother in
the dining room. All the while Toots kept searching for a flashlight and
looking out the windows. He saw Gaillard run from his car, carrying his
boy. Toots found a light and started to lead his family to the cave with
the Thompsons, but by then it was too late. The tornado was on them.

Storm Report from the National Weather Service (excerpt)

Eight Miles West of Arkansas City, Kansas,

approximately 30 miles south of Udall, Kansas

Date: May 25, 1955

Time: 2158 to 2215 CST (9:58 to 10:15 p.m.)

AN ELDERLY COUPLE, MR. AND MRS. POST, REPORT THAT
THEIR POWER FAILED AT 9:58 PM (TIME ASCERTAINED FROM
A STOPPED ELECTRIC CLOCK) FOLLOWED IN ABOUT 5 MINUTES
BY HAIL AND A TERRIBLE ROAR. THIS WAS FOLLOWED BY A
QUIET LULL WHICH LASTED PROBABLY LESS THAN A MINUTE.
THE STORM STRUCK AGAIN, BLOWING DOWN SEVERAL LARGE
TREES.... THE COUPLE WAS IN THE HOUSE THE ENTIRE
TIME LOOKING OUT THE WINDOWS. WHEN THE INITIAL
ROAR WAS HEARD, ONLY BLACKNESS WAS VISIBLE TO THE
SOUTH. AFTER THE TORNADO PASSED OVER, IT WAS CLEARLY
VISIBLE TO THE NORTH AGAINST THE BACKGROUND OF
ALMOST CONSTANT LIGHTNING FARTHER TO THE NORTH.

THE EARL BENNETT FARM IS LOCATED TWO MILES FROM
THE POST FARM. MR. BENNETT WAS ROUSED FROM BED
BETWEEN 10:10 AND 10:15 PM BY HAIL, SOME AS LARGE AS
HEN'S EGGS. THIS WAS ACCOMPANIED BY SEVERE CONSTANT
LIGHTNING. THEN THE STORM STRUCK, DESTROYING
SEVERAL OUTBUILDINGS.... THIS WAS FOLLOWED BY A
LULL WHICH LASTED ABOUT HALF A MINUTE. STRONG WIND
AGAIN STRUCK SUDDENLY.... LOOKING OUT TO THE NORTH,
MR. BENNETT SAW THE TORNADO FUNNEL BACK-LIGHTED
BY CONSTANT LIGHTNING. HE DESCRIBED THE FUNNEL
AS HANGING DOWN FROM A BLACK CLOUD AND GYRATING
SLOWLY BACK AND FORTH. HE ESTIMATED IT TO BE ABOUT A
QUARTER OF A MILE IN DIAMETER IN ITS LOWER PORTIONS.

EARLIER IN THE EVENING, GAILLARD AND BETTY JO THOMPSON HAD stood at their back door and watched the storm strengthen. Even in the dark, they could see hail bouncing on their sidewalk, pelting the yard. "There goes my tomatoes," Gaillard said. It was a beautiful patch of the Sioux variety he had planted over a month ago. Now he'd have to plant again. He wondered about his birds too—seven pheasants, plus a brood of banty hens sitting on seventy pheasant eggs about to hatch.

After the hail, the rain and wind intensified. Trees bent and twisted. One gust broke a huge limb that jabbed into the ground. That triggered Betty Jo. "I'm going to the cave," she said. "You can stay here if you want." She hurried into the bedroom to rouse Sawny. The child was a big girl, maybe 60 pounds to her mother's 145, but that didn't slow Betty Jo. She hugged her close and ran out the door. Gaillard thought he better go, too, so he woke Clinton and searched for his son's shoes—under the bed, in the closet—nothing. He never did find those shoes.

The wind picked up speed like somebody pushing on the gas pedal. Out the door with the boy in his arms, Gaillard immediately became soaked. But the house door wouldn't stay shut. Gaillard reached back, grabbed the knob, and slammed. Did it again. And again. He had to slam it three times before it finally stayed closed.

He expected to find Betty Jo waiting out of the rain in the car, but it sat empty. Gaillard panicked. He had to find Betty Jo. And Sawny. And he had to get his boy to the cave. It was their habit to drive the short distance, so that's what he did, he drove the 150 feet across the street and parked beside Toots's car and truck.

Betty Jo stood on the cellar steps waiting, Sawny with her. Gaillard could barely see them through the rain. Betty Jo had carried Sawny all the way, avoiding the full ditches and falling tree limbs.

Gaillard knew the cave was far safer than his car, so he grabbed his son and ran. He didn't shut the door. The wind no longer gusted. It blew straight and hard, harder than any he had ever felt, harder than even the typhoons he had sailed through in the navy. It blew so hard that as Gaillard ran to the cave, the wind about blasted his feet out from under him. He didn't know if he could make it.

Severe Weather Warning #3

"Teletype" posted from the National Weather Service, Wichita, KS

Date: May 25, 1955
Time: 10:10 p.m.

REVISED FORECAST FOR WICHITA AND VCT . . .

NOT TO BE USD AFTER 4.30AM

THE FOLLOWING IS AN EXTENDED TIME ON SEVERE WEATHER

FORECAST ISSUED EARLIER. . . . BOTH TIME AND AREA EXTENDED.

SCTD SEVERE THNDERSTROMS AND ISOLATED TORNADOES

EXPECTED TO CONTINUE IN AREA 30 EAST OF EMPORIA

TO RUSSELL AND SOUTH TO 10 MILES WEST OF FT. SILL

OKLA TO ARD UP TO TULSA AND BACK TO 30 MILES

EAST OF EMPORIA. ABV IS CURRENT TO 0300C

WICHITA IS INCLUDED IN AREA ABV.

HERE IS ALL THE INFOMRMATION I HAVE ON TORNADO AT

BLACKWELL OKLA. BLACKWELL OKLA HIT BY TORNADO. . . .

NEED AMBULANCES FROM ALL TOWNS AROUND.

WHEN THE ELECTRICITY CUT OFF AT THE COMMUNITY BUILDING, the women didn't panic, but their anxiety rose. In the dark Cleo Tschopp played a few tunes she knew by heart on the piano, others singing along. Then she suddenly remembered her diamond ring, which she rushed to find in the stage's dressing room. On the other side of the great room, the cleanup crew searched the kitchen and found candles and matches. They at least had light, and this light drew in others.

Beth Morgan's father and Cleo Tschopp's husband had been across the street at Eddie's Pool Hall, passing the time while waiting on their wives. Like the rest of the town, the pool hall had lost power, so the two men decided to run through the pelting rain to join their families. After they dried off, the women fed them leftover cupcakes.

The now fourteen people waiting out the storm in the Community Building stood by the windows trying to gauge its intensity. Lightning flashed continuously, blinding them, so they simply had to listen—to the pounding rain, the boom of thunder, and the whine of the wind through the electric lines.

Allene Holmes jingled her car keys—she wanted to get home and trade her heels and fancy dress for something more comfortable. But Mr. Morgan saw the keys and told her: I don't want you driving home right now. Just wait till the weather settles down. So she put the keys back in her purse and listened to the storm.

In the great room, everyone gathered; a young girl clung to her mother and began to cry. Beth realized they needed some distraction, a song to help forget for a moment, so she and Allene ventured onto the stage with a candle to find songbooks.

As they stepped off the stage, something fell from above—a ceiling tile. Someone yelled, Is that a train? since the tracks cut right through town. But to the bride's sister, this sounded like a hundred trains, not just one. Another person yelled, No, that's the wind. To Allene it was the loudest noise she had ever heard, so loud she couldn't think—no, *this is a tornado*; no, *how am I going to get home?* No thoughts, just feet moving, hands seeking shelter.

After supper at the Atkinson's and after her boys did their usual rough-housing, Nina bathed Stanley, the youngest, and put him into bed, with Gary soon following. Bobby stayed up a little longer to try to cool off by the water cooler, what his parents called the swamp cooler because it threw out so much humidity. His parents had just bought a TV, and Bobby liked to watch the news at 10:00 p.m. with his dad; tonight the weatherman predicted a chance of thunderstorms but said nothing about tornadoes. Then Bobby, too, headed to bed, passing the mantel with the quart jar of alcohol holding his adenoids, his father's finger, and Gary's big toe. Sometimes he held the jar up to the light, swirled it a little—to remember or simply to admire.

Bob Sr. stayed up to watch Tennessee Ernie Ford, who came on after the news. Four years earlier, in 1951, Bob had been diagnosed with cancer of the sinuses. The doctors used heavy doses of radiation, but they only gave him a few years to live, if that. He always worried—what would happen to his wife and boys after he was gone? How would they manage? And yet here he was, in 1955, thirty-six years old and surprised to be sitting with Nina. Surprised to find himself alive and healthy enough to hum along to "Sixteen Tons."

Bobby and Gary and Stanley all slept in the same room, with a window between the two older boys. From his bed Bobby could see the water cooler, and some nights he could listen to Tennessee Ernie Ford, but not tonight. The wind grew louder and more intense. The rain banged hard on the roof. He heard his parents' low voices but couldn't make out their words.

Then the water cooler blew straight across the house. Bobby heard it slam into the kitchen. When he felt the house lift, he shoved open the window screen and dove to tuck himself against the foundation.

2 The Weight of It

MAY 25, 1955

10:35 P.M. TO 10:38 P.M.

TO BOBBY ATKINSON IT FELT LIKE TWO TORNADOES. THE FIRST ONE, probably the front wall of the tornado, blew over him with a great force, wind strong enough to rip off his clothes. But there was little debris with it, and he wasn't badly injured. And then the wind stopped. There was noise but not on top of him. He got on his knees to look around. The house was gone. Just simply gone. Lightning illuminated the empty foundation, the splintered and leafless trees. Where were his parents? His brothers? He didn't hear their voices. He didn't hear any voices.

After a few moments, the eye of the tornado moved to the northeast, and the rear wall of the funnel slammed into him. To Bobby it felt like somebody shooting a shotgun at close range, right at him, over and over, while someone else kept hitting him with a baseball bat. Something pummeled his hand, then both arms. Something else stabbed his back and stayed there. Then a rock or brick—some hurled object—hit him on the back of the head. Then only darkness.

When Mayor Rowe realized his family wouldn't make it to their cave, he yelled for everyone to get down on the dining room floor. Cover your heads, he shouted. Lola gathered Jan underneath her, Toots held Gary underneath him, and Pat climbed in between her parents.

Then it sounded like a bomb exploded right on top of them. The bricks and boards that had been their house became shrapnel raining down, and it didn't feel like it would ever stop. Pat and her mother prayed aloud, but the noise smothered their words. They called for Toots, but he didn't respond. Pat couldn't feel him moving beside her, didn't know if he was still alive. In all the chaos Gary slipped out from under his father's body. When the boy stood up, a fence wire pierced his neck. He screamed in pain and then disappeared.

Toots started moving. Something had hit him on the back of the head and knocked him unconscious for a minute or two or three—he didn't know. When he woke, the sound of the tornado had started to fade, so he called. Lola? Pat? You all right?

We're here, Lola yelled over the thunder, but I can't move my legs. I think they're broken. And I don't know where Gary is.

Lola, Pat, and Jan were pinned under the remains of their house, and he had to get them out. And he had to find Gary.

Gaillard Thompson barely made it to the cellar. He hauled his son down the steps, put him on a bench next to Sawny, where Betty Jo hugged them both, then Gaillard started back up to shut the door. But it was too late. The tornado was on them, deafeningly, horrendously roaring. It blew the cave door shut, then it blew an oven and refrigerator, a mattress and tire, tree limbs and shingles, all of this hurled *through* the wooden door.

The family cowered in the cave's corner. The parents covered their children. They pressed into the corner of the cement wall to become as small as they could.

Lightning illuminated the cave like daylight, so intensely did it strike, so continuously. Gaillard felt the tornado pass over, the weight of it bearing down, the vacuum of it sucking through his ears, hurting them. Then dead calm. No air, all of it sucked away. The center of the funnel on top of them. How long that lasted, who knew? Maybe a minute, probably less. Time stilled in a place like that. It stopped long enough, it seemed like you could poke your head out and look around, but Gaillard knew to wait, to not let his family move, to hold them close. The children sobbed. He felt Betty Jo shiver. His stomach roiled. Rainwater pooled in the cave, deep, up to his calves, and he wondered how much more would come in.

Then the other side of the tornado struck. More debris flew over them. More dropped on top of them. But that all stopped when the whole side of Earl Rowe's house slammed down like a giant door, covering the cellar.

At the wedding shower, another ceiling tile fell and hit one of the women. More tiles started dropping, as the storm sucked them off and threw them down. The roof opened. A great wind filled the giant room; it snuffed out the candles. Lightning punctuated the complete darkness, while the sound of a hundred locomotives bore down. Everyone knew then—knew what they had not wanted to know, wanted to *not* know even in that moment—the tornado was upon them.

One of the men yelled, The bathroom. It was in the southwest corner and supposedly the safest part of a building during a tornado. The group ran toward the small space, hands searching for the door, hands on shoulders, reaching for other hands, bracing against walls. As soon as Beth entered, the only window in the bathroom broke inward. Rain and glass showered down. Everyone screamed. They turned, mothers picking up crying children. Someone yelled, The kitchen, so that's where they headed. Beth reached for her parents, her best friend, but found nothing; she kept moving. In the great room, lightning flashed, and she glanced to the stage, where she and Allene had stood ten minutes earlier. The whole roof had come down on top of it.

In the kitchen they fell to the floor between counters and cabinets, bodies squeezed together. The roar traveled over them. The bride's sister couldn't breathe, the air pressure so great she felt her lungs might collapse. The window in the outside door shattered, and a fist-sized shard of glass sliced into Aileen Holtje's back. On the other side of the room, Beth felt something hot on her leg, she didn't know what. Something heavy like a cement block fell on Allene's back. Dishes and pots fell over everyone. A door fell on top of Cleo, and she screamed, "God help us." Then she thought, "Well, whatever it is, it's here," and whispered, "God, please save us." All the fear Cleo felt suddenly dissipated, transformed into a calm resignation. Then the walls sheared away and disappeared.

Water gushed, hailstones pounded, and without moving, everyone was suddenly outside.

In the darkness, on that kitchen linoleum, soaked by rain and covered by debris, fourteen people kept their faces down, their arms over their heads. Mothers covered children; husbands hugged wives; everyone prayed.

3   What the Lightning Revealed

MAY 25, 1955

10:39 P.M. TO 11:35 P.M.

Severe Weather Warning #4

"Teletype" posted from the National Weather Service, Wichita, KS

Date: May 26, 1955

Time: approximately 10:15 to 1:00 a.m.

POLICE DISPATCH REPORTED UDALL

KANS FLATTENED BY TORNADO.

AMBULANCES REQUESTED FOR TORNADOES

AT BOTH UDALL AND ROCK KANSAS.

THESE ARE ABOUT 30 SE OF WICHITA....

OCCURRED ABOUT 11.45 PM

MORE INFO ON BLACKWELL OKLA TORNADO...

OCCURRED ABOUT 9.50 PM

DESTROYED 12 BLOCKS NORTH END OF CITY.

RAINFALL SINCE 6.30 PM.... 1.23 ...

MAKING A TOTAL OF 2.11 TODAY.

POLICE DISPATCH REPORTS UDALL ALMOSTLY

COMPLETELY OBLITERATED.

REPORT FROM BLACKWELL ... XXX SEVEN KNOWN DEAD.

NUMBERO OF INJURIES UNKNOWN TO PRESENT TIME.

NEXT TO THE FOUNDATION OF HIS FAMILY'S HOUSE, BOBBY ATKINSON regained consciousness. Cold rain and baseball-sized hail pounded him back awake. Even though the tornado had moved on, the sky still boomed with thunder, and lightning's bright flashes revealed the destruction.

Somehow Bobby crawled to his father's car, a Chevy, not far away. All the windows were shattered, the glass covering the seats, but the top provided cover, so he slid inside. Hail dented the roof and hood deafeningly loud, like a million ballpeen hammers.

Bobby drifted in and out of consciousness. He wondered about his parents, his younger brothers. He tried to get a sense of his injuries— the broken bones in his arms and hand, a ripped-up back, probably a concussion, and who knew what else. With his good hand, he touched the back of his head, his fingers sticky with blood. He reached around to feel what had stabbed him in the back. His fingers found a 2x2, with at least eight inches of wood sticking out. Again, his hand came away sticky and red—no wonder he couldn't get enough air.

But what haunted him, what he couldn't shake, was the loneliness.

He remembered the civil defense drills at school, how they had practiced "duck and cover" in the hallways and under their desks, how they single-filed to the fallout shelter. They watched movies of Bert the Turtle telling them what to do. Or another movie showed the mushroom cloud, and then afterward, the camera panned slowly over a destroyed landscape, the long shot implying, This is what it might look like when you emerge after the bomb.

That landscape lay before him now. With every lightning flash, Bobby witnessed a destruction worse than even that movie. No buildings. Only a few trees, their bark blown off, white limbs jagged like lightning. And no people.

Bobby wondered if he was the only one left alive.

When the rain suddenly poured over those gathered in what remained of the Community Building and the tornado had moved on, Thelma Morgan called for her daughter. Beth answered, Here, Mama. Beth called for her best friend Allene, the Holtje sisters called for their mother and each other, and on and on, everyone calling, checking, amazed—*I'm alive* and *We're all alive.* Anybody hurt? someone asked. The bride had glass in her back, and another woman had burns from the hot water tank. Allene had trouble standing—she knew whatever hit her had broken a bone—but she could walk. The women from the wedding shower miraculously stood in the remains of the kitchen, most of them uninjured and all of them now soaked and cold.

The tornado had caved in the main exit, so they climbed over the rubble, helping each other over the busted bricks and boards. Beth lost her shoes. She yelled, but the men called, Hurry, you don't need them. She scrambled into the street. Her feet were tough from going barefoot, but those Sunday shoes had been her favorites, white and comfortable.

The group started down First Street, keeping close together, Allene hobbling, her tailbone sharp with pain. The rain pounded their heads and backs; lightning illuminated their way. Cleo Tschopp yelled, "We can't cross the wires." The electric wires were down everywhere. Her husband reassured her, saying the electricity had cut off, remember? Still, they snaked this way and that, holding hands, helping when someone stumbled. The water came to their ankles and then up to their knees. Not only had the storm dumped inches of rain, but, they soon learned, the water tower two blocks away had fallen over and flooded the street.

They heard a peculiar sound, what Cleo thought almost sounded like a warning whistle, like another tornado might be bearing down on them. She turned to look back, wondering where they could hide. And in turning back, she felt the full force of the wind and rain together. It felt as if someone had poured a bucket of water in her face, and she gasped for breath. One of the others realized the sound was a horn, a car horn. They saw several cars, ones they had driven, some with doors open and trunks up, dome lights on, roofs sunk in, and on one a beam across the hood, shorting the wires and causing the horn to blare.

The fourteen people slipped past the many demolished cars, the rubble heap of Atkinson's Grocery, past what remained of the pool hall. Beth's father wondered about the other men, those he had been playing pool with just a few moments ago.

They came to the long string of brick buildings on First Street and found shelter under the entrance to the Oddfellows Lodge. Much of the rest of the business district had blown away, but the brick archway had held and gave them some dryness. People from other parts of town also gathered. Some had little clothing on, the tornado having ripped it off. They seemed numb, except for their shivering. They said the water tower was gone and so was their school.

Beth thought of that new high school building, those solid walls, where she had looked forward to spending her senior year. She wondered where she would go to school, but then a gust of rain blew into the archway, and she huddled closer to her mother. All this time the bell at the railroad crossing went on and on, *ding-ding, ding-ding*. Like something else might come down the tracks.

Toots Rowe felt the immense pressure in his ears ease as the tornado moved to the northeast, but that didn't ease the pressure of so much debris that smothered him and his family. Rain and hail pummeled his face as he started digging, throwing off the bricks, boards, and nails, whole walls, the remains of what had been his house. And where were his wife and two daughters? They had been right beside him, but he couldn't see them.

Once freed, Toots dug for the others. Pat, his eldest daughter, cried out to God, and that voice in the dark was the only sound Toots could hear over the rain and thunder. He found the edge of a flattened wall, lifted with all his strength, and Lola, Pat, and Jan crawled out.

Where's Gary? Toots asked. No one knew, so Toots yelled over the thunder and rain for his only son. He kept at it, hollering: Gary, Gary. Where are you? Finally, a minute or two later, a small voice called back. Toots ran to find his son covered by tin and boards piled at the base of what remained of a neighbor's house. He dug to find Gary. Blood spurted from his neck. Toots picked him up and ran back to his family. Then all of them hurried to the cellar to get out of the hail and rain. What they found was the side of their house covering the cave.

Gaillard! Toots yelled. Are you in there? He had to call a couple of times, and his voice carried to the Butchers' house, a few lots away. Mrs. Butcher called Toots by name, yelling for help, but Toots couldn't go over there, not yet. He needed to stop the blood that flowed from his son's neck. He needed to get his family safe.

Finally, Gaillard responded.

A wall of my house is covering the cave, Earl hollered. And this hail is about to beat us all to death. There's a pickax in the back corner, he told Gaillard. Chop us a hole so we can get out of this hail.

Gaillard made a slash or two with the pick, busting open a hole so that Toots could lower his children and wife down. Then he dropped down through the hole, and all of them were out of the hail and wading in water. Mud and rain covered the Rowe family, such that Betty Jo didn't recognize them for a moment. Then she pulled them close, lifting the kids up onto a makeshift bench, where the adults hugged them to try to keep them warm.

They had no light, but lightning flashed so much that they could inspect Gary's neck. Blood still seeped from around the wire that protruded a few inches, and the boy looked pale. Gaillard took off his T-shirt and wrapped the wound to staunch the blood. But how do you do that with a fence wire sticking out? They did the best they could.

As they waited out the storm, Earl told of standing at the kitchen door and watching Gaillard run from the car. I didn't think you made it, he said, because just as you ran by, all our windows started popping out. He told Gaillard that they all fell to the floor, then the storm took the house clear off of them. And in all of that, Gary had panicked and somehow run away.

The make-do wound dressing wasn't working. The cloth quickly soaked with Gary's blood.

4   Hit by Emptiness

ONE OF THE FIRST NOTICES OF THE TORNADO THE OUTSIDE WORLD received occurred at 11:35 p.m. An off-duty police officer named Thompson had just passed through Udall when he and his car were struck by the tornado. In his words, the tornado "blew my car clear around back toward Udall." Luckily, it didn't turn the car over. Thompson watched as the powerful wind destroyed a nearby barn and collapsed a garage onto two vehicles. The officer ran to the farmhouse to find the woman inside "cut up pretty bad." He decided to return to Udall, a quarter-mile away, for help, and that's when he saw the total destruction of the town. Two survivors rushed to his car, afraid another storm might come, so he took them back to the farmhouse.

From there Thompson sped to Belle Plaine, nine miles to the east, where he used the town marshal's radio to send out word to the Wellington police, to the sheriffs in Sumner and Sedgwick Counties, as well as to the Kansas State Highway Patrol. Calls quickly spread to physicians and nurses, ambulance drivers and more rescuers.

Another cry for help occurred at roughly this same time. In Mulvane, nine miles to the north, a trucker brought in a man who had had his throat cut. At first the physician thought the injury was from a traffic accident, but soon he learned of the tornado. The doctor sounded the air raid alarm, packed what medicine he had, and headed to Udall in an ambulance, with others behind.

One other call for help came miraculously from an anonymous teenage boy from Udall who had survived the tornado. He told an interviewer: "As soon as the wind died down and I could get my little brother and sisters out of the cellar, I went to the highway and hitched a ride to Winfield. I got there about an hour after it happened. I went to the police station. There weren't any warnings about [the tornado] when I got there." His alarm sent the Cowley County sheriff's patrols to Udall, and this Sheriff's Office also was the first to notify the Kansas National Guard.

For at least an hour, maybe two, Bobby Atkinson lay in that beat-up, windowless shelter of a car, drifting in and out of consciousness. Then, at some point, a beam of light shined in on him. *Help*, he thought. And *Thank God, another person.* The flashlight blinded him, but Bobby recognized the voice. It belonged to an older man, a relative of one of Bobby's neighbors, someone Bobby used to deliver papers to. The man asked if Bobby had seen his kinfolk, and Bobby said no.

And then the man left.

He saw the blood, saw Bobby's injured head and arms, and he simply moved on.

In that empty car, Bobby felt a different kind of shock.

As more people gathered under the archway, the adults from the wedding shower realized they needed more shelter. They saw a light in a house across the tracks, a block away. That's Lora Grant's house, someone said. She's lit her old lamps, someone else said. The kerosene lanterns shimmered a promise of shelter from the wind and rain, so Beth's dad, Cecil Morgan, ran across the tracks to check. When he came back, he told them that Lora Grant had one dry room, the bathroom, and she said to come on. The group hurried that way, meeting two men from the Santa Fe work train who offered them shelter in their bunk car. Cecil Morgan kindly thanked them and pointed to the Grants', saying they hoped to find safety there. Many in the group feared another tornado might strike the town again. They hoped a bathroom would be safer than a railcar.

The rain had yet to slow, soaking the wedding shower party even more. They shivered as they stepped over the railroad tracks, past the crossing sign, the *ding-ding* blaring into their ears.

Lester Grant, Lora's husband, met them. Part of our house is still standing, he told them. And we have blankets, so come on.

He told them how he and Lora and their disabled renter, John Arbuckle, had made it to their shelter in the backyard, and then, when the tornado passed, they had pulled debris away from the house's door so they could get dry. Now he helped people climb over a pile of boards that used to be the front porch. Half of the house was gone, but the remaining rooms still had a roof.

Lora Grant came to the front entrance to see eighteen people dripping wet and frightened. Come on in, she yelled over the thunder, and they crowded in with other neighbors who had already found this shelter. At the back of the house, she entered the bathroom, opened her linen closet, and said, "Get in here and get dried off."

The women wrapped themselves in towels and huddled together in the six-by-ten-foot space. Beth, Allene, and others stood in the bathtub, while the Grants brought them blankets and coats, especially for those barely clothed. Sixteen women crammed into the tight space, jostling to try to make more room. They listened to the thunder, to the rain pounding the roof. Someone began to pray, and others joined. Then someone sang "Bless This House," and others lifted their voices. One woman made a joke about not having much house to bless, and others laughed. The tension eased and the singing resumed. Next came "How Great Thou Art" and "The More We Get Together, the Happier We Will Be," the melodies drifting over the debris, calling in other survivors. The women passed the hours, filling the small space with songs.

Meanwhile, Thelma's and Cleo's husbands headed back out. They worked their way over the rubble without a flashlight, only the occasional lightning to help them navigate. Within a half-hour they came back. They spoke the names of the dead they had seen, the living rescued, and the houses destroyed. They told of the survivors crowded into a two-story, concrete chicken house that somehow still stood. Beth's dad told Thelma, You have a house, but there are some problems. Beth was relieved—the house she had known all her life had survived the tornado.

Allene Holmes asked about her grandmother, who lived just across the alley nearby. The men said the house still stood, but the roof was gone and the cellar full of water—and it had no people in any of it, dead or alive, as far as they could tell. Allene worried even more.

After an hour or so, the hail stopped; the lightning and thunder still boomed and roared but farther to the northeast. Rain continued, but all of it seemed a little quieter, except for that *ding-ding, ding-ding*. Toots and Gaillard couldn't figure it out. Then Gaillard realized: the bell at the railroad crossing. It filled the whole town, and it wouldn't stop.

Lola kept checking her son's neck, Toots watching best he could in the dark of their cave. The boy's skin had turned pale. Finally, Toots said, "We got to get Gary to the hospital."

Gaillard climbed out of the cave, while Toots lifted the others up. Through the chopped hole, Gaillard gently pulled Betty Jo and Lola, Sawny and Clinton, Pat and Gary and Jan, then he gave a hand to Earl, and all of them huddled on the saturated ground. The children were barefoot and afraid, so the adults carried the four youngest.

"Let's go over to my house," Gaillard yelled over the thunder. "The rain's started to slow."

"You ain't got no house," Toots said.

Enough lightning flashed that Gaillard could see across the street. The emptiness hit him. And the closeness of it all, how they almost didn't leave, almost didn't make it.

They walked closer, and sure enough, no house. Nothing but foundation and the roof. It lay on the back of the lot. Where had that part between gone, the middle part, the one you lived in—where had that gone?

"You still have your tree," Toots said. But when they got closer, they realized the maple was upside down, roots poking the sky like branches.

And neither man had a car anymore. The tornado had lifted Gaillard's

Chevy and smashed it down on top of Earl's Chevy. His pickup was demolished as well.

So, the two families started walking north, toward Highway K55, to see if they could find shelter and help. The lightning illuminated their way, and all they could see around them was rubble. Pat walked gingerly through the water and debris, afraid of nails and live wires, so she followed her father's footsteps. He limped—the tornado had driven an eight-penny nail into his leg, near his knee—but still he moved quickly enough that Pat worked to keep up.

When they came to the main road, a brand-new Chevrolet pulled up. It was Benny Weaver, a car dealer from nearby Belle Plaine, a friend of Toots. How can I help? Benny asked.

Toots nodded to Gary. We need to get him to a hospital.

Benny told them to get in, and the father and son sped off to Winfield.

Soon after, a farmer rode into town on his tractor, pulling a wagon. He lived four miles away and had heard about the storm and came to help. Betty Jo and Lola climbed aboard, while Gaillard lifted the Thompson and Rowe children onto the wagon. The farmer took them out to Lola's brother's, the Satterthwaite's farmhouse, about a half-mile east of town. The tornado had hit there too, shifting the house off its foundation. But everyone could get inside and be dry. And they had electricity still, so Emma Satterthwaite turned on the stove and made tea and hot chocolate, a small comfort amid so much loss.

Aunt Emma put Pat and the other children in beds and covered them with blankets. But Pat couldn't stop shaking—she was frigid with shock, and like her parents and kinfolk, she was worried about her brother and her grandparents. No one knew if the elderly Satterthwaites had survived. They lived just a few houses away from the Rowes. Pat couldn't dare believe that their house had survived. But had they?

At the Grants' house, through the long hours of the night, the bridal shower women kept singing hymns from the tiny bathroom. The house became stuffy, with so many people, so they opened the window, and their hymns carried across the small town.

Then Allene Holmes heard her father calling her name. She broke down crying and yelled back and climbed out over the broken porch to hug him.

Mr. Holmes had come to town with his son, first searching for his oldest daughter, Betty, who lived on the northwest side of town. They found her alive and tucked into the neighbor's cellar with her two small children. During the storm an older woman had died in that cellar with them, probably from a heart attack, so everyone was shaken by both the storm and her death. Betty and her brother took the children to their family farmhouse in the country, while Mr. Holmes continued to search.

At the Community Building he stumbled over debris to discover no people and no bodies. Next Mr. Holmes climbed into the remains of his mother's house, to again find nothing. Had he lost both his youngest daughter and his mother? He called and called into the night to finally hear Allene call back from the Grants' house. Waves of relief washed over him. Then the two of them slipped and stumbled over the debris until they came to their car a mile away.

After he drove Allene home, Mr. Holmes insisted she go to the hospital, so she and her mother headed south while he returned to Udall to help with the rescue. Allene's mother wanted to take her to the Winfield hospitals, but finding the way blocked, she instead drove to Wellington. There, an X-ray revealed Allene had a broken tailbone, probably from part of a cement block wall falling onto her. The doctors said there wasn't much they could do, just make sure she rested. She and her mother drove back to their farm, the rain coming down through the long night but the lightning lessening.

Meanwhile, in Udall, Mr. Holmes helped dig the wounded and dead out of the rubble, working with others through the night and for most of the next day to search house by house, block by block.

Storm Report from the National Weather Service
Udall, Kansas

Date: May 25, 1955
Time: 2235 to 2238 cst (10:35 to 10:38 p.m.)

UDALL, KANSAS, ABOUT 30 MILES SOUTHEAST OF WICHITA,
UNDERWENT ALMOST COMPLETE DESTRUCTION FROM THE
TORNADO WHICH STRUCK ABOUT 2235 CST. MOTORISTS . . .
REPORTED . . . THE TORNADO FUNNEL APPROACHING UDALL.
IT STRUCK THE SOUTHWEST CORNER OF THE TOWN FIRST,
TRAVELING ALMOST DUE NORTHEAST WITH DESTRUCTION
OCCURRING OVER THE ENTIRE WIDTH OF THE TOWN ABOUT
THREE-FOURTHS OF A MILE. THE ONLY HABITABLE STRUCTURE
LEFT . . . WAS A FRAME DWELLING WITH ONLY MINOR DAMAGE
ON THE EXTREME NORTHWEST EDGE OF TOWN. EXCEPT FOR
A FEW OTHER DWELLINGS . . . THE ONLY BUILDINGS . . . NOT
COMPLETELY LEVELED WERE A FEW TWO-STORY MASONRY
BUILDINGS FROM WHICH THE UPPER STORY HAD BEEN
REMOVED. EVIDENCE OF ROTATION . . . INDICATED A SOUTHWEST
TO NORTHEAST FLOW. . . . DESTRUCTION REQUIRING IMMENSE
FORCES . . . DID YIELD INDICATIONS OF CYCLONIC ROTATION.
A MUNICIPAL WATER TOWER IN THE NORTHWEST PART OF
TOWN WAS TOPPLED TOWARD THE SOUTHWEST. THE CENTER
OF ROTATION PASSED ACROSS AND ALMOST [AT] RIGHT ANGLES
TO A TRAIN OF RAILROAD CARS ON A RAILROAD SIDING. THE
CARS TO THE NORTHWEST OF THE CENTER WERE BLOWN
OFF THE TRACKS TO THE SOUTHWEST AND THE CARS TO THE
SOUTHEAST OF THE CENTER WERE BLOWN TO THE NORTHEAST,
ALTHOUGH SOME CARS BETWEEN (OVER A DISTANCE OF
ABOUT 1½ CITY BLOCKS) WERE STILL ON THE TRACKS.
SOME EVIDENCE WAS FOUND OF "EXPLOSIVE" EFFECTS. A
CONCRETE BLOCK BUILDING ABOUT 30 FEET BY 40 FEET
HAD STOOD IN THE SOUTHWEST PART OF TOWN AND
WAS APPARENTLY NEAR THE PATH OF THE CENTER OF

THE TORNADO. ALL FOUR WALLS HAD FALLEN OUTWARD,
LEAVING THE FLOOR AREA RELATIVELY CLEAR OF DEBRIS.
EYE-WITNESS ACCOUNTS WERE NOT AVAILABLE ... UNTIL
SEVERAL DAYS AFTERWARD BECAUSE OF UNDERSTANDABLE
CONFUSION AND THE SHOCK THAT MOST SURVIVORS SUFFERED.
MR. WHEELER MARTIN, A SURVIVOR FROM UDALL, REPORTED ...
A "ROARING NOISE" AT ABOUT 2220 CST FOLLOWED BY HAIL
AND RAIN. THE WIND WAS FROM THE SOUTHWEST AND
GETTING STRONGER. AFTER A FEW MINUTES, THE HOUSE
BEGAN TO SHAKE. AT 2235 CST IT "COLLAPSED." THE HAIL
CONTINUED FOR SEVERAL MINUTES. BEYOND UDALL, THE
PATH OF MAJOR DESTRUCTION ENDED. SPOTTY DAMAGE
EXTENDED FOR 18 MILES EAST-NORTHEAST OF UDALL.
A CAREFULLY CONDUCTED SURVEY OF DAMAGE ... REVEALED
THAT AT LEAST FROM THE TIME THE TORNADO CROSSED
U.S. HIGHWAY 166 AND THROUGHOUT ITS NORTHWARD
TRAVERSE THROUGH UDALL, A CONTINUOUS PATH OF
DESTRUCTION WAS APPARENT. [BEFORE UDALL] THERE
WAS SOME "SKIPPING" BUT THE GREATEST SKIP WAS ...
3½ MILES. THIS EVIDENCE TOGETHER WITH THE RADAR
EVIDENCE STRONGLY SUGGESTS THAT THIS ONE STORM
HAD A CONTINUOUS PATH FOR MORE THAN 50 MILES.

5 Something Shifted Inside

MAY 26, 1955

2:00 A.M. TO 5:00 A.M.

ON THE GLASS-COVERED SEAT OF HIS FATHER'S CAR, BOBBY ATKINSON listened to the rain on the car roof, and he waited. No one else shined a flashlight on him, no rescuers called his name, so he kept waiting, drifting in and out of consciousness. He wondered what he should do. How long should he wait? How long *could* he wait? Would anyone else come searching? The darkness and long empty hours made it seem unlikely. And every breath hurt.

To the north, a half-mile away, he saw lights at the edge of town. He guessed they were cars on Route K55, one of the main roads into Udall. He watched them flicker. A few cars seemed to turn and park facing the town, toward him, shining their lights onto the ruins like beacons. So Bobby slid out of his shelter into the cold rain. One leg was so sliced up he couldn't walk, and both arms were broken, plus his right hand was mashed and mangled. He was losing blood, he knew, and the pain kept ratcheting him back to clearheadedness. He began to crawl.

Debris covered every surface: bricks and splintered boards from houses, churches, schools; shards of glass from so many windows; the hulking metal frames of cars; toothpicked telephone poles smelling of creosote, their lines snaking through the water. And water covered so much, sometimes just puddles, sometimes in streams a foot deep, water black as the lightless night, water that smelled of gasoline and who knew what else.

A block from his house, at what had been the circular intersection of First and Broadway, Bobby's good hand touched a twisted, metal I beam. Instantly, he knew where he was and what it was—a leg of the water tower, the tower he had climbed and sent signals from, the big U-D-A-L-L hot from the sun. He slumped his body over the leg and then the next, over the wrist-thick cables that had braced them together in giant x's, cables he and his friends had slid on down to the green earth. For a moment he rested, breathing hard and wondering about his friends—Wilmer and Truman and Dale.

Bobby crawled over the third tower leg, skirting the crumpled tank. Then, when he slid over the last I beam, lightning flashed, and he saw a hand connected to a wrist and a forearm but nothing else. Just half of an arm lying there beside the silver I beam.

Where was the rest of the body?

Bobby kept moving.

After he made sure his and Toots's families had found shelter outside of town, Gaillard returned to search for others. He heard the railroad crossing bell before he even got out of a borrowed car. It unsettled him more than he wanted to admit, but he kept moving. Lightning flashed enough to overwhelm him with the destruction.

Gaillard headed west, scrambling over rubble. As a councilman, he knew he had to turn off the gas mainline for the whole town. A small shed protected it, but his flashlight showed no shed; all of it had been blown away by the tornado. Somehow, miraculously, a piece of debris had hit the big lever and turned off the main valve. Gaillard checked to make sure, clasping the emergency cutoff in place. No gas leaked, and none had leaked that he could tell. If it had, any spark from wire or lightning would've exploded into block upon block of fire.

Gaillard stumbled down First Street toward where the tornado struck first. His flashlight illuminated the remains of the Methodist church, a single wall of the parsonage, nothing whole. He found a neighbor who had crawled under his oak table—the whole house gone, except that table, and somehow the man had survived.

Then Gaillard came to a friend sitting at the edge of his yard, Ben Rudd, a retired widower who liked to wear a straw hat on his morning walk to the P.O. Are you all right? Gaillard called out, and Ben said yes, so Gaillard walked on.

He came to the grade school—nothing but scattered bricks. The same with the brand-new high school.

Nearby he found four people lying by the road—a man, a woman, and two children—all of them at odd angles, close to each other, touching, all of them completely naked. Gaillard bent down and found no pulse in any of the bodies.

He breathed hard.

The Karnes family. George, the father, a fellow councilman and manager of the grain elevator, he and his family, newly come to town. Now gone.

Something shifted inside. To Gaillard this felt worse than anything he had seen in the war, worse even than the bodies burned and floating in the sea. This family. These bodies. These children.

Gaillard turned and started walking back.

He found Ben Rudd again, still sitting in his yard. This time, though, Ben didn't respond to his shouts, so Gaillard stepped closer. He saw no blood, but when he touched the old man, he felt only cool skin. No warmth, no pulse. Ben Rudd was dead.

Gaillard started hiking—almost running—back to his family, his breath coming in gasps. He needed to leave. He needed Betty Jo and Sawny and Clinton. He needed to hold them. He'd take them to his father's farm. They would be away from this and safe, he hoped.

With the help of his friend, Mayor Rowe had gotten his son to a Winfield hospital seventeen miles away. There the doctors removed the wire from Gary's neck, and Toots's brother and sister-in-law came to stay with the boy. On Toots's ride back to Udall, he thought about his wife and kids and trusted they had found shelter somewhere close and safe. And he worried about all the people of his small town but especially Lola's parents, Ben and Lydia Satterthwaite. They were eighty and seventy-five-years old, respectively, and lived just three blocks from his home, near the water tower. He couldn't imagine their house surviving the storm.

When they parked at the edge of town, Earl and his friend headed into the rubble, one flashlight between them for some illumination. But the mayor of Udall had trouble navigating—there were no landmarks, no streets or intersections or trees or houses or the water tower that he had looked at every day. All he saw in every direction was flatness, all of it punctuated by two sounds—a car horn that blared unceasingly because a brick wall had collapsed and crushed the car's roof onto the steering wheel; and the continuous *ding-ding, ding-ding* of the railroad crossing, lights blinking, bells going off, and the arms down.

The rain lessened as they climbed over or around banks of boards. A half-mile in, they came to the Satterthwaites' lot. Nothing remained of the house, and rubble filled the basement. Lola's brother, Ira, was there also. He'd come to town to search for his parents.

Two years earlier Toots had helped the Satterthwaites build a small, cinder block shelter in the southwest corner of their basement. The Satterthwaites had called it their cubbyhole, and that's where the men hoped to find the elderly couple.

The men dug with their hands, calling for Ben and Lydia. Finally, Toots heard, Yes, we're in here. The three men dug faster until they could open the door.

Because they kept hearing rain, hail, and thunder, the Satterthwaites hadn't tried to get out, so they didn't know they were trapped. And they didn't know the freight train they heard passing through was really a tornado. Shocked, they climbed out of the remains of their house. Their son took them to his home, where their granddaughter Pat was overjoyed. She clung to her grandmother so hard, she didn't want to let go.

More people heard about the tornado and came to Udall, searching for survivors. Within a half-hour after the storm, someone parked a car so the headlights beamed over the wreckage to serve as searchlights, and by midnight dozens of men had arrived, neighbors and strangers, firemen and police. One of the first was Kansas State Highway patrolman Charles

Miller, who had received word of the tornado at 11:45 p.m. and arrived in Udall by midnight. He, too, shined his headlights into the middle of town. He tried to radio for more help, but static electricity from so much lightning made radio use impossible, so he started to search.

The chaos startled him, not only of the remains of the town but also the rescue effort. No one was in charge. As he stated: "People would come up to me and ask what to do. I didn't know who was in charge and I didn't know what had been done. . . . No one seemed to have any authority." One man didn't want to drive an injured person to the hospital—because the available vehicle wasn't his car. But Miller convinced him to go, so he took off to Winfield in a stranger's car carrying an injured survivor.

Another rescue worker overwhelmed by the destruction was Roy Harris of the Sumner County Sheriff's Office. The day after the storm, he told a reporter that the "sight was the worst I ever want to see. If hell is anything like that I am going to be a saint from this day forward. There were no lights, no nothing, and it was raining. In the darkness—dark as the inside of your hat—you could hear people screaming, moaning, calling for their families. My God, my God, it was terrible."

Thompson, the off-duty Wellington officer who had first called for help, quickly returned to Udall, and he, too, like Patrolman Miller, grew frustrated with the lack of organization. The ambulance drivers, for example, were all parked in a row. The drivers went out to help with the search, while others filled their cars. When an ambulance was full of injured townspeople, often the drivers couldn't be found and the vehicle was blocked by the other, later-arriving ambulances. Men had to go out yelling for all the ambulance drivers to return so the casualties could be carried away. At one point it took thirty minutes to get an ambulance out of the mess. As Officer Thompson later stated, "No one was in charge," and it remained like that until the National Guard and the Red Cross arrived.

When the Cowley County sheriff got word of the disaster, he called in his best dispatcher, Fred Satterthwaite. Fred lived in the county seat, Winfield, but he had been born in Udall. His parents and grandparents still lived there, and Lola and Toots Rowe were his aunt and uncle. The sheriff told Fred that Udall had blown away in a tornado and that he was to get on the radio and call everyone he could. But first Satterthwaite wanted to check on his parents and grandparents. The sheriff told him he'd have other officers see about them, that he needed Fred to stay at his post and get to work on the radio. Satterthwaite called every department in the state of Kansas for assistance—the National Guard, McConnell Air Force Base, the Red Cross, and all the fire and rescue departments throughout the region. An hour or so later, the Sheriff called Fred to tell him his parents and grandparents were all okay. Fred stayed at the switchboard all night, coordinating rescue efforts, relaying calls for help, directing where he could from afar. He didn't leave his post until eleven the next morning.

Fred didn't know until the next day that his wife had also been assisting the rescue efforts. She was a nurse, and after he left, another nurse called her to help. The two rode to Udall in an ambulance to find a town shattered and in total darkness. People stumbled toward their lights, and the nurses did what they could. Mostly, they loaded the wounded into vehicles and rode back and forth to the area hospitals, tending to people while they raced down the long country roads.

The National Guard commander in Wichita received the phone call from Fred Satterthwaite shortly after midnight. He immediately drove to Udall to assess the damage. When he saw the extent of the destruction, he worked through the lightning-caused static on his mobile radio until he reached others and ordered all available men, trucks, and equipment to come at once. Other Guard companies from surrounding towns also mobilized, so that between 1:00 and 1:30 a.m., over three hundred men arrived in Udall. In addition to helping with the search and recovery of injured and dead, the Guardsmen gathered and secured any valuables found in the rubble, and they set up roadblocks at the main roads to control the flow of onlookers and ambulances.

The Wichita Red Cross received word of the disaster around midnight, and the local manager quickly sent rescue and medical teams. They were already en route to Blackwell, Oklahoma, to help with recovery from the tornado, which had touched down there before striking Udall. The Red Cross team switched destinations and arrived in Udall with medical staff and supplies by around 3:00 a.m. Because communication was so difficult, with lines down and lightning causing static interference, the Red Cross manager called ham radio operators in Mulvane, who also soon headed to Udall.

Satterthwaite or the Red Cross also notified the McConnell Air Force Base commander, who mobilized his Disaster Unit. By 2:00 a.m. three air force ambulances carrying twenty-two airmen were headed to Udall. Two hours later two other convoys left McConnell. One headed to Winfield to help set up a temporary shelter in the National Guard Armory. This included trucks hauling cots, mattresses, and blankets. The other convoy headed to Udall with its cargo of heavy machinery and searchlights. In all, the Red Cross immediately sent 25 medical persons and the air force 150 men. Some of these rescue workers were World War II veterans; they said Udall looked worse than anything they'd ever seen in combat.

Civil defense patrols joined the search, and they and firemen from Wichita, Winfield, and other towns brought huge spotlights, illuminating sections of the devastation. The movie giant Columbia Pictures was shooting the film *Picnic* nearby, and the director sent a pair of large spotlights. But all these lights only did so much; they couldn't reach the darkest corners.

A northbound Continental Bus arrived in Udall on time for its scheduled stop at 11:59 p.m., only to find blocked streets and no town. Several passengers got off to help rescuers. When the driver knew he couldn't wait any longer without getting into trouble, he beeped his horn to signal to his riders it was time to keep going. One man didn't reboard, choosing instead to stay in Udall to help through the night.

Another of the first to arrive was Oliver Stone, a former Udall resident. As he scrambled over debris, he spotted an infant lying in the street, alive but barely. He wrapped the child in his coat, feeling the cold fingers and nose, the wet skin. How long had it cried in that torrential rain? Probably several hours. The baby died on the way to the Winfield hospital.

Rescuers pulled Toots's neighbor Mrs. Butcher from under her house. She was severely injured, as were two of her children. Nearby they found the bodies of her husband and two sons, one of them fifteen-year-old Wilmer, Bobby Atkinson's friend.

Through the chaos and rain and lightning-shattered darkness, men gathered the bodies, dead and alive, and carried them to the edge of town. Often the cries of the injured called out. On the north side of town, near where the ambulances gathered, six bodies lay in ditches. As the rescuers worked to save the living, they had to pass these dead bodies for several hours. Finally, some men found blankets to cover the remains.

As one rescuer described the night, "[It] was raining so hard we couldn't see or couldn't breathe or anything else when we started rescuing people. . . . There wasn't much we could [do], only to start covering them up and keep them as dry as possible. . . . There wasn't much to do anything with or to put them into."

The living found room in a railroad bunk car turned into a first aid station, or they piled into automobiles that sped them to area hospitals. A farmer drove his flatbed truck to town, and this became the crude repository for the dead. When there was no more room, one of the National Guard trucks started to fill with more corpses, until it reached capacity at twenty-four. There, on that truck, Toots saw a coworker, a man he had planned to carpool with to the oil rig the night before. Eventually, Toots would learn that every one of the seven men in Eddie's Pool Hall had been killed.

All during that long night, no one knew how many people were missing, and often the rescuers didn't know to which hospital the living were being sent. As Toots and others searched, newcomers approached to ask, Have you seen my mother or aunt, my brother or son? Do you know if they survived? Sometimes the rescuers could answer; often they could not. So the newcomers either joined the search—a new flashlight bobbing with the others, a new voice calling out—or they returned to their cars to travel the long, straight roads to a hospital in Wichita or Winfield, hoping the rescuers had told them right, that their loved ones were among the living.

After Mr. Holmes found his daughter, Allene, he returned to look for others, his friends and neighbors. Yet several times he wasn't sure he wanted to go on searching. Often it took two men to carry the heavy bodies, the searchers scrambling backward and sideways through debris. The southwest part of town, near the schools, where the tornado hit first, had the most casualties, and it was at least a half-mile from the main gathering place. They used tarps to carry the corpses between them. Then they had to heave the weight of the dead onto the flatbed truck.

The hardest to carry were the children. They weighed the most in memory. Mr. Holmes found a young boy, maybe six years old. Clothing gone, his arms and legs mangled, and his head. . . . How do you carry a child whose head is almost severed from his body?

Another child, an infant, was found by a railroad worker named George Curtis, a World War II vet and part Choctaw Indian. As Curtis later told a reporter: "I took the baby and handed him to some people in a car. The baby was crying. The mother was dead."

Curtis also told the reporter that he saw many bodies ripped apart by the tornado. He had been a machine gunner in nine South Pacific battles. In all that combat, he had never seen anything like this destruction.

Curtis belonged to a crew of gandy dancers, men who worked for the Atchison, Topeka & Santa Fe Railway, building and maintaining the tracks. For several hot days in late May, these men had lifted steel and swung sledges to lay a side rail for the grain elevator. Twenty-eight of them, along with their three cooks, slept in three old coach cars. The foreman slept in his own car. By ten thirty at night, most were asleep, with a few reading or listening to the storm. They all woke to the roar of the tornado.

Their work train had several cars—a coal car plus others holding equipment and supplies. To the north of the bunk cars, the tornado twisted six of these cars, including the coal car, off the tracks toward the southwest. To the south of the bunk cars, the tornado twisted two more cars off the tracks in the opposite direction, toward the northeast. And it toppled the eight-story Udall elevator across the railroad. A massive part of this structure crushed these two railroad cars, one of which held the foreman. Yet in the middle of this work train, the three bunk cars still stood erect. The tornado blew out the windows and tore open the doors, but every one of the thirty-two men survived, including the foreman, who managed to crawl out of his car.

Anyone hurt? he called out over the thunder and wind. A few of the men had cuts from glass; otherwise, they all were fine. The crew split into smaller groups and spread out to search for others. They had only a few flashlights, but they found more in one of the blown-out stores. Soon they heard cries for help from above what used to be a restaurant. It was an older couple, the owners, who lived on the second floor. The outside fire escape was twisted, but a few of the gandy dancers climbed up to free the couple from the fallen walls and debris. They helped them back to the bunk cars, which quickly became shelter for many of the injured. The railroad workers built fires in their stoves and covered the naked with jackets and blankets. They threw mattresses against the open windows to keep out the cold rain. They made coffee for the growing number of stunned townspeople who stumbled to their cars.

Another survivor who quickly became a searcher was Gene Beard. He and his wife rented an old house on the north edge of town. When the tornado struck, they frantically slipped between the mattress and springs of their bed, their only shelter. In all the storm's roaring, they felt the house shake and shift, and they heard the windows shatter. They also heard booms and cracks as debris flew overhead. Somehow they survived. When the worst seemed to have passed, they crawled out and shined their flashlight beam over the wreckage. Right above their bed, the light revealed a sharp-edged disc blade. The storm had hurled it through the outside wall to lodge in this interior wall right at head height. It could have easily decapitated one or both of them.

Their house was too damaged to remain in it, so they hurried through the rain to the house of a neighbor, Mrs. Kennedy, which was still standing. Many others gathered there as well.

Soon afterward, Gene's friend Jay Lacey showed up. He lived in the southern part of town, where the damage was the worst. He was bleeding badly from deep wounds, and his leg was broken. By sheer will he had managed to limp the three-quarters of a mile to Mrs. Kennedy's. Jay's wife, Jewell, and their two-year-old daughter were still back at what remained of their house. Because Jewell had several large cuts and she was eight months pregnant, she couldn't climb over all the rubble. Jay asked Gene to return to his house to bring her to Mrs. Kennedy's, so Gene and another friend headed out through the wind and pounding rain. Even with a flashlight, they stumbled and fell, and everywhere they heard people moaning and screaming for help.

The men found Jewell and her daughter, but Jewell was hardly able to walk. Gene picked her up, her pregnant body heavy in his arms. The other man carried the child, all four of them drenched and weaving through the rubble by the light of the constant lightning. They walked northward, maybe hiking a mile, to the flashing lights of an ambulance that carried the two away.

Gene choked down his fear and headed back out into the destroyed town. He was a veteran of the Korean War; he had already experienced horror. It hadn't been too long since he had returned from a hospital in Japan, where he spent three months recovering from a severe neck wound he had sustained while fighting in heavy combat. In his words, he "wasn't ready for any more activity right then," and yet, as he carried Jewell through that rubble, he had heard all those other people calling out, and he knew he had to try to help. So he turned around and headed back into the town's remains. He found Ben Rudd, the retired farmer Gaillard had also spoken to, maybe just minutes earlier. Gaillard had thought Rudd not badly wounded and moved on. Gene, though, found Ben Rudd lying on his side struggling. He leaned down to talk to him, to try to help, but instead, he witnessed Ben Rudd breathing his last breath.

Gene turned and found other men nearby working to rescue a young woman named Marilyn Foote. She screamed in pain, part of a roof covering her. When rescuers lifted the roof and pulled her out, they found a board had punctured and shattered her leg. Two stretcher-bearers carried her north to an ambulance.

Gene Beard worried about his parents. They lived two miles north of Udall on an isolated farm. He borrowed a car and drove out to find the windows dark but the buildings all standing and undamaged. He had to yell and bang on the door to wake them. He told them of the tornado, and they didn't believe him. His mom even asked if he was drunk. When they realized the truth, Gene's dad wanted to check on his friends, the Harveys, who lived on the south side of Udall. Gene and his dad drove back to Udall and climbed through the rubble to find Ed Harvey in shock and hurt but not badly. His wife, Anna, though, lay on the ground, naked and mangled. Gene found a rug and covered her from the pouring rain. And then the three men crouched beside her as she breathed her last.

Gene carried Anna Harvey's body, while his dad helped Ed navigate through the debris. They came to the main intersection, where search-lights illuminated the area, and an ambulance took Ed Harvey away. Gene asked a group of men where he should put Anna Harvey's body. They pointed to an army flatbed truck. On it the dead bodies were piled up like cordwood. He tried to gently lay Anna's body beside another. That other body, Gene realized, was Eddie Taylor, the pool hall operator and friend, a World War II vet who walked with a cane. Just that morning Gene had seen Eddie walking in town, and they had waved to each other.

And now Eddie was gone.

That night Gene Beard witnessed the deaths of nine people.

Every ambulance in Wichita, except two on reserve, headed to Udall. Other towns also sent emergency vehicles, filling the countryside with the sounds of sirens all night long. Private vehicles also carried the wounded, and at one point a bread truck served as an ambulance.

The closest hospitals to Udall were St. Mary's and William Newton, both in Winfield, over seventeen miles to the south. Most of the wounded were taken there, but no system existed in the effort to rescue survivors, and no one recorded who went where. Drivers had to decide where to go based on what they heard about the status of hospitals or what they thought of the roads—which hospitals were overcrowded?— which roads were passable? Only streets in the larger towns were paved, so all roads from Udall were gravel or sometimes slick mud. As a result, some ambulance drivers took survivors to St. Luke's Hospital in Wellington, twenty-three miles to the southwest, or north to the three hospitals in

Wichita, twenty-eight miles away. In total that night, seven hospitals received over three hundred Udall survivors and dead.

A friend of Gaillard Thompson named Bob Clements worked for a mortuary in Wichita. When Clements heard of the tornado, he drove his ambulance to what was left of Udall. He found the gathering point near the railroad tracks, where men helped him load the injured into his vehicle. They just kept loading and loading into the back and front, as many as would fit.

Finally, Clements headed south toward Winfield. He was driving down County Road 3 at a good clip when he came upon a farmer's grain bin sitting in the middle of the road. He braked hard and swerved, the moans rising from the back. He made it around the debris but barely.

In Winfield, Clements pulled into William Newton Hospital, next to two other ambulances, with another right behind him. The orderlies and nurses helped him unload—unconscious children; crying children; naked, moaning men; silent, shocked women. As the staff pulled the last person out, the orderly in charge said, Nineteen. Clements had transported nineteen people.

Inside the hospital, they had trouble finding enough space for the injured. So many already filled all the rooms that the orderlies had to settle them in the halls. There were at least one hundred injured, someone told Clements as he headed to his ambulance to drive that long dark road back to Udall.

Once or twice more through the night, Beth Morgan's father and his friend came back to their families at the Grants' house to report what they'd seen—this house was gone or so-and-so's was nothing but a slab of cement. As the rain eased, others arrived to collect their families. But then Mr. Morgan didn't return. Soon the only people left from the wedding shower were the bride-to-be, Aileen Holtje, her mother and two sisters, and Beth Morgan and her mother.

Aileen's father showed up, worried and looking for his family. On his farm he had lost a huge grain bin and several trees, but he had no idea there'd been a tornado, not until he made it through several flooded streams to find a flattened Udall.

Since Mr. Morgan was still out searching, Mrs. Holtje told Beth and her mother to come with them to their farm. When the group walked out of the house, the night had quieted. Mist rose in pockets. No sound of the thunder lingered. The Morgan women traveled in a crowded car several miles out into the country, where they stayed until the next morning.

6   Bigness of Heart

AFTER THREE HOURS OF CRAWLING THROUGH A HALF-MILE OF DEBRIS, Bobby Atkinson made it to the White Eagle Service Station. A man Bobby recognized as a customer at his family's grocery stood by the road. He was a farmer roughly his father's age named Roy Cole. He had come to town from his home a few miles north to find his daughter, Marlene, who lived near the Methodist church. She sat in the back seat of Roy's brand new '55 Buick, holding a towel to the side of her head.

Roy looked at Bobby. "Get in there," he pointed to his car. "I'll take you to the hospital."

Bobby shook his head, which throbbed at the movement. He held up his bloody hand. "I'm not getting in that brand-new car and messing it all up."

"Just get in there before I beat your ass," Roy said. So Bobby did. With Roy's help, Bobby dragged his leg into the back seat, beside Marlene. All he had on was the waistband of his underwear, so he tried to shield himself.

"I lost my ear," Marlene told Bobby. She held the towel away from her head to reveal the bloody hole.

"Sorry to hear that," he said.

"You're looking a little rough too," she said as Roy slammed his door and drove.

Because of the two-by-two in his back, Bobby couldn't lean against the seat, so he rode to Winfield hanging onto the front seat right beside Roy. And Bobby held onto the seat with his good hand as tight as he could as

Roy pushed the gas to the floor and pinned the speedometer at ninety. When they got to Winfield, Roy backed off a little, but still, they flew down Ninth Street at eighty miles an hour. Bobby thought he was going to die before he even got to the hospital.

But they made it, finally, to St. Mary's Hospital in Winfield, at 5:30 a.m., seven hours after the tornado.

Dorothy M. Bixler, administrator and head nurse at William Newton Memorial Hospital, got the call to report to work immediately after the first load of victims arrived at 11:45 p.m. This was everyone's first knowledge of the tornado, and she, like so many other nurses, doctors, and staff, rushed to help. Bixler arrived at the ER in ten minutes, and the second load of patients arrived five minutes after her, right at midnight. For the next four and half hours, a continuous stream of vehicles brought more and more victims.

As Bixler later told a reporter, "These patients were cold, wet, muddy, and in a stunned, shocked condition." The staff covered all of them with blankets as the doctors evaluated them. They sent some to surgery, some to beds to be monitored, and the less injured were transported to a nearby Red Cross shelter. Area motels also opened their doors for the newly homeless.

Every available person associated with the hospital was called in, including all volunteers and graduate students. Every available bed was filled and every available space filled with beds and patients, including surgery, recovery, lounges, and hallways. The total number of people who came through the Emergency Room that night easily exceeded 100—of whom 70 were admitted to the hospital—more than doubling its patient count. The hospital's official capacity stood at 100, yet by early morning it had admitted well over that number, and its records showed they had 129 patients.

At one point early the next day, the doctors ran out of X-ray film, so they called the state patrol and requested that they bring more film from a hospital in Wichita with great urgency.

By 5:00 p.m. the next day, the last operation ended. Doctors and nurses put down their instruments and rested. They had performed surgeries for seventeen continuous hours.

In the Emergency Room of St. Mary's Hospital, the triage doctor assessed the wounded as they arrived, while nurses and orderlies moved them about. The doctor saw Bobby Atkinson's back and all the blood and yelled a code that made the orderlies come scrambling with a gurney. Again, Bobby couldn't lay on his back, so they gingerly helped him onto his side. Every time the two-by-two jostled or bumped against something, Bobby bit his tongue to hold back a scream.

Bobby barely registered the hallways—how they were lined with people, wounded lying on pallets on the floor.

In the operating room, a nurse started an IV, and the anesthesiologist did his work. Soon Bobby drifted off to numbness. The two-by-two board had nearly gone all the way through his body, so the surgeons cut and pulled it out. But they could do little for Bobby's punctured lung and kidneys and five broken ribs. These the body would have to slowly heal by itself. The doctors focused on the debris-gouged back, quickly cleaning and threading over one hundred stitches to piece his back together. Several wounds—like the two-by-two puncture—were too deep, so these they sutured only partially, leaving small holes for the wounds to seep and drain. They would suture them all again later.

Doctors covered the hole in Bobby's fractured skull with a metal plate. They cleaned and stitched his lacerated leg. They set, pinned, and put casts on both arms, so that he had casts from shoulders to fingers, right and left. His right hand was so mangled that the doctors only put a temporary cast on it. When they finally finished, the surgeons had spent eight hours working on Bobby.

The morning after, the sun rose into a clear sky. A few strands of fog went from blue to pink to white as the sun gradually burned them away. Puddles held the sky's colors—first the mercury of early dawn, then the sunrise's brief rainbow, ending in the plain reflection of a cloudless sky.

Slowly, the searchers' flashlights blinked off, Toots Rowe still among them. The men shared information—where they had searched; who they had found, dead or alive; who was still missing; and where they needed help. The moisture from the storm turned into humidity, turned into sweat. Rain slickers got thrown aside, gloves put back on if they had them; most did not.

The sun revealed so much more than their flashlights and spotlights. As one journalist wrote, "Anything could be found wrapped around trees—cars, clothing, pieces of roofs, and furniture." Pianos had keyboards but nothing else. Bedsprings hung from branches. Massive trees looked like they'd been cut at the ground with a chainsaw. The ones that still stood had few limbs and no bark. All that remained of the elementary school was the entrance. The brand-new high school was not much better. Cars lay upside down or on top of each other or flattened under buildings. The frame of one pickup hung in a cottonwood. No one knew the whereabouts of the rest of the truck or its owner.

A reporter asked Toots how he felt. "It still all seems like a dream," he replied. "I still can't believe that it's all happened—that so many of my friends and neighbors are dead or injured, that we don't have a town to live in, that a number of them probably still lie buried beneath the rubble." He paused. "My house just floated away. I don't know where it is." He looked around. "There's nothing left." He repeated, "There's nothing left."

In that brief confession, Toots captured the shock that everyone felt.

The shock also soon carried a certain smell. Toots and the others had to work around the bodies of dead cows and other livestock, some flat on their sides, others in contorted positions. There were many, all carried by the tornado and dropped along its path—some right in town, others far out in fields. Rain had slicked their black-and-white hides. Soon they would bloat. Soon the stench would be unbearable.

Other animals somehow survived the storm, including chickens that were completely de-feathered. A veterinarian assisted by a young airman from McConnell tried to help the animals that they could. They pulled splinters of wood from hides or cleaned wounds where chunks of flesh had been gouged out. Some cattle even had horns broken off by the tornado. On most of the wounded animals, the vet applied a liquid antiseptic and then moved on. Some animals had to be put down.

A block from Toots's house, the eight-story Udall elevator lay across the Atchison, Topeka & Santa Fe railroad tracks, crushing two railcars.

Bulldozer operators had started working to clear the tracks in the early-morning hours so that by sunset the next day the first train was able to travel through the town but at a much slower rate.

Other power equipment soon arrived—bulldozers, shovels, and cranes from area towns and private excavators, from McConnell Air Force Base and the Kansas Turnpike Authority. Many of the operators wanted to start right in, but Toots Rowe said not yet. He wanted to make sure no bodies, dead or alive, might still be buried in the rubble, especially of the homes. So all day Thursday, the dozen or so bulldozers idled or worked on clearing streets already thoroughly searched by the crews of volunteers.

At each homesite, whatever searchers found that might have any value—furniture, clothing, books—they placed at the front of the lot for the owners to collect. More valuable items, such as car keys and eye-glasses, safe boxes and jewelry, and especially wallets, purses, and money, filled a guarded truck. Individuals wanting to make a claim had to prove their identity and identify what they had lost. Mayor Rowe believed that no looting had taken place, but others weren't so sure.

Meteorologists knew the Udall tornado would rank as the worst yet in state history. One National Weather Bureau expert at the time even said, "This storm far eclipses anything in Kansas." The previous worst storm in terms of casualties had happened in Sedgewick County, near Wichita, in 1917. That tornado killed twelve people, and like the Udall tornado, it also occurred on May 25. And this 1955 storm didn't just hit Udall. Across the southern plains that night, storm cells spawned several tornadoes that killed over one hundred people.

Another Weather Bureau official, Victor Phillips, chief meteorologist for the Wichita office, toured Udall the day after the tornado. He told a reporter: "I don't see how the town can survive. The schools are gone and there's not an undamaged building left. . . . I don't see how there will ever be a town there again. It will take a complete rebuilding."

On the Weather Bureau's part in predicting the storm, Phillips said, "I think we did an excellent job last night in disseminating the storm information." He pointed out that TV and radio outlets have the burden of getting word out about severe weather—and, he emphasized, people have to take storm warnings seriously. The reporter didn't question why the Weather Bureau waited to include Wichita in its storm warning area until later in the day. Nor did the reporter question why none of the warning areas had included Udall.

Phillips's confidence in the Weather Bureau's work belies an interesting history, especially when it comes to tornadoes. In the mid-1880s Sergeant John P. Finley of the U.S. Army Signal Corps (the Weather Bureau's predecessor) studied tornadoes in hopes of being able to forecast them. He organized over two thousand "reporters," who sent him information about severe, tornado-causing storms. He then mapped and plotted weather patterns. Finley began issuing "alerts" but only for a few years. His superiors, bowing to political pressure, decided "the word 'tornado' provoked undue fear amongst the public." So Finley's work halted, and "little progress was made in the understanding and forecasting of severe local storms in the United States during the first part of the 1900s." It seemed the Weather Bureau believed if they didn't say this word, maybe they wouldn't have to deal with these storms or a paranoid public.

The Weather Bureau banned the use of the word *tornado* for several decades, until 1938, when it officially changed this policy. But the fear pervaded, and "few forecasts made mention of tornados during the 1940s." Eventually, forecasters in the air force had success. In 1948, for the first time, they predicted a tornado. That pushed the Weather Bureau to improve, and finally, the word *tornado* became more widely used.

But the success in prediction still had, and has, a long way to go. The second Severe Weather Warning issued at 4:36 p.m. on May 25, 1955, did use the word *tornado*, but the head weatherman admitted later that the bureau had waited to use the word because they didn't want panicked Kansans calling their office and jamming the lines. And the area of this second "warning" did not include the town of Udall.

While the Weather Bureau's official surveyed the destruction on the day after the storm, the Red Cross established a temporary headquarters in what remained of the Udall bank. There it began to compile a list of the survivors and the dead. By 10:00 a.m., May 26, Southwestern Bell, the phone company out of Wichita, installed two temporary phone lines to the Red Cross field office. One phone was for public use, including journalists, who shouted their reports as fast as they could to their editors. The other line went directly to the main Red Cross office in Wichita. This caused some controversy and jealousy among others who wanted to use it but weren't allowed. The Red Cross field manager in charge maintained that this direct line was needed in order to organize the lists of the missing and dead and to aid the wounded as best possible. Even with these lines, though, shortwave radio operators connected to other ham radios in Winfield and elsewhere, helping to compile lists of casualties from hospitals and send them back to Udall. Slowly, the lists of dead and survivors grew, as did the list of the missing. One official said it might take two days before everyone was accounted for.

During this immediate time after the tornado, the Red Cross also set up its many committees to handle various logistics. In Wichita this included a Blood Service unit that accepted blood donations and sent them to surrounding hospitals. In Udall more and more Red Cross social workers arrived to set up field tents and administer relief. They served as messengers for storm victims to connect with their families. The social workers also registered and interviewed storm victims, assessing what they had lost and what they needed. Some survivors found this process cold and uncaring, especially when compared to how the Salvation Army treated them, but the Red Cross maintained this process was needed to root out fraud, to address the greatest needs first, and to serve the whole community fairly.

The Salvation Army arrived in Udall by 2:00 or 2:30 a.m., right after the storm, and like everyone else, it assisted immediately with the search and rescue. As more and more of the missing became accounted for, its focus shifted to helping with recovery. By early Thursday morning, both the Red Cross and Salvation Army had set up canteens on opposite sides of First Street. In addition, the Salvation Army began dispensing clothing, bedding, and furniture to tornado victims. Unlike the Red Cross, however, its workers asked no questions; they just gave food and other items to anyone.

Udall city clerk John Arbuckle had been paralyzed in a swimming accident as a teenager, so he used crutches to get around. He rented a room with Lora and Lester Grant, and the three of them had survived the tornado in their cave. Arbuckle's sister came to Udall shortly after the storm to take John to her house in another town, but as they were driving out of town, John saw Toots searching through the rubble and rolled down his window. They greeted each other, talked about how each had survived, then John asked the mayor what he was going to do.

"This is my home and I plan to live here," Toots said, unequivocally, no hesitation. "I'm going to rebuild and stay."

"Well, if you are, then I am too," Arbuckle said. "I'm staying too." He got out of the car right then, using his crutches to maneuver over the debris. He couldn't help with the search, but he could still be a record keeper, a source of information on the dead and injured. Toots found him a place to sit near where bodies were being collected, and the city clerk went back to work.

Another friend of Toots's and also a city employee, Wayne Keely, met Rowe during the search. Keely was the city marshal—he knew and loved this town. The two men shook hands, and Keely told of how he had gone to the store to buy a soda for his daughter when a friend walked out of the pool hall and said that the severe weather warnings had been called off. The bright moon lit Keely's way home, but when he looked to the southwest, he could see the storm clouds rolling in. He wasn't sure he believed whoever had called off the storm warning.

For a while Keely watched TV with his daughter and her friends. Then he heard the roar. He yelled for everyone to get into the cave, and he closed the cellar door just before the tornado hit. As they sat in the dark, his wife lit a candle. They listened to the storm above, the pounding rain and hail, the ripping, smashing wind. Slowly, the candle's flame grew taller and taller. Keely guessed it reached ten inches before it flickered out.

Keely's wife asked if it was the train whistle they were hearing. Wayne shook his head and said the train had already traveled through; it was a tornado. As it passed over, Keely's daughter feared the cave would collapse on top of them, it was shaking so much. Dust filled the small space, making it hard to breathe.

Then the roaring subsided, and Keely opened the cellar door, shoving boards and bricks out of the way.

"What's it look like?" his wife asked.

"I don't think there's ten people left in Udall alive," he said. Nothing was left. In the lightning flashes, he saw no houses, few trees. He could see all the way to the other side of town, over twelve blocks away. Right beside him, the remains of his house had crushed his police car. And in his front yard, the tornado had hung the frame of a Chevy pickup twenty feet high in the fork of what remained of a tree. The truck's body, as a *New York Times* reporter later described it, "was wadded up like tinfoil."

Keely had a sense that others would want to know what time this happened, so when the lightning flashed again, he looked at his watch. It read 10:38.

After the storm Toots and Keely stood amid the rubble, both wondering how they had survived. Then Toots told of how he and his family had dug out of their collapsed house and climbed down into the cave with the Thompsons. We were lucky, the men agreed. Very lucky.

The two men talked of who had been killed, neighbors and friends. Keely talked about how hard it was trying to identify people because of the extent of their injuries. "People you'd known all your life, you couldn't tell who they were," he said. And sometimes the living were so covered with mud that the only way to identify them was by the sound of their voices.

Then Toots asked Keely, "What are you going to do?"

Keely said, "I'm gonna build somewhere else."

"The hell you are," Toots answered. "You're gonna build right back here."

Keely eventually agreed.

Many, like Arbuckle and Keely, heard Toots and stayed on because of him. They picked up his words—*I'm going to rebuild*—and made a refrain of hope, resilience, and determination.

7 People Will Return

AT ST. MARY'S HOSPITAL, BOBBY SLOWLY WOKE FROM HIS SURGERY. He felt pain all over but numbed pain, pain nothing like what he had felt right after the storm. Both arms felt heavy, and he couldn't move his legs, and the thin blanket didn't keep the cool air off his body. But he was alive, he knew that much.

As the orderlies wheeled him toward his room, Bobby saw others lying on gurneys lining the long hallway. The tornado had injured so many that the hospital had run out of rooms. On one gurney, Bobby recognized a schoolmate with matted blonde hair—Barbara Braddy. In that moment of recognition, he also saw her leg, the stub of it. The bloody huge knuckle of her knee.

In his room someone told him that Barbara had lost her little brother. Bobby wondered about his own brothers, Gary and Stanley. Wondered where they were. If they were alive.

That first night Barbara Braddy screamed and cried and moaned. All night long she filled the hall and all the rooms with her wails.

Beth Morgan and her mother woke early the next morning in the Holtje farmhouse. As they ate breakfast with Aileen and her family, they talked about Beth's father, Cecil, and Aileen's fiancé, Roy. They still hadn't heard from either one.

Because Roy worked at the Arkansas City newspaper on the other end of the county, Aileen expected that he would've heard about the tornado shortly after it happened. But he'd have no idea if Aileen was alive—the phone lines were down and would be for days. Had he gone to Udall to find the rubble heap of the Community Building? She hoped he would come to the farm. Shortly after breakfast, he did.

Roy had gotten off work at midnight and driven the thirty miles north to Udall, meeting ambulance after ambulance racing the other way. He knew it would be bad, and still, he was shocked. Even in the dark, he could see how complete the tornado's destruction had been. The rubble of the Community Building revealed no bodies, but he couldn't be sure because the debris was so thick. He heard rumors that all the women at the wedding shower had been killed. At dawn Roy left Udall and drove to find Aileen, her sisters, and mother cut and bruised but alive.

For Beth and her mother, it'd been over twelve hours since they last saw Cecil. What had happened to him? Had he gotten injured while trying to search for others?

Beth's oldest sister lived on the other side of Udall. Mr. Holtje offered to take the two Morgan women there—maybe Beth's father was there, and it would be a good place to stay. As they traveled northward on County 16, they came within sight of the town. Out of habit, they looked for the water tower, only to register the empty space and the loss of trees no longer lining the streets. Then they saw the twisted I beams of the new high school's gymnasium, the pile of bricks where Beth had hoped to graduate the next year. The car filled with silence.

When the National Guard had arrived in Udall that night, the soldiers quickly took over the search and rescue. By dawn they had made most of the searchers leave. This angered many who had worked all night to rescue others. These were friends and neighbors helping each other, yet here came strangers pushing them out. We don't want any looting was their rationale.

So that morning, at the edge of town, Mr. Holtje had to stop the car; army trucks blocked the road. Three National Guard soldiers greeted them. No, they said, you can't travel through town. You'll have to go around.

Mr. Holtje headed west and north on country roads to arrive finally at Beth Morgan's sister's. The tornado had broken out windows and ripped off the front porch, but everyone in her sister's family was alive and unhurt. Yet no one knew anything about Beth's father. They didn't know if he had continued searching for survivors in Udall or if he had been hurt and gone to a hospital. It was unlike him to not send word. Finally, after further searching, a friend told them he had had a cut on his head and had been taken for stitches to the Emergency Room at the Newton Hospital in Winfield.

At some point in the middle of that first day, Mr. Morgan arrived at his older daughter's home in the country. He was exhausted and soaked and had white gauze wrapped around his head to cover a cut above his eye. It was shaped like the corner of a cement block, he told them, one from the Community Building. And oh, he was happy to see them all. He fell asleep quickly, and when he woke a few hours later, he and Beth's mother drove into town to assess the damage of their house. They hoped the National Guard would let them enter. And no, they said to Beth, you don't have shoes, you can't go along. You might cut your feet.

Late that first evening after the storm, Beth Morgan's parents returned from Udall; the soldiers had recognized Cecil Morgan and allowed them through the blockade. Her parents avoided telling her of the deaths, instead focusing on what they had found. Because their house sat in the northwest part of town and out of the fiercest winds, it had survived, they told her. The wind had broken out every window, blown off all the shingles, and shifted the house on its foundation. But it was salvageable, her dad said. Rain had poured through the open windows and soaked the new living room furniture. Her mother had saved up her teacher's salary and had only just bought the sofa and chairs. But, she said, they could be saved. They'd have to repaper the walls, a job they had just completed. Her mother's new sewing machine, her first electric one, was a muddy mess, but it could be cleaned up, they hoped.

They decided to repair their home. The house Beth had known all her life was one of the few still standing in Udall after the storm.

"Looks like someone stole my Indian pennies," Beth's father said. He had had a quart jar full of them. Another can of coins had survived the tornado sitting right beside the penny jar, so he couldn't imagine the storm taking one and not the other. But why would a person take one and not the other as well?

Then Mr. Morgan said in surprise, "And right in the middle of the living room floor sat a roast pan from Mrs. Binford's five houses away."

"Your favorite skirt," Beth's mother told her, "the one I made with box pleats, the one I'd just ironed—it's gone," her mother said. "I'm sorry." She had hung it on the outside of the closet, and the tornado had torn it away. The rest of her clothes in the closet survived, but the skirt was gone.

Her father also told her about Mary Taylor, the neighbor who baked cakes and pies and lived across the street from the Morgan's with her family, including her son, Eddie, the pool hall owner. The Taylor home was a large two-story house with a barn in the back, where the Morgan's kept a horse and two cows, cows that Mr. Morgan milked twice a day, every day, sharing the milk with the Taylors. And Mrs. Taylor, the telephone operator, the friend and neighbor Beth had wanted to spend the evening with, to learn her new summer job—

"Well," Mr. Morgan paused, "the telephone building is gone, and so is Mrs. Taylor."

"But," he added, "her house survived."

Joe Morris was the Cowley County coroner, and Udall was in his jurisdiction. With his brother, Paul, Joe also owned and operated the Morris Funeral Home, one of two funeral homes in Winfield. When they heard about the tornado, Joe sped in their ambulance to Udall, where his car quickly filled. He made the thirty-two-mile trip to Udall and back three times in the night, carrying injured early on and then, later, the dead.

Paul stayed in Winfield to take care of the bodies. All night they came. One National Guard truck brought in twenty-four corpses, which alone overwhelmed the capacity of both Winfield funeral homes. Yet the corpses kept coming. By the next day sixty bodies filled the two mortuaries.

The Morrises needed help, so they sent out an emergency call. Soon other morticians arrived from across the region, from Topeka to the north and Tulsa to the south, driving hours to bring their skills as well as much needed embalming supplies.

As they worked through the next days preparing the dead for burial, the Morris brothers tried to interpret the story of the dead—how did they die? And who exactly were they? When a family member came in to search for loved ones, Joe or Paul took them to the rows of bodies, lifting each sheet to reveal a cold face. If one corpse proved to be a missing parent or child or relative, the Morris brothers tried to comfort the family. The morticians also, tactfully, had to encourage those who had lost family members to bury their dead as quickly as possible. "It isn't a lack of respect," Paul Morris repeatedly told the families and a reporter. "It's in keeping with the whole emergency." Digging so many graves and organizing so many services would take time and coordination.

He also told the reporter that a day after the tornado, only thirty-four of the sixty bodies had been identified.

The morning after the tornado, Gaillard, Betty Jo, and Gaillard's mother parked at the edge of what remained of Udall. Nothing looked the same. No water tower, no grain elevator. For a while Gaillard felt disoriented. All the familiar landmarks had disintegrated.

As they walked, they came to a house still standing, a large two-story on the corner of First and Clark. The Seamans had lived here for many years, Betty Jo's aunt and uncle. They ran out and hugged Betty Jo and shook Gaillard's hand. They had survived the storm in their house, they told them, even though the tornado had shifted it far off its foundation. The house looked precarious, like it might shift some more, yet people milled about inside. Gaillard nodded to the others—some he knew, many he didn't—rescuers and reporters and who knew who else.

Toots Rowe was there, and Gaillard was glad to see him. Toots told him about Dick and Mammie Stone, Gaillard's cousins and good friends. Instead of running to the neighbor's shelter, the Stones had stayed in their house. "Mammie got a piece of pipe driven into her," Earl said. "That's what killed her." Dick was in the hospital.

Betty Jo's aunt and uncle Sadie and Henry Storey also didn't make it, Toots told them. The Storeys had just retired from farming and moved to Udall a year or so ago to a house with wide porches just west of the water tower. The shadow of the tower covered their house every morning as the sun rose. Little was found of the house; the storm had so demolished it. Searchers found their bodies near the high school gym, several blocks away.

And the tornado had killed both of Gaillard and Betty Jo's neighbors Emmie Foulk and Cynthia Walker, the woman bound to a wheelchair who lived under Emmie's care. Emmie had taught Gaillard and Betty Jo's daughter, Sawny, how to make rag rugs. They had been good neighbors, and Emmie had been Toots and Lola's close kin. The searchers found the women's bodies lying against the foundation of Emmie's house.

In the few blocks right around the Rowes' and Thompsons' houses, the tornado had killed twenty-six people.

For a moment Gaillard and Toots stood in silence trying to comprehend so much loss. Then Gaillard told his friend he was sorry to hear of so many but especially of Emmie Foulk.

The Thompsons walked on, crossing the train tracks with the railcars twisted and lying on their sides, past the rubble of the downtown stores. The town was quiet. No car motors, no hum of electricity through the lines, no wind in the trees—because there were no trees.

The Thompsons came to their lot, only a bare slab of foundation, the house roof on the ground, the rest of the house blown away. They spread out, searching. On the backside of the roof, Gaillard's mother found the pheasant rooster, stunned but alive, so she carried him under her arm. A newspaper reporter took her picture and later, incorrectly, wrote that this was her only possession. Another reporter from the *New York Times* asked Gaillard about his experiences. Gaillard told him: "That wind looked like somebody was pushing it. My house blew up in three directions when it hit." Then he added: "All I have now is two hacksaws and a hammer. Everything else is gone."

On top of the remains of his house's roof, Gaillard also discovered his Winchester shotgun. It had come through the storm in perfect condition, like someone had found it and laid it there. Gaillard had bought the gun when he was fifteen so he could hunt ducks on the Arkansas River. One time he sat at the river's edge on a horseshoe bend, when the ducks came up behind, a whole flight of teal. He shot two with one shot, just like that. But they dropped on the far side of the river, one hundred feet away, and the water was high, five feet deep. He wanted those ducks, so he pulled off his clothes and swam, and just like a dog, when he retrieved them, he put their necks in his mouth so that he could swim back. On shore he shivered in the cold wind, before hurrying home with his Winchester and the two ducks.

When he returned from the navy, Gaillard went out hunting with the Winchester again. Once more, he shot a duck that landed on the wrong side of the river. This time he could wade across to retrieve it, but as he pushed through the roots and rocks, he cut his toes and tripped hard onto his knees. Then and there he decided duck hunting wasn't worth all the aggravation.

The gun had sat in a closet for almost a decade. And then, beside the remains of his house in the center of this shattered town, Gaillard held it once again and wondered why it had survived and so much else had not.

They found nothing else. So they walked, trying to take in the totality of so much destruction, so much open sky. They saw the flattened Community Building, and Betty Jo wondered about the women at the Holtje wedding shower. Had they still been in that building, or did they escape? Across the street, at Eddie Taylor's pool hall, a small crowd had gathered. The county highway department had brought in a bulldozer and power shovel to slowly remove the wood and rubble. People might still be underneath all of that, Gaillard realized, men he knew. Dead or alive, he didn't know.

Then the Thompson clan came to the remains of the water tower, its crumpled I beams, the flattened bell of its tank. The tower had fallen to the west, straight up First Street. It had hit no houses; it just fell down the middle of the street.

The tornado's aftermath revealed a bizarre randomness, like the water tower falling down the middle of the street or Mrs. Taylor's house surviving while she died at work a few blocks away. The *Wichita Eagle* made a list of these occurrences, under the headline "Miracles and Oddities"—some of which read:

"Three large Mobil Oil Storage tanks north of the community building survived the tornado intact."

"In the rubble of a Udall house, a refrigerator stood untouched. A vase holding a rosebud atop it stood upright, the water unspilled—but the doily beneath it was gone."

Then there was this from the *Winfield Daily Courier*:

"While on duty the local [National] guardsmen observed many . . . evidences of the strange and enormous force of the tornado. On the floor of one home which had been entirely swept away, there was left one piece of furniture, a small table. On it was a bowl and in it were goldfish untouched and apparently the water hadn't even been spilled."

And there was this: On the evening of May 25, 1955, Harold Mettling kissed Cora Morton good night on her porch in Winfield. She was a college senior, he had been her teacher at Udall High, and after four years of courtship, they were engaged to be married in a few months.

After the kiss, Harold headed back to Udall, where he rented a room within walking distance of the high school. Lightning punctured the black night, and his headlights revealed sheets of corrugated metal in the road. When he got to the edge of town, debris blocked the road, and he realized what had happened. He grabbed his flashlight and stumbled through the rubble. He found a street corner but couldn't tell which one it was—no landmarks existed, no church he had attended, no school where he worked, no houses of children he had taught. Rain pelted his coat as he played the light over a bathtub, a stripped tree, a beaten-down chimney.

Then he found where he had lived. His landlady was away visiting friends; he was thankful for that because only one wall of the house remained—the south wall, his bedroom wall—and it lay flat on the ground. When he climbed on top, he found his bedroom window still had its glass. And under that shining surface, he saw the small cardboard box that held the wedding ring he planned to put on Cora's finger. The box, the papers inside, the ring—all were dry. He pried open the window and lifted out the gift. It fit deep into his pocket.

The ring still rides on Cora's finger.

When darkness fell on May 26, the day after the tornado, Toots was so exhausted he had trouble focusing. He had been awake for almost twenty-four hours, and not just awake but frantically scrambling over rubble searching for anyone still missing.

Now, though, with the horizon the color of blue milk, it was time to rest. He shouted out to the others to call it a day, to go home—wherever that home might now be—and to rest for the night. They had rescued the living, sent them scattered over the region to so many hospitals. But some people were still missing, and Toots and the others expected to find more bodies under the rubble the next day.

In his tiredness, his wounds throbbed. The hole in his leg—a deep puncture the size of a nail—seeped and stained his pants. And the back of his head ached where a brick had knocked him out. But he couldn't sleep, not yet. And he had to stayed focused.

The mayor stood in the middle of his dark little city, between the remains of the Community Building and the pool hall. A breeze rocked a tin sheet of roofing somewhere out in the rubble, but otherwise the place was silent and empty. No trees caught the wind. No leaves blocked the clear night sky. The stars blinked on above, like every night, when someone flipped that switch, but before him, no house lights or streetlights or headlights. He felt a sudden loneliness as these last twenty-four hours—the whole of it, the enormity of it all—settled in.

Two men joined Toots, Kenneth Lake, regional administrator of Civil Defense, who had driven all day from Denver, and Brigadier General Howard S. Searle, state Civil Defense director, who had come from Topeka at the order of the governor.

Toots told them what he could about the number of dead and injured. All the while, though, he knew their ultimate question.

After some silence, one of them finally asked it. Do you want to rebuild?

Yes, I want to rebuild. We have to rebuild.

Lake and Searle glanced at Rowe, tried to see his face in the darkness.

But there're no people, one of them said. You can't have a town without people.

People will come back. Just give us the money for schools and utilities and churches. You'll see.

But why do you want utilities? Or schools? There's nobody here.

They'll come back, Toots said. Look, we have a new water and septic system, so we just need the electric lines restored. We can reuse the schools' foundation. Same with the churches. You help us, and the people will return.

Even in the emptiness, Toots felt the spirit of so many. He couldn't walk away and bury it all.

You give us those things, and the people will come back.

The Civil Defense men agreed to help and said they'd start the paperwork in the morning. They also advised him to call the governor of Kansas, Fred Hall, and gave him the number. Toots headed out, driving the seventeen miles to his brother's house, wanting to fall into an exhausted sleep.

Away from Udall, though, Toots realized he couldn't sleep until he had made that phone call. Late that night, Earl Rowe dialed the Kansas governor.

Yes, I've heard about the awful devastation, the governor said, and yes, all the citizens of this great state are praying for you. And we're going to help you rebuild.

Toots asked Governor Hall to request federal funding to help with the utilities. The governor then sent a telegram with the mayor's request to President Dwight Eisenhower, himself a Kansan.

Toots also realized he needed to make a second call to reach his boss, Mr. Shawver, owner of Stelbar Oil Corporation. Toots liked Mr. Shawver, knew him as fair and honest.

I'm sure glad to hear from you, Mr. Shawver said to Toots. Glad to hear your family is all okay and the same for Gaillard's. It's a miracle, all of you somehow alive.

And yes, he said, you take off. You don't need to be out drilling for me; you have more important work to do. And don't worry about your paycheck either. I'll cover you for six weeks, how's that sound?

Then Mr. Shawver asked where Toots and his family were living, and after Toots told him, Shawver said, You know I have that ranch out near Douglass, and it has two houses on it. You and your family go live in one and tell Gaillard to take his family out to the other. You stay there as long as you need, till you get your new houses rebuilt.

Toots leaned against the wall. Such generosity. He thanked his boss, gave Lola a hug as he told her the news, and then fell asleep.

At the St. Mary's Hospital, Bobby Atkinson had trouble sleeping—he couldn't move; the white casts on both arms worked like lead weights pinning him down; plus, the doctors had ordered him to lie on his back so that his wounds would drain. Every hour the nurses rolled him on his side so they could change his sheets. Bobby couldn't see the blood-soaked linens, but he smelled them, and they smelled like death.

It took a day, maybe longer, for Bobby's aunt and uncles to find which hospital he had been taken to in the mayhem after the storm. Finally, they came into his room and held his good hand as he drifted in and out of morphine-induced sleep. They must've told him about his father so beat-up by the storm as to be unrecognizable. But he was alive and in good care here in the same town but at a different hospital. At some point they had to tell Bobby that his mother had been taken to a hospital in Wichita and that she was in even worse shape than his father. And at some point Bobby had to learn that his two little brothers—Gary and Stanley—were gone. They were killed in the storm.

The day after the storm, the soon-to-be Mrs. Aileen Holtje Wittenborn and her sisters and parents drove the few miles from their farm back to the Udall Community Building. They had hoped to carry home some wedding shower gifts that might've survived the tornado, but they were still shocked at how few remained. They found an electric mixer, a waffle iron, and a red, blue, and yellow plaid linen tablecloth. The mixer and iron still worked; the tablecloth had holes from where debris had ripped through it, but it was something, and so Aileen held onto it. Everything else, including all the fine glassware and crystal with the tulip design that so many friends had bought for her, all had been broken into shards and scattered or blown away.

Gone, too, were several students Aileen had taught. So many were so young—Gary Atkinson and Dickie Braddy and Paul Butcher, Mary Horn and Clinton Turner, Patricia Boyd and Maxine Karnes and Michael Woods, and the Kennedy siblings, Lea Ann and Harvey Ray. Of the twenty-two children ages sixteen or under who died in the storm, Aileen had taught eleven.

8   Overwhelmed

BEFORE THE TORNADO, THE UDALL CITY COUNCIL CONSISTED OF SIX men, Gaillard Thompson, Cecil Morgan, Raymond Wall, Dick Stone, George Karnes, and Earl "Toots" Rowe, with Toots serving as mayor. Three, Karnes, Stone, and Wall, were now either dead or in critical condition in the hospital. The others, Thompson, Morgan, and Rowe, were all homeless but alive, with few injuries. They held an emergency meeting on May 27, the first of several they would hold over the next months.

Even before the storm, council members were active and took their job seriously. In the early 1950s they realized sanitation in their town was not adequate. Some citizens still used outhouses, and others had septic systems that kept clogging, so they put to the Udall citizens a referendum—do you want a new sewer system? When the votes were tallied, the majority said no. Earl and Gaillard and other councilmen pondered this for a month or so. Someone else's septic system clogged. They passed by someone's outhouse every day. They realized they needed the new septic system, whether the citizens agreed to it or not. The laws regarding sanitation gave them the authority, so the councilmen voted to go ahead. The only person who really opposed the plan was the banker, who hired a lawyer to try to stop the town from moving forward, which didn't work. They told him he could take the new system out of his house after a year if he so chose. He never did.

Toots, Gaillard, and the council created a better water system shortly after they completed the septic system. The old city well was so full of lime, it turned peoples' pipes white, and the water was hardly fit to drink. In fact, infants couldn't drink it unless it was boiled. Toots convinced the other councilmen that they needed a new well, deeper and three and a half miles to the west of town. They laid a five-inch delivery pipe, and that served the town with much better water.

Soon after the storm, the city council met around a table under a tent. They could hear the work of men sifting through the rubble, of more bulldozers being unloaded from trucks, of National Guardsmen giving directions. Still stunned by so much devastation, the councilmen learned during their meeting that Dick Stone had died. He had survived the tornado with serious, but not life-threatening, injuries. On the night of the tornado, though, in all the rushing around in the hospital, the medical staff had forgotten to give him a tetanus shot. A few days later, Dick Stone died of lockjaw. He was buried beside his wife, who also died in the tornado. So, with Dick Stone and George Karnes dead, one of the council's first orders of business was to appoint Max Carlton and Lionel Kehr, longtime residents of Udall, as their replacements.

Then the council voted to give everyone in town three days to clean up whatever they could from the remains of their houses. After this, bulldozers would begin working on the lots. The councilmen also realized they needed to hire surveyors to reestablish property lines.

Toots and the other leaders feared if they waited much longer, the volunteers would disappear. People from all over were coming to help— and they wanted to get to work right away. In the Mennonite community, for example, the calls went out in the middle of the night right after the tornado to members across the region. By early morning of the twenty-sixth, over one hundred Mennonites were searching the rubble for victims and valuables. By the next morning over three hundred Mennonite men came and, by Memorial Day, over five hundred. The three days' time for Udall citizens to salvage what they could seemed like a long enough window, and no one complained.

The council decided to clean the streets immediately and to make the school football field the dumping grounds. Trucks hauled load after load of what once were houses to the field. There bulldozers pushed everything into a pile so massive, it would take days to burn.

While Toots worked in town, Lola took their three children to a nearby farm, the Barnetts'. a mile south of Udall, where the tornado had done little damage. There the Barnetts made their homestead the center for relief distribution. Marie Barnett was president of a sewing club, and in that role she asked volunteers to help with donations. People first brought clothing and food salvaged from the Udall stores and homes. Then donations began to arrive from all over the country. The Barnetts received some directly, while others were sent to a college in Winfield, where the Red Cross, college students, and Girl Scouts sorted the gifts and sent the most needed to the Barnetts.

In Barnett's barn, volunteers sorted and distributed men's clothes. In the garage, they strung lines to hang women's garments, and in neat piles, they arranged the children's outfits. The rooms overflowed. Two days after the tornado, the Red Cross was so overwhelmed by donations that officials stopped accepting anymore. Any unusable clothing was sold in Wichita, with the proceeds going to buy towels and other items many of the families no longer had.

At the Barnett's homestead, Lola sent her teenage daughter, Pat, off with the youngest, Jan, telling them to find what they could and mind their manners. Then she took Gary with her to the men's barn to find anything that might fit Toots. He had changed once, into clothes borrowed from his brother, but he needed more pants and shirts. When she found what she hoped would fit, she headed to the garage to search for outfits for Gary and herself. She didn't search alone. The volunteers, many of them friends, rummaged through the piles, holding up pants and shirts against Gary, fussing over him as he silently, bashfully, took in their attention. They even found him a pair of shoes.

Lola tried to thank them all, and the children did too. But the volunteers waved off the kindness and helped carry sacks of clothing out to Lola's borrowed car.

As Toots and Lola and others went about the business of remaking their lives, they also kept up with the Red Cross's three lists: the list of the dead (so many gone); the injured (in hospitals over a wide region); and the list of the missing (what happened to them? were they dead or alive?). One particular family on the missing list, the Lannings, made the Rowes and others pause. Norman Lanning was the well-liked music teacher for the high school. He and his wife and three small children had lived just a few houses from the Rowes—Lola had even seen Markita Lanning return from the bridal shower just minutes before the tornado struck. Yet afterward, nothing remained of the Lannings—no house, no car, no bodies buried in the rubble. Of the structure they called home, only the staircase remained—all walls and roof and everything inside, gone. Had the family been blown far out into some field? Had they survived and left town to stay with a relative or friend?

Finally, forty-eight hours after the storm, Norman Lanning showed up in Udall. He and his family had survived by climbing into a closet under their stairwell—all five of them crammed into a tiny space underneath the massive, blasting tornado. When the air pressure had returned to normal and the roaring faded, Lanning opened the closet door to find nothing remained. The bright lightning showed the kitchen was now an empty slab of concrete slick with so much rain. He looked around for the other rooms, the other furniture—nothing. Their car had been demolished, so the five of them started walking out of town. They found shelter at a farm a half-mile to the northwest, where the farmer and his family took them in. Eventually, the Lannings had gotten a ride to Markita Lanning's parents' home eighty miles away.

On the morning of May 27, thirty-five men from the Wichita Association of Home Builders arrived in several vehicles, including trucks hauling lumber and roofing materials. They came to erect a temporary headquarters, a place for the rescuers and rebuilders to gather, plan, and share information. The men cleared a spot along First Street, unloaded the materials, and set to work. They used the forty-by-eighty-foot foundation of the Community Building as their base, and within six hours, they had the walls up and the roof completed.

At three o'clock that afternoon, they had a "ceremony" in which the Builders Association president handed the keys to the building to Toots Rowe. The ceremony lasted only a few minutes, and one newspaper reporter quoted Mayor Rowe as saying how wonderful this building was. "Yesterday," Toots continued, "the people I talked to were kind of undecided about whether or not it was even worthwhile to try and build again. Today we have our first new building, and everyone is looking forward again."

The photograph of the occasion showed Toots wearing coveralls and a fedora over his tanned face as he shook hands with the Builders Association president. Toots's son, Gary, stood beside his father, wearing a ballcap tilted back and giving a perplexed look at the two men. The bandage around his neck was visible, as was a small circle of blood that had seeped through.

The new building created enough dry area for several agencies: Civil Defense would handle government moneys to rebuild schools and utilities; the Reconstruction Finance Corporation, the federal government's lending branch, would make low-interest loans for homes and businesses; and the Red Cross and the Salvation Army would handle donations and furnish emergency aid. Insurance agents set up a table to help their policyholders file claims. A Volunteer Labor Office was created to coordinate the work of the hundreds of people offering to assist in the aftermath of the storm. Pat Hurd, the owner of Udall's phone cooperative, installed several temporary lines, and the city of Winfield's utility company strung emergency power lines to provide electricity. City clerk John Arbuckle set up his own desk—a table, really—and started back to work for the citizens of Udall. And in a back corner, behind a counter set up to divide the room, Toots Rowe set up his own table-turned-office desk for his mayoral duties.

The first day after the tornado, volunteers and Udall citizens had carried out their work in a somber tone. Rescuers searched for the bodies of living or dead and shared information in hushed voices. There was no joking, few smiles.

The second day had a much different feel. The dead had been dispatched to morgues, and the wounded were recovering in hospitals, so the focus shifted from rescue to cleanup and reconstruction. Both the Red Cross and Salvation Army set up canteens to take care of feeding the soldiers, airmen, Mennonites, and other volunteers. As one observer noted, the "atmosphere was one of festivity," especially during mealtimes. The Red Cross had set up on a more trafficked street corner, so the Salvation Army felt the need to draw in the workers by shouting out their wares—coffee and sandwiches, ice cream and "ice cold pop." They also hung a canvas awning to shade those who stopped by. The Red Cross soon did the same. One Salvation Army volunteer found cases of still-intact sodas in one of the destroyed grocery stores. He carried them to the Salvation Army cooler, and they quickly disappeared into the hands of volunteers.

The festive, competitive mood also carried over into larger concerns. After the contractors of the Wichita Home Builders finished building the temporary city hall, their labor union counterpart, the Construction Trades Council, joined the cause. The trades council proclaimed it would donate labor and materials, as well as $40,000, to rebuild a permanent Udall City Hall and fire station.

All through this busy day of directing volunteers and talking to journalists, Toots kept looking for a special guest. He had been told to expect Kansas governor Fred Hall sometime later that afternoon, that he would be flying from Topeka to Strother Field, a small airport a half-hour south of Udall. Around 4:00 p.m., a state police car pulled up with sirens blaring. The trooper had had to drive on the highway shoulder much of the way to get around the traffic jam of onlookers.

Toots in his khakis towered over Governor Hall in his suit and tie, but the shorter man, with his large round glasses, was a practiced lawyer and debater and thus had a commanding presence. The two men shook hands and greeted each other as the press and volunteers gathered around them. When the photographers were ready, Governor Hall held out a telegraph to Mayor Rowe. Hall then proclaimed to the crowd that the telegraph was from President Eisenhower himself. Governor Hall read aloud the president's note: "I am deeply concerned with the hardship and suffering caused the people of Kansas by the tornado, and as you suggested I have today declared a major disaster under authority of Public Law 875, in those areas of the state which have been damaged. I have allocated to the federal Civil Defense administration such funds for federal assistance as are necessary to supplement state and local efforts." Hall clarified that their fellow Kansan had already approved $250,000 of federal aid for the Udall rebuilding effort and that more money would be available if needed. These appropriated funds were to be used to rebuild schools, streets, and utilities not covered by insurance money.

Toots, happy and overwhelmed by the generosity, thanked Governor Hall and President Eisenhower. Then a Red Cross official reported the damage figures to Governor Hall. At least 192 buildings in Udall, most of them houses, had been destroyed. Some homes were still standing, but their damage was so extensive that they were unlivable and would have to be demolished. Several people were still missing, so the total number of dead had not yet been determined, but they expected the figure to be over seventy-five, maybe even close to one hundred. According to this official, "Approximately 50 per cent of the families in town lost one or more members of their families."

The governor acknowledged so much loss, and as he started shaking hands and thanking the large group of farmers-turned-rescuers in their overalls and worn caps, a man came running into the crowd. He shouted that there might be a child's body under the school rubble. The missing boy's dog seemed to be on a "death watch" near this pile of bricks, so maybe the boy's body was underneath. Seventy-five men left the governor and hustled the three blocks to where the school had stood. They pulled up bricks and formed lines to hand them off, with shouts of encouragement and questions going back and forth.

Mayor Rowe and Governor Hall followed the men at a slower pace as Toots gave his guest a walking tour of the tornado's damage. Near the school where the searchers worked, Toots pointed out the twisted remains of a pickup truck hanging onto a bare tree. Over the din of the bucket cranes and bulldozers clearing streets, they viewed the new high school, now flattened. They paused by a stop sign where the tornado had wrapped a fencing wire around and around its post. The two men gazed over the block upon block of debris, stepping over one leg of the fallen water tower, passing the brick archway on First Street, where so many had found refuge after the storm, before coming back to the freshly built shell of the new city hall. Governor Hall praised the quick work of Toots Rowe and so many other fellow Kansans, told Rowe to keep in touch, then headed back to Topeka.

Not long after, the searchers finished clearing the mass of bricks. The ground lay bare, and the boy's dog had disappeared. There was no body.

Allene Holmes climbed a hill between her home and Udall. The year before, her father had helped build K15, a new state road that shortened the trip from Udall to Wichita to about a half-hour. When Allene reached the summit, that new road was bumper to bumper as far as she could see, cars full of people coming to see what the tornado had done. She had heard that the traffic jam was seven miles long, and it was taking those driving from Wichita over three hours to reach Udall. She had also heard about several accidents, including one that involved eight cars. At the town's edge, volunteers held out buckets, and every car stopped to give what money they could to help the little city rebuild. In one day the total donation reached almost $7,000.

On the Sunday after the storm, officials allowed some sightseers into town. But it became too problematic—too many people getting in the way of all the work still in progress—so they again shut off access to the town. The tourists had to stay on K15, looking at the devastation from a distance. Eventually, in the days ahead, the visitors could also stop at a few vendors selling postcards with photographs of the destroyed city. But now, with so much traffic, Allene wondered how the funeral processions could make it through.

While she looked on, Allene watched a train approach from the north. She was used to hearing trains barreling through Udall, blowing their horns at all the road crossings. This train, though, did not barrel along. Instead, it crawled. The passenger car's windows were filled with gawkers.

Just like the people lining the roads, the train's engineers and crew and everyone onboard wanted to witness the aftermath. Even the air above the town filled with airplanes, some of them flying low over the devastated village to give gawkers a good view.

At some point in those first days, Allene's father told her about their car, which she had driven to town for the bridal shower. He had found it exactly where she had parked it, across the street from the Community Building. In those dark hours after the storm, he had peered inside, searching for her.

You know, Allene, he told her later, that tornado threw bricks and blocks at the car, smashing the hood. And it drove a board through the driver's side window and out the windshield. If you had been sitting there, your head would've been cut off.

For years afterward, her brother Ray teased her about "totaling" their car by parking it in the path of a tornado.

The evening of May 27, two days after the storm, Toots returned to his brother and sister-in-law's house in Winfield in time for a late supper with his family. While they ate, they heard the boom of another storm. The lightning intensified, and it seemed to be aiming right for them, or so thought Pat, Toots's eldest daughter. She stood at the dark window looking out; she tried to pray; she tried to stop her hands from trembling. Every time lightning flared, she jumped. Were the tornadoes following her?

Her uncle and aunt didn't have a storm cellar, so when hail pounded the roof and the wind beat the rain against the windows, the two families— four adults and three kids—rushed across the backyard and alley to their neighbors' cave.

They weren't the only ones. It seemed like the whole neighborhood had come to this one cave. Twenty or so people crammed into the small cellar, all of them standing with no room to sit. Toots held tiny Jan in his arms, and Lola kept her hands on Gary's and Pat's shoulders. The air hung heavy with staleness and smelled of earth and so many bodies. There was little talk. The Rowes and others stood in the dark and listened. Even though most of the neighbors in the cave were strangers, they knew who Toots and his family were. Even in the dark, they could see the white bandage wrapped around Gary's neck. They, too, hoped they might survive like this family if another tornado struck.

Nearby, in the two Winfield hospitals, patients heard the same storm, and they also heard trucks with speakers driving the streets, booming out warnings, telling everyone to seek cover. The tornado victims who were able got out of their hospital beds and insisted on leaving the building. Children crammed themselves into the corners of their rooms. Nurses and doctors had to reassure everyone it was all right—they didn't need to leave the building or their beds. They were safe.

About an hour later, the storm passed. A tornado never came. People tried to settle back into their hospital beds. And Toots Rowe and his family, like all the others in that cramped cellar, filed up the steps to return to their homes and try to get some sleep.

9 So Many Dead

AS UDALL BEGAN THE LONG PROCESS OF RECOVERY, IT ALSO BEGAN the long process of grieving, of putting its dead to rest. The *Wichita Eagle* subtitled one Sunday article "Continuous Services Scheduled Today." The next day the same paper subtitled a different article "Prayers and Bulldozers"; it began, "Prayers and the chug of bulldozers were mixed Sunday as this small Kansas town buried its dead and started to live again." Funeral notices filled the newspapers, with titles like "Double Services for Storm Victims" appearing in the *Winfield Daily Courier*, next to another article also about a double burial. The Winfield paper noted that there were nine funerals for tornado victims on Saturday and ten more on Sunday.

On Sunday the Salvation Army asked everyone to halt work for a short memorial service held on the newly cleared site of what had been the Baptist church. Enough of Udall's streets had been cleared to allow people to gather, most of them men already sweaty from a few hours of labor. They held their hats as a prayer was said, along with a brief sermon. Then the Salvation Army's band played several hymns. There was no echo, no buildings for the notes to bounce against. When it came time for the last song, a trumpet player stepped forward alone. He played taps, and the haunting notes floated over everyone to disappear over the plain. The quiet only lasted briefly. Soon the dozers and cranes started back into the work with a grinding roar.

The next day both the *Wichita Eagle* and the *Winfield Courier* ran small articles announcing the death and funeral arrangements for Bobby's mother, Nina Alina Atkinson, age thirty-five. She had been rushed to St. Joseph Hospital in Wichita during that long night after the tornado, where her father finally found her. He, along with several of her siblings, tried to be with her and her husband and one living son spread across three different hospitals separated by an hour's drive. A hospital spokesman said, "She suffered severe injuries to her head and lungs as well as deep wounds to her legs and multiple bruises." Nina never regained consciousness, and she died on Sunday, four days after the tornado, at 5:00 p.m. The family had already made funeral arrangements for the two youngest boys, and now Nina's funeral would be combined with theirs. Bobby learned of his mother's death that Sunday evening. Because of the casts on both his arms, someone else had to wipe the tears from his eyes.

There were so many dead. Columns of names filled the papers: Emmie Foulk, age seventy-nine, Lola's aunt Emmie, who operated the elderly care home across the street from the Rowes; Stella Kennedy, seventy-three, who lived near the Atkinsons, and her great-grandchildren, Billy, six, and Lester, five, who had come to town for a week of Bible School; Gaillard's friends Ora and Mary Clodfelter, seventy-nine and seventy-six, respectively, who had lived in Udall for forty-nine years, he having come to Kansas as a child in a covered wagon in 1875; and the Kennedy siblings, Lea Ann, eight, and Harvey Ray, four, both ripped from their father's arms by the tornado while being carried down into the storm cellar.

The Udall Methodist minister, Reverend Giles Stagner, conducted many of the funerals, including those for Nina, Gary, and Stanley Atkinson. Reverend Stagner and his young family had been visiting his wife's family two hours away that night, so the tornado destroyed their parsonage and belongings, but the Stagners had survived. Reverend Stagner immediately returned to help the families who had lost so much. For the funerals he wore a white shirt, dark pants, and a dress coat that was too large, all borrowed from others since the storm had destroyed his own clothing. At the double funeral for Henry and Sadie Storey, Reverend Stagner preached to the mourners that it was futile to question the tragedy or

God and that they should have faith and continue living. "In my Father's house are many mansions," he might've read. And "though I walk through the valley of the shadow of death, I will fear no evil."

There were so many bodies that they filled a temporary morgue. Teams of morticians—some traveling from afar and others coming out of retirement—readied the corpses. A monument company donated gravestones for all those killed by the tornado, while volunteers dug the graves, most in the graveyard just a half-mile east of the decimated town. "At the cemetery," the Wichita Eagle author stated, "it was a common sight to see a service in process, a grave being closed and a fresh one being dug all at the same time."

Because the tornado destroyed Udall's churches, many services were held graveside. As funeral processions traveled through the town, the bulldozer operators stopped their machines, and volunteers and workers, who some days numbered over two thousand, lined the streets. The town became quiet as the hearses drove through the rubble.

Allene Holmes and her family attended many funerals. Every time Allene put on her Sunday dress and her best shoes that, even after many attempts to clean, still showed smudges and scratches from the storm. At each grave she stood beside her brother and parents and watched the body be lowered into the ground. At Hazel Standridge's funeral, Allene remembered one basketball practice when she and the other players were so hungry that Mrs. Standridge, the school cook, allowed the girls to make mayonnaise-slathered cheese sandwiches in the kitchen. And as the casket of Mrs. Standridge's son, Truman Turner, was lowered, Allene remembered her schoolmate's heavy black eyebrows and quiet manner.

Five people in that family were buried that day—Hazel Standridge; her sister Alpha Lawson; and three of Mrs. Standridge's children, Truman, sixteen, Clinton Wayne, nine, and Donnie, four. After the storm, Earl Standridge had found the bodies of his wife and two stepsons, but he couldn't find Donnie. He visited the hospitals in the surrounding cities, hoping he was alive, then he went to the mortuaries. Two days later the father discovered his youngest son in a funeral home. His face and body had been so mangled as to be almost unidentifiable.

Sometimes the death toll was even worse than the Standridge's; sometimes the tornado killed whole families, so extended family came from out of town to arrange and attend the burials. Or if the people were newly moved to Udall, like the Karnes family, their relatives took the bodies back home.

Nina Atkinson and her two youngest sons—Gary, age twelve, and Stanley, age five—were buried on Memorial Day, the Monday after the tornado. Bobby couldn't attend his mother's and brothers' funerals, nor could his dad. They both were still in critical condition in separate hospitals, so Nina's father and siblings made the arrangements.

For Allene Holmes's younger brother, Ray, the hardest funeral was for his best friend, Gary. No longer could he help his friend deliver newspapers. No longer could they ride their bikes together or climb the water tower or trick other kids into riding the Holmes's pony that always ran back to the farm. No longer could they trade punches or jokes or secrets. No longer could they do anything together.

Just as there were so many dead, there were even more survivors with incredible stories.

On the evening of May 25, Clara Lacey was home alone with her two boys, Rick, age five, and Rock, just a toddler, a year and a half—home alone and pregnant with her third. Her husband, Ray, worked the swing shift at the Coleman plant in Wichita. He usually left for work by three in the afternoon and returned around twelve thirty at night. The young couple had just moved into a new house in Udall six months earlier, in time for Thanksgiving. They had also built an attached garage for their yellow Mercury. That evening it wasn't Ray's turn to drive in the carpool, so before he left, he pulled their car into the garage for the night.

To help with expenses, Clara worked part-time at the telephone company, trading shifts with Mary Taylor. Pat Hurd, her boss, even put in a daybed so she could tend her young sons while she worked. Just the day before, she had sat at the switchboard plugging in lines, connecting people.

Clara was in her second trimester, and for months her hands had been too swollen for her engagement and wedding rings. So she had set them aside on the kitchen windowsill. That morning after she did the dishes, she picked the rings up to see if she could get them back on. They slid down her finger just right.

For a while after supper, Clara watched the boys run around outside, letting them play and wear themselves out. The Laceys had a big lot and also owned the empty lot next door, so the older boy would run out to an old fence and turn and run back. The toddler tried to keep up.

The couple did not have a TV, and Clara was usually too busy minding the boys to listen to the news on the radio. She didn't hear a weather forecast that day, but as evening came on, she watched the skies grow darker and darker. Clouds rolled in to block the night sky, and the lightning and thunder flashed and boomed continuously.

Clara put the boys to bed, and around ten o'clock, she went to bed herself. But she couldn't sleep, not with so much wind and rain.

The hail came hard, popping against the house, and soon the electricity cut off. Clara rose and found a candle. She set it on a little table in the hallway and lit it. For a moment she stood in the doorway watching her boys sleep. The pounding hail intensified, like it might break the windows. She grabbed the youngest out of his crib and laid him beside the older boy on his bottom bunkbed. Then she laid on top of them. She watched the candle as it wavered. A roaring blast slammed shut the bedroom door, and Clara knew the candle had fallen onto the floor. She was sure the house would catch on fire.

Then some part of the disintegrating house struck her hard on the head and knocked her unconscious. The world went black.

When she woke, she was disoriented and wet and cold, but she could tell she had somehow landed against the fence in the lot south of their house. She still had the smallest child in her arms. Rick, the older boy, had landed farther away, in a field. He walked along the fence to find her. All three of them had landed over one hundred feet from the house.

Clara hugged Rick and Rock tight.

"Mama, what are we going to do?" Rick asked.

"Don't worry. Somebody will find us," Clara said.

The Walls lived next door, their houses separated by less than thirty feet. The Walls' house still stood. After the worst of the hail and wind had stopped, Sonny Wall had stepped out to look around. He ran back in and yelled to his wife: "Ray and Clara's house is gone! It's just gone!" He had thought it was just a bad storm. He hadn't realized there had been a tornado.

Sonny grabbed a flashlight and went searching. He found Clara clutching the two boys. He picked her up and told the boys to follow and got the three of them into their house. The two little boys had a few cuts but were okay; Clara, however, was bleeding and in a lot of pain. They put her in their bed until they could get her to a hospital.

Sonny's folks lived in the south part of Udall, and when he went to check on them, he found their house completely gone too. But his parents were alive, so he brought them back to his house. When his mother saw Clara, she said, "I came to spend the night and you beat me to it!" Clara tried to smile.

Eventually, they got Clara to a Winfield hospital, where the doctors determined she had a skull fracture and many bruises and abrasions. She still had her boys, and she still had her wedding rings, but no one knew if the baby she carried inside was unharmed.

Meanwhile, in Wichita, Ray had heard nothing about the tornado. During a break he had stood in the factory's door to watch the lightning show to the south. But he had thought it was just another summer thunderstorm.

Driving home, he and his coworker came through Mulvane, the town north of Udall. A policeman waved his flashlight and flagged them down.

"Where you boys heading?" he asked through the window.

"Well, we're going to Udall."

"There's no use going," the officer said. "It blew away."

Ray was terrified. What about Clara and the boys? What about his brother and his wife who lived nearby? They drove as fast as they could on the muddy roads.

It was pitch-black when they got to the outskirts of Udall. Ray stepped out of the car and into ankle-deep water. The water tower to the south had blown over, and all the water had pooled on the streets.

He waded through Udall to find an empty slab of concrete where his house once stood but no Clara. He looked in the car still parked where he had left it. Despite all the walls around it being blown away, the car hadn't moved. In his flashlight beam, Ray could tell the car was no longer yellow. The wind had blasted off all the paint. Inside the car was empty—still no Clara.

Ray banged on his neighbors' door, and the Walls brought him in out of the rain. They told him everyone was alive, that Clara was in a hospital and the boys were with some friends. Ray headed south to Winfield to check on his wife. There he found Clara bruised from head to toe. Her face was so banged up, she had a hard time smiling, but she did when she saw him.

Ray also found his brother and sister-in-law—Jay, with a broken femur, and Jewell, like Clara, pregnant, bruised, and concussed. But everyone was alive and going to make it, and the hospital staff had put Clara and Jewell in the same room, so there was that small comfort too.

The next day Ray returned to their home to search for anything he could save. There was very little. And yet all the houses around looked untouched; the Walls' house to the north, and the one across the street, Charlie Selvage's, both still stood, as did one catty-corner. It was like a little tail of the tornado had spun around and destroyed their house and only theirs. But he had walked through other parts of the town, and he knew that wasn't true.

When he went back to visit Clara, Ray said, "You know the car was in the garage and it didn't move. Why didn't you get in it?"

"Ray, we are all alive," she answered. "I did everything right."

Yet she worried about her two boys, wondered if they truly were okay. The hospital didn't allow children to visit, but Clara's parents talked to the nurses, her dad insisting a visit from the boys would help Clara heal. The next day her parents snuck the two boys up an outside stairway and into her room. Clara smiled and cried at the same time when she saw Rick and Rock, and her dad claimed he could see her improve immediately.

Over the many days in her hospital bed, Clara heard about the deaths, especially of so many young children, like the two sets of Kennedy kids and the Atkinsons, playmates of Rick's. She knew how lucky she and her boys had been. Just as easily it could have been them. It didn't matter that all their belongings were gone. That didn't matter at all.

A few of their belongings were found, though. When the Mennonites cleaned up Clara and Ray's lot, they found pennies, lots of pennies, probably from the boys' piggy banks. And then one day Ray came into the hospital carrying an envelope that he placed in Clara's hands. Inside were two photographs, one of each boy, Rick and Rock. The pictures were creased and torn, but still they showed the boys' beautiful smiles. A farmer to the northeast had found them in one of his pastures. The tornado had carried them ten miles away.

The doctors kept Clara in the hospital seventeen days. Because of her head wounds and pregnancy, she still needed care and bedrest after her release, so she stayed with her parents several miles away from Udall. It was at least a month before she was well enough to ride in a car and return to Udall. By then the town had been cleared, and people had started to rebuild. Clara cried at the great expanse of empty lots. So much destruction, so many lives lost.

While Clara healed, Ray and his father-in-law started to rebuild on the old foundation. But first they built a storm cellar, which the old house did not have. Clara demanded that, and Ray agreed. The factory where Ray worked, Coleman, donated money to help, as did Ray's many factory workers. And many others gave clothing and furniture. On one of his visits, Clara's father told her, "I'll build you one more house, but you have to take care of this one!" Her boss, Pat Hurd, said the same thing as he hooked up their new phone, the first dial phone in Udall. "Clara," he said, "I'm going to give you one more phone. You take care of it!" The Laceys moved back into their new-again house in November 1955, in time for Thanksgiving.

Four months after the tornado, Clara returned to the hospital to give birth to their third son. All those months she had worried, and finally she had an answer to her question. Yes, he was all right. The tornado had not harmed him. The nurses wanted to call him Tornado Pete, but Clara and Ray named him Ron. Her sister-in-law and good friend Jewell also gave birth to a healthy child. At least four pregnant women survived the tornado and gave birth to healthy babies.

In February, nine months after the storm, a doctor cut into Clara's ankle to dig out whatever debris kept bothering her. He expected to find a splinter. He found a one-inch-square piece of wood.

One of her doctors later asked Clara to tell her whole tornado experience story again. Afterward he said: "You know, you had four lives in your hands—yourself, the two boys and the pregnancy. You had four lives in your hands." She never had thought of it that way.

And, she realized, it was probably best that she hadn't.

Another survivor story: Jerrold Hoffman was new to town, having moved to Udall six months before the tornado to live with his sister's family and work on the railroad. In those six months, the twenty-year-old had fallen in love with and planned to marry Sally Ann Hurd, who was the daughter of Pat and Martha Hurd, owners of the telephone company. The evening of the tornado, Jerrold and Sally Ann had driven the few blocks from her house to the store downtown to fetch milk and razorblades for her parents. When they got back, they had a little time before she had to go inside, so despite the ominous weather, they parked beside her house and stayed in the car to talk and kiss.

Soon hail began to batter Jerrold's car, pinging the metal like hammers. The wind howled, and a washtub banged hard against the car. In his headlights, Jerrold could see the Hurd's house moving. He pushed Sally Ann down onto the seat and laid on top of her. He stomped hard on the car's brake, but the car kept moving no matter how hard he pressed. A power pole with a huge transformer fell right beside them, just missing the car. The car windows shattered, and a rain of water and glass poured in. Jerrold looked up and into the tornado, and in all the lightning streaking in arches, he saw tiny twisters that bounced around like snakes. Then it was only rain—cold and dark.

Pat Hurd crashed through a house window right before the tornado hit, and after it passed, he climbed into the car with Jerrold and Sally Ann. Martha Hurd was with a neighbor—they hoped she was all right.

They waited for the wind and rain to ease—the wind did, but the rain continued hard and long. After an hour they walked downtown to find no landmarks, just a mad chorus of horns blaring under the hoods of so many brick-crushed cars. Had Jerrold and Sally Ann stayed downtown, their car would've been crushed like so many others.

Jerrold searched for his family, who lived just a few blocks away. When he found his brother-in-law, he recognized him only by his high voice, his face was so covered by mud. He and his family had survived in their storm shelter.

Pat Hurd found his wife in a nearby car with her friend, both of them alive and well, and Pat was anxious to find Mary Taylor, his friend and telephone operator. He had been talking to her right as the tornado hit. Her last words to him were that the Weather Service had given an all-clear— and then the phone line was cut off. They never found Mary Taylor's body until the next day, buried in the cinder block rubble of the telephone office.

Jerrold saw many dead that night of the storm: two children lying side by side on a foundation; another carried by a young man, the child's head at an odd angle; and Truman Turner, Sally Ann's classmate, who had no marks on his body and yet he was dead. All the while, the horns of the cars buried in the rubble honked until the batteries died. Then it was only the blackness of cold rain.

Beside the new City Building, the Red Cross and Salvation Army quickly set up mobile canteens, and throughout the first days, all three build- ings filled with activity. An estimated two thousand people worked on the cleanup, and hundreds more gave blood or donated money, heeding the calls from local papers that "all hearts and purses will be open to a stricken people" and that "Udall as a community vanished in a matter of seconds. Her people must not be abandoned in their sorrow."

With so many people pouring into town, the canteens kept busy serv- ing free coffee, donuts, and sandwiches as well as hot meals. While the Red Cross provided the food, the National Guard did most of the cooking, serving, and cleaning. On their busiest day, they served seventeen hun- dred meals for a noontime dinner. Many of the ingredients were donated from local grocers, dairies, bakers, and others. One dairy stationed a milk truck full of water by the canteens. A Wonder Bread delivery agent even stopped by to donate four hundred loaves of bread.

The City Building didn't serve food, but it did offer hope or answers—or just more questions. It was the central place for people searching for relatives or friends. As one newspaper stated, "'Have you seen or heard anything of . . . ?' was the almost constant, tearful, hopeful query of weary survivors with blood-shot eyes, most of them still dazed, as they haunted the headquarters for information on loved ones." Phone calls from all over the world poured into the City Building, one even from Australia. People wanted to learn more about their relatives or simply wanted to offer encouragement and prayers. Most of these callers asked for Mayor Rowe, and most of the time he was too busy, so someone else would take the call and relay the message to Toots.

The new City Building also served as the gathering place for volunteers offering to help. Sometimes as many as fifty people crowded into the small room. Those who had come to donate blood were encouraged to go to Wichita or Winfield.

With so much aid coming in, Toots began to distribute the good news. A few days earlier, he told his neighbors and friends he was staying, they better do the same. And now he could tell his citizens there would be money to help—from the Red Cross, insurance, and donations. When he told one woman that her house would be rebuilt, she sat down and sobbed. Another woman laughed and hugged her husband with joy, some good news amid so much bad.

In one corner of the City Building, Toots set up a table of lost and found items, a place for the cleanup crews to deposit small valuables for the owners to find, if the owners had survived. The most common items were lost glasses and dentures, and these personal necessities showed up all over the town but especially in the debris piles of the three elderly care homes, where residents had set aside their teeth and glasses for the night. Many of these stayed on the lost and found table, unclaimed.

The living still needed to keep on with the business of living, and those in charge of the cleanup needed to work together to make this rebuilding possible. Men and women from various organizations met at the new City Building on the Saturday morning after the storm. Mayor Toots Rowe presided over the group sitting around a long table. The aid groups had had some difficulty with duplication of work during the past days of cleanup. This meeting, everyone hoped, would dispel some of that confusion and establish plans for the days ahead, including a scheduled meeting every morning.

The group determined that the National Guard would remain in charge of security until the threat of looting had disappeared. The Guardsmen would also handle the clearing of all streets, school buildings, public spaces, and some individual lots, while private contractors and volunteers would clear most of the private homeowners' lots. This work of clearing debris they expected to complete within a week.

The Red Cross would continue interviewing those left homeless, evaluating their needs, and setting up finances, if needed. The Red Cross would also keep working with the Salvation Army in feeding workers and families, along with the soldiers and airmen. And the Red Cross would continue to collect donations, which in a few days' time exceeded $85,000.

The leaders discussed the need to complete the water connection between the mainline and town and to rebuild another water tower soon. They also noted that electrical crews were in the process of replacing poles and stringing new lines, and power would soon be restored.

Civil Defense affirmed their role in helping the city leaders handle state and federal money and paperwork. John Arbuckle, the Udall city clerk, reported on the estimated total for all the damage—$15 million. He also reported on the donations coming in, including more than $14,000 from Beech Aircraft and its employees. This and other donated moneys were deposited in a special account at the local bank. Tracy Hilderbrand, the banker, lost his house in the storm and part of the bank, but he still found his safe and all deposits accounted for, so within a day after the tornado, he opened his bank.

The other aircraft manufacturer in Wichita, Boeing, also donated money and more than ten tons of clothing, canned foods, and furniture. Coleman, another manufacturer in Wichita, employed people who lived in Udall, and it, too, donated immediately and generously to help victims recover. But $15 million was a huge amount—could all the donations, grants, and insurance cover it? Toots believed so, and others followed.

After the meeting, Toots kept busy. In his makeshift office, he gathered the stack of applications he knew he'd be filling out in the coming days. He also started contacting surveyors needed to remark the property lines for each house. Outside Toots talked to reporters, planned where next the crews of volunteers would go, and oversaw the clearing effort. When he could, he joined the other men as they searched the debris.

Near what used to be the feedstore, someone showed Toots a gander they had found. It had poked its head through a pile of boards, and once released, it quickly found water to ease its days-long thirst. A black pet rabbit also survived the tornado, along with roosters that pecked at scattered grain.

And then a cry went up from what used to be Lawrence Kennedy's lumberyard. One of Kennedy's relatives, searching for whatever could be salvaged, found a full box of dynamite, sold at the store to farmers wanting to blow up stumps or prairie dog colonies. The man gently carried it to a cleared area and yelled for everyone to stand back. A National Guardsman, an expert with explosives, came forward to investigate. He found the sticks in good condition and not a threat, so he carried them off to a secure place. He also told a reporter that "a sudden sharp jar could have set them off." All the while, a bulldozer worked on the next lot. Had it run over that box of dynamite, there would've been more names to add to the list of the dead.

Two or three days after the storm, Allene Holmes visited Bobby Atkinson in the hospital. Her mother took her and a few other kids, Bobby's friends. They found the Winfield Hospital so crowded that Bobby was in a bed in the hallway. He had so many broken bones and bad cuts and bruises, Allene could hardly look at him. On his back she saw the raw, exposed muscles, the skin flayed away in a hole the size of two hands. His arms were up in traction. Doctors and nurses rushed by to treat the other wounded. Allene, her mother, and friends did not stay long. They said hello to Bobby and to Johnny Boyd, who had a broken arm and leg and cuts and bruises all over—and who, like Bobby, had lost his mother and sibling. Then the visitors quietly left.

Three types of people started to stream to Udall—gawkers, helpers, and reporters, who sometimes gawked and sometimes helped. They had much to take in. Men swarmed over the whole town, including National Guard soldiers, air force servicemen, local contractors, and sometimes as many as five hundred Mennonites in one day. Their work progressed steadily, with dust filling the air, along with the *clack-clack* of dozer tracks and the constant grind of large engines. Five days after the tornado, they had cleared whole blocks, the debris hauled to the growing pile on the high school football field.

Toots Rowe became the unofficial spokesman for the city, so usually reporters started with him, and often they included his family. Journalists came from all over the country, and their stories were distributed all over the world. Newspapers in New York City, Miami, Seattle, San Diego, Chicago, Los Angeles, Denver, Honolulu, and Paris, France, ran articles, usually front-page coverage with photographs of the destroyed town.

One reporter, a woman from the *Winfield Daily Courier*, asked Toots's daughter Patricia what she missed most that the storm had taken. Pat couldn't decide between their dog, Corky, or her new Brownie Camera. She had loved both and now had neither. She had received the camera as a Christmas present the year before, and she often had taken silly pictures of the dog sitting with his tongue out and ears pointing up. She knew the family dog was gone. She had asked her dad about him the previous evening, and he had just shaken his head. We found a lot of animal bodies, he told her. I doubt Corky made it.

The next day a Guardsman spotted a muddy dog limping into town. He carried him to the city hall, where the dog saw Toots and tried to jump out of the man's arms. This yours? he asked, and Toots said yes, as Corky licked his face. No one could believe it. How far had the tornado blown the poor dog, and how had it survived? But there it was, muddy and happy, sore, with cuts, but otherwise healthy. That night the family and dog had a happy reunion.

Hollywood came to Kansas a few days before the tornado. Cast and crew flew into Wichita to make the movie *Picnic*, written by a Kansan and set in Halstead, sixty miles north of Udall. As soon as they started, a thunderstorm delayed the schedule, knocking over props. They picked up the next day, Rosalind Russell and other stars moving about the town's park or participating in the movie's watermelon- or pie-eating contests. The local townsfolk baked thirty cherry pies for the scene, and the director shipped in eighty-four watermelons, big doings for the whole region.

That night the tornado struck Udall, and Columbia Pictures sent spotlights to help with the search.

Rosalind Russell wanted to do more, so on Sunday, May 29, four days after the tornado, she appeared at the local Wichita Indians minor league baseball game. Admission prices had been doubled, with all proceeds going to aid the tornado victims. Before the game started, Russell walked to a microphone on the infield and waited for the crowd to quiet. She wore white gloves, a long dress coat, and open-toed heels, her whole appearance the definition of elegance. She thanked the crowd for coming, for supporting the people of Udall with their extra admission money, and she presented a check for $1,000 from the director of *Picnic*, also for Udall relief.

Then Russell stepped away from the mic to take off her gloves and coat and stand in a strapless dress, shoulders exposed, pearl necklace and pearl earrings, pillbox toque hat, and lots of lipstick. She was a comedian as well as an actress; she knew how to ham up the first pitch. She also knew how to throw a baseball. Her windup was slow, her mouth wide open and challenging. Even in heels and a dress, she leaned back on her right leg, right hand on the ball in a fat baseball glove. She held the baseball with fingers forked like she'd done this before. And for a moment, the crowd and players forgot the tornado.

At her sister's home, Beth Morgan kept busy—it helped her forget. She gathered eggs, picked green beans, and took care of her three small nieces and nephew. She also hauled water. Her sister's house didn't have indoor plumbing, but it had a storm cave, and Beth visited it often.

Beth's parents found a car—a nearby dealer loaned it, for as long as they needed, he said. For days after, they helped with the search and cleanup. But still, they wouldn't let Beth ride back to town. Oh, we forgot your shoes again, they'd say. She believed it the first day but not the second or the sixth, especially after they brought her a change of clothes from her old closet. Finally, a week after the storm, they brought her shoes and took her to town for the first time.

Beth first noticed the absence of the National Guard, who had pulled out the previous evening, June 1. They had cleared the streets and many blocks of homes, and the traffic they had monitored had slowed. This left much still to clear, a need met by Mennonites and other volunteers still coming by the carloads, though lessening some, especially as many of these men were farmers and the harvest of winter wheat was about to begin.

With the streets mostly cleared, the men and their bulldozers, cranes, and dump trucks pushed and scooped and hauled off what remained of the buildings, moving from debris-filled lot to debris-filled lot across the village. Some houses still stood, but most of them had walls caved in or roofs blown off, so they had to be torn down and rebuilt, the damage was so bad.

On Beth's street the two-story house across from hers was coming down, as were several others nearby. Only eight or so houses had somehow made it through the storm—like a large two-story on the northwest edge of town, by the park; Charlie Selvage's house directly across from Clara and Ray Lacey's now-empty lot; and across the street from Beth's, the telephone operator's, Mary Taylor's house.

Allene Holmes still hurt from where the tornado had hurled debris onto her. Her cracked tailbone made it painful to sit, and she had several cuts that throbbed, the worst in her knee. After a few days, when the throbbing became more intense, she scratched off the scab and asked her dad to help. The wound on her knee had become infected, so first he squeezed out puss. He kept squeezing until finally out came a thick splinter, over an inch long. When it popped out, he held it up and said, Well, look at that.

Bobby Atkinson's family visited him as often as they could. His Atkinson grandparents had also survived the storm but were now homeless, so they stayed at another son's house in Winfield. From there they could check on Bobby and his dad as well as start to rebuild their Udall house and the grocery store. Bobby's uncle Richard reopened the family grocery about a week after the storm in a Quonset hut behind what remained of the store. Bobby's grandmother told the *Winfield Courier* that a surprising amount of food was left undamaged by the tornado. She also listed the many kindnesses that people had offered, including another store moving a refrigerator railcar onto the Santa Fe siding in Udall so that cold goods could be stored and sold from it.

On one of their visits with Bobby, his grandparents told him about what they found after the tornado. That night they had gone to bed as usual, and like every night, they put their glasses, dentures, and watches on the bureau nearby. When they heard the tornado, they rushed to their storm cave, where they listened to the howling wind. An hour later they opened the door to find their home destroyed.

They returned the next day to search for whatever might be salvaged. There in all the splintered boards and busted bricks, they found both sets of their glasses, both dentures, Grandpa Atkinson's wallet, and both of their watches. His grandmother's watch still ticked along with the accurate time.

Gaillard and Betty Jo Thompson and their two children stayed a couple of days and nights at his parents' farm a few miles outside of Udall. They had only the clothes on their backs. For their kids that meant just their pajamas and no shoes. Nothing else. The family borrowed a car and traveled to Winfield to shop for clothes.

Then Mr. Shawver, Gaillard's boss and the owner of Stelbar Oil Corporation, invited the family to stay in one of his summerhouses near the town of Rock. The Thompsons, like Toots and his family, were overwhelmed by the kind gesture, and the two families stayed there all summer, until their houses were rebuilt in Udall.

Gaillard kept working on the oil rig, while Toots took time off to rebuild

Udall. One day shortly after the storm, Gaillard ran into one of his cowork-
ers, a friend named Walker who lived in a house trailer at the edge of
Udall. Sometimes the two men liked to share a drink, especially around
Christmas, when the company gave every worker a fifth of whiskey and
a ham.

After the tornado, Walker told Gaillard about his trailer. The wind
had lifted one end, then the other end. Then the tornado lifted the whole
trailer and threw Walker and his wife into the backyard. When it passed,
she was hanging around Walker's neck, and neither one had a stitch of
clothes on. But they made it. Eventually, they moved to town to make
their home in a new brick house.

A post office, in many ways, makes a town a town. A crossroads becomes
more than a crossroads; it becomes a destination—for packages, for
postcards, for people. You'll find me here, says a return address. This is
my home. Even if you no longer have that home.

Like all the other downtown businesses, the Udall Post Office had
sustained heavy damage. The tornado had ripped off the roof and shattered the windows, scattering shards of glass everywhere. The building
was not a safe place. Yet miraculously, W. H. Lawrence, the postmaster,
said they didn't lose any mail, "not even a postcard." They gathered up
what they could and moved to a safer building, what used to be someone's
house. They put out a hand-lettered sign saying, "U.S. Postal Service,"
and only missed one day of mail delivery—Thursday, the day after the
storm. By Friday, Lawrence and his assistant, Mrs. R. L. Harris, were
back to collecting, sorting, and sending out mail.

Fortunately, all Udall postal service employees survived the storm,
including both rural carriers. One of these carriers was Roy Harris, who
used to be postmaster and had lived in Udall many years. He and his wife
were on vacation when the tornado struck. Afterward, when he talked with
Mayor Rowe and learned that most of the city records were destroyed,
Harris created a three-page list of peoples' names. He mentally went up
and down each street and wrote who had lived where before the tornado.
This list built on memory became the city's new census.

The other rural carrier was Hugh Atkinson—Bobby's grandfather—who lost Nina, his daughter-in-law, and Gary and Stanley, his grandsons. And Hugh Atkinson was still unsure if his son Robert and other grandson, Bobby, would survive.

As the country and world learned of the tornado, mail arrived in great canvas bags from all over the globe—from France and England, Italy, Australia, Canada, Japan, and every state of the Union. Even the mayor of Hiroshima wrote to ask how he could help. The long summer days gave Lawrence and Harris light to sort the mail before the electricity was restored as they worked from 5:00 a.m. to 7:00 p.m. to keep up with the influx of mail in their makeshift quarters. There was so much mail that they hired Beth's father, Cecil Morgan, to help.

The postmaster told a local reporter that "the mayor has been getting the most mail," some simply addressed to "Mayor, Udall, Kansas." Each letter affirmed Toots Rowe's belief that even though the physical structures of Udall might not exist, the town still lived and would live for many more lifetimes.

Udall received so many gifts from so many people—personal checks of a few dollars or Ruritan Clubs sending $100. One donor stands out. The town of Hebron, Nebraska, sent a check for $1000 to Earl Rowe to help Udall recover. And then, a few months later, the town sent another check for over $900 to the Mennonites, who used it to buy blankets for the Udall survivors. The town of Hebron was not wealthy—it was like so many other midwestern towns, struggling to survive. But two years earlier, in 1953, it too had been decimated by a tornado, and it had received great help. So knowing they could never repay all that they had been given, the people of the town gave what they could to another town in need.

Years later, Udall did the same. Jerrold Hoffman was mayor of Udall in 1966 when an F5 tornado plowed through Topeka, 150 miles away. Hoffman put out a call to his fellow Udall citizens, and as he said in an interview years later: "It wasn't very difficult to get a busload of us to go up there and clean up. We did that. No question about it, a full busload spent all day up there. It was a dirty job."

The same happened in 1990 with Hesston and again in 1991 with Andover. Udallians gathered their tools and drove to help their fellow tornado-stricken Kansans. They wanted to say, We've been through this too, we've experienced unbelievable destruction, we've lost family and friends, and we're here to help.

After the 2007 Greensburg, Kansas, tornado, a group of Udall citizens, including Beth Morgan Evans, made several trips across the state. They remembered the decimation of their own huge elm trees that used to shade the streets. As Clara Lacey once told a reporter, "It was years before we had any trees and birds again." They knew Greensburg would also need new trees, so they drove 150 miles with donations of money and truckloads of trees; planting all the trees took four trips.

For Beth Morgan Evans, it felt right to help Greensburg, like she and her town had been helped. But it was also unsettling to again be surrounded by so much destruction. On one of the trips, Beth had to leave early; the Greensburg devastation called up her own horrible memories.

On Wednesday, June 1, 1955, almost a week after the storm, Toots called a meeting with all the leaders of the various organizations helping Udall, followed by a press conference at the newly constructed city hall. In addition to the Udall City Council and school board members, the roster of attendees included national and military leaders from Civil Defense, the Red Cross, the Salvation Army, McConnell Air Force Base, and the National Guard. For many of these officials, it would be their last meeting in Udall. Their work was almost done, or they were handing over duties to local and regional officials.

During the meeting, the group established a building code committee to make sure that new construction was done safely. They also talked about money—what had been allotted, what was still needed—for major public structures such as the schools. Insurance would not cover all the loss, so the city council and school board hoped to secure funding from government sources. Federal money was already committed to replacing the municipal infrastructures and buildings.

At the press conference after their meeting, Toots and others reported on their progress as well as answered questions. The mayor was the first to speak. He told the small crowd of journalists: "Yesterday I gave out four permits for rebuilding homes. The town of Udall is on its way back." Over the next days, Rowe expected up to sixty new houses to be "under construction almost immediately" along with several structures in the business district. Toots was certain that the town would rise again from its own ashes—"bigger and better than ever." He assured all that the rebuilding would be well planned, "nothing haphazard . . . nothing that we won't be able to live with in years to come." And the mayor said, "We'll build again, not with our loved ones who are gone forever, but with those who are left. The town is here and here it will stay."

After Toots, the regional Civil Defense chief talked about the federal money promised for infrastructure and the need for more. The National Guard spokesman explained that the majority of lots and all the streets were cleared, and most of the Guard's heavy equipment would be leaving in a day or two. The local Civil Defense was taking over emergency policing duties, and the Red Cross and Salvation Army were still busy processing applications and meeting the needs of so many families, as many as 750 in the region. The Red Cross announced that donations for the Udall disaster had exceeded $85,000, with contributions coming from as far as New York and Los Angeles. This money would go to help private families and individuals with medical as well as rebuilding costs. But, they added, the Red Cross had already spent $5 million for relief in the region, which was $1 million more than it had budgeted. So the relief organization needed many more donations. The Red Cross also noted that it had served 18,000 individuals at its Udall canteen, that sixteen hundred pieces of heavy equipment had been used in clearing the debris, and that a total of 143 patients from the tornado had been treated in eight hospitals across four counties.

The National Guard commander wanted to dispel one rumor about the soldiers' work: no bodies had been buried in the ruins by their equipment.

"To my knowledge," the Kansas National Guard commander, Colonel Goodvin, said, "the last of the injured were removed Thursday morning and the last of the dead Thursday afternoon, the day following the storm." He assured everyone that the Guardsmen had taken great precautions to find everyone, injured or dead.

Mayor Rowe and Red Cross officials addressed the confusion from the missing persons list, explaining how it had initially been compiled mostly from inquiries from concerned relatives. And now, with a week's time to check and verify, there were no more missing people—they were either dead or alive. Toots said, "I think everyone living here at the time of the storm has been accounted for." He offered revised casualty figures—79 dead, 118 major injuries, 104 minor injuries, 143 hospitalized.

Lastly, Toots thanked all who had donated money to the Red Cross or directly to Udall. The town had set up a separate fund just for these gifts, and he urged anyone in the disaster area who was in need to contact him or the Red Cross. Toots ended by saying, "The funds are here to be used." The energy focused on rescue, recovery, and cleanup now turned to rebuilding.

The official list of the dead showed how vulnerable the young and the old are in a natural disaster. Roughly a third of the people who died in Udall and the surrounding area were over the age of seventy, farmers who had sold their farms and retired to town or elderly people living in one of the three care homes. Almost another third of those who died were under the age of sixteen—Bobby Atkinson's younger brothers, the school principal's only son. One family, the Kings, who lived ten miles south of Udall, near Oxford, lost five children to the tornado. The father was sick with tuberculosis and being treated in a sanatorium three hundred miles away from the family and their farm, so the mother was by herself with their ten children, ages eleven months to twelve years, when the tornado struck.

A few days after the storm, Ruth King gave her account of that night to an official from the National Weather Service. Around five thirty that evening, they heard the weather broadcast on the local radio station—severe storms but no warnings of tornadoes. She put her children to bed around nine, and she and her eldest daughter soon followed. But neither could sleep. The rain grew harder, and the flashes of lightning and booms of thunder "were almost simultaneous." Then came the hail and stronger wind. Ruth got up to close a window and was too anxious to go back to bed, so she sat with a light on, trying to calm her nerves. Her daughter called to her that the wall beside her bed was shaking. That was about 10:10 p.m., and before her daughter could finish talking, a north window shattered.

Ruth King's "first inclinations were to get her little children as far away from windows as she could, so she grabbed the two babies and put them on the floor in the bedroom near the center partition and away from all windows. Two of the bigger children laid down beside them." She "ran back to get another little boy, age five. Her twelve-year-old daughter got the little six-year-old boy, and they were about halfway to where she had put the other children when the southeast corner of our house started flying to pieces." The next thing she knew was "rolling over and over with the little boy in her arms." There had been "no warning rumble . . . immediately before the tornado hit." She only heard lumber and other debris flying overhead, and she screamed for God to have mercy on them. "The wind was so strong, though, it literally tore the words out of her mouth." Then some debris knocked her unconscious. When she woke, she was "being whirled around," and she wondered about the child she had just held in her arms. Where did he go?

The tornado dropped Ruth on the ground in front of the family car. As she hit the earth, she watched the car go straight up into the air and disappear. Soon two of her children found her sitting up, saying, "I can't believe it," over and over. They huddled together and wondered about the other children, so they started searching. They found the car, over three hundred yards away, and Ruth told her children to get inside while she searched more. She called and called, two more answering, so she could carry them to the car. She found one child, dead and lying between the house and car, then she found two more of her children dead and lying on the foundation of what had been the barn. She couldn't find the other two.

When the morning sun finally rose, some neighbors came to check on the family. Ruth had cuts and needed to go to the hospital, but she wouldn't leave until she found her other two children. Their bodies were located under all the rubble of the house, where she had told them to lay down in that brief moment before the house collapsed.

The five children were buried three days later, on Saturday. Mr. King was able to attend, but Ruth was still in the hospital. The children who died were Nancy Faye, twelve; Ronnie Wade, six; Billie Wayne, five; Victor "Vickie" Alan, three; and Barbara Ann, eleven months.

On one of her first days back in Udall, Beth Morgan walked the streets, keeping out of the way of all the workers. On the other side of First, Martha Hurd, one of the telephone company owners and a woman Beth had only spoken to a few times, came rushing across to her. "Oh, Beth. We heard you were killed and here you are," she said as she hugged her. "I'm so glad to see you," she repeated. Beth hadn't realized until she returned the hug, but she was glad to see her as well.

Mrs. Finn, a neighbor who lived across the street, greeted her the same way. Beth knew Mrs. Finn had always feared storms and that she swore that if she died in one, she'd die with her clothes on. Well, the rescuers found me, she told Beth, sitting in my wheelchair, right in the middle of what used to be my house. And I had my clothes on.

These joyous greetings continued for all the survivors over the next several weeks, sometimes even at the many funerals. Acquaintances or close friends, it didn't matter, the happy surprise at surviving and finding other familiar faces alive called for a warm handshake or hug, a pause to say: It's good to see you. It's good to be alive.

10 Distributing Kindness

IN 1955 ST. MARY'S HOSPITAL IN WINFIELD WAS A NEW THREE-STORY brick building with its own cadre of medical staff. But local family doctors performed operations there as well. Such was the case for Bobby and his doctor, Dr. Grosjean. He checked on Bobby daily, making sure he stayed on his back so his open wounds drained properly. The three huge gouges seeped so much that every hour throughout the day and night the nurses changed his sheets and dressings. By the end of the second week, the seeping had stopped, so Dr. Grosjean decided it was time to operate again.

The morning of the surgery, a nurse pushed Bobby and his bed down the hall to the elevator. She punched the button for the lower floor, waited for the doors to slide open, then his body jiggled and bounced as she rolled his bed into that big coffin-like space. She didn't get on the elevator. The doors closed, and Bobby rode down alone. He stared at the ceiling. He heard the gears spool out the cables to lower him. Again, like right after the storm, he felt an immense wave of loneliness roll over him. Then the elevator stopped, the doors slid open, and another nurse pushed him out. He still felt alone, but at least now he could look out the windows of the hallway before entering the operating room.

The anesthesiologist covered Bobby's mouth and nose, then Dr. Grosjean set to work. First, the doctor took out all the old stitches on Bobby's back, before reclosing the wounds with over 150 new stitches. Then he focused on Bobby's hand, the one most smashed by debris. He inserted steel pins through several fingers. On one mashed knuckle, the doctor used rubber bands that, in the weeks ahead, slowly pulled the knuckle into place to once again be set in a cast.

When Bobby woke, he was back in his room, and after a nurse checked on him, he was again alone. No one in his family could be there to comfort him, and the pain was immense.

One nurse, Ruth Comstock, became especially adept at changing his bandages on his back while he lay on his side. She also worked on the puss-filled welts of imbedded splinters and rocks. As gently as she could, she prodded and squeezed to dig these out of Bobby's head and back and legs.

Because of the casts on both arms, Bobby couldn't do anything with his hands, including feed himself. So, for every breakfast, lunch, and dinner, a different Girl Scout volunteered. The food was good; he had the appetite of what he was, a fifteen-year-old boy, and he would eat just about anything. But he wondered about how the young Girl Scouts fed him. They just shoved in the spoons of mashed potatoes or the forks of hamburger steak. They never turned the utensil slightly in his mouth—just straight in and straight out—and often the food dribbled down his chin. Bobby got frustrated and tried to ask them to roll the spoon, but they never did. And he was too grateful to complain.

Toots and Lola Rowe owned a 190-acre farm about one mile west and north of town; they had lived there for several years when they first got married. Toots enjoyed the place, and since he worked the nightshift on the oil rig, he often spent time, in the afternoons or evenings, planting and cultivating and harvesting as the seasons progressed. After the tornado and all the immediate work of rescuing the living and finding the dead, he took a break and drove out to the farm. He wondered how it had fared.

It hadn't. The winter wheat he had planted in the fall and watched come on in the spring—all of it about ready for harvest—now was gone. The barn where he parked his tractor and equipment—gone. The tractor and plows and drill and sprayer—all destroyed.

Given what he had seen over the past week, it didn't surprise him. And yet it did. He lit a cigarette, let out a long exhale, and headed back to town.

By Thursday, June 2, the National Guard commander in charge of cleanup was able to tell reporters, "Ninety percent of this tornado-ravaged town can be rebuilt on areas now cleared of debris." All the heavy equipment from so many different organizations and all the donated energy from so many volunteers had cleared the tornado's destruction in one week's time. They had hauled away what once was a town to a massive heap on the demolished high school's football field. Now it would sit until ideal weather to burn. Plus, some plots of the town still needed the slow, careful attention only possible with manual labor, meaning more debris still had to be collected. For the most part, though, the big equipment began loading up and leaving.

As the demolition crews headed elsewhere, the construction crews started arriving. In the temporary City Building, city clerk John Arbuckle had never processed so many building permits in such a short time— forty-five permits totaling $293,000. And this was just one week's worth of permits, with more still coming. The local paper listed all the names of individuals with permits, including the estimated cost of the new home. Some of those filing for three-bedroom frame homes were Wayne Keely, the town marshal, $8,850; Gaillard Thompson, $8,883; and Earl Rowe, $11,850. Mrs. Willis, the woman the Atkinson boys feared when they delivered papers, filed a permit for a two-bedroom home for $5,000, as did the telephone company president, Pat Hurd, $11,000. Arbuckle issued several one-bedroom home permits, including one to Toots's neighbor Grant Gearhart for $7,000. As the money became available through bank loans, insurance payments, and government grants, people acted quickly. They wanted new houses soon; they wanted home.

The Red Cross processed requests and distributed food and money. The Salvation Army gave out food, clothing, and used furniture. And though the citizens of Udall appreciated both organizations, neither was nearly as well liked as the Mennonites, who brought one more item of special importance: kindness. They knew that yes, these survivors needed a great deal of physical help, from clearing streets and rebuilding houses to simply finding suitable clothing and the next meal. But they also needed attention beyond the practical; they needed a handshake and a smile, a gentle hello, and how are you?

The Mennonites came by the hundreds, carloads of men from all over Kansas and Oklahoma and as far away as Nebraska, Indiana, Ohio, and South Dakota. Often the closer volunteers finished their morning milking chores to board the back of big trucks they then filled with debris from Udall. The church also purchased a school bus to help with transport, and then in Udall this bus also served as a field office for the Mennonites, a place to store equipment as well as a first aid center.

During the first week after the tornado, the National Guard prohibited most Udall citizens from entering the city limits because they couldn't distinguish between legitimate Udall homeowners and potential looters. But the Mennonite leaders had worked with Toots Rowe and the other recovery leaders so when each man showed his Mennonite Disaster Service Member card, the National Guard let him in. By the end of the first week, close to two thousand men had passed through these checkpoints. One Mennonite overheard a conversation between two Guardsmen as he made his way through their roadblock. "Who are all of these people?" one Guardsman asked. The other answered, "All I know is they're Mennonites, and they sure are on the ball."

They were on the ball because they had learned the power of community service during World War II. As conscientious objectors, the Mennonites had refused to fight, yet they wanted to serve, so the federal government established the Civilian Public Service and put these and other co's to work. The government gave them no wages and little support, and yet the Mennonites found their physical actions a better witness than words. After the war, the church created the Mennonite Disaster Service to continue this work.

In Udall the Mennonites began searching through the debris with some trepidation. When homeowners were absent, how could the volunteers determine what in the rubble of a house was valuable or not? As they debated how to proceed, they watched the National Guard's bulldozers. The young operators in their hurry pushed everything away, and in the early stages of the cleanup, they even unintentionally smashed dead bodies. The Mennonites figured people would be quite happy with their more conservative, feet-on-the-ground approach. The National Guardsmen saw how well the Mennonites worked and quickly showed respect, holding off on the bulldozer and crane operations until the men had given an area a thorough search.

Slowly, they worked, some crews roving over the town to hotspots where they were immediately needed, other crews working lot by lot. The adults wished for more trucks, tractors, and chainsaws, and over the next days, they brought their own if they could. Some of the Mennonites were young, just graduated or still in school. These teenagers were excited by the offer of free food and pop as well as a chance to be away from the farm. Often they were amazed at what they found, like a newspaper driven through a tree like a nail. Many worked for ten or more days, loading their truck with boards and bricks and then riding to the football field to unload it all by hand onto the debris pile, again and again.

The Mennonites and other searchers found all manner of items, from eyeglasses and dentures to small safes and undamaged furniture. They even found a wallet holding $700. They piled the furniture and clothing at the front of the lot for the owners to pick up when allowed. The smaller and more valuable items the Mennonites tried to label by lot number, then they deposited these in a special truck the soldiers guarded. Sometimes they learned that the owner was in a hospital. Then the Mennonites would get permission to store what they found in their own homes until the owner came home and their possessions could be delivered.

Sometimes the Mennonites found severed arms or legs, body parts the morticians would come to carry away. And sometimes the Mennonites helped dig the graves.

One day, while the Thompson clan worked on cleaning up their house lot, Gaillard met his neighbor, Grant Gearhart, the town mechanic. The Gearharts lived right across the street from the Thompsons, next to the Rowes. Because Gearhart's house was built with cement blocks, it had survived, but it was torn up too much to salvage; the family planned to tear it down and rebuild.

Gearhart always liked to prove his toughness. One time he went to the doctor to have his hemorrhoids operated on. The doctor wanted to deaden the skin around the piles, but Gearhart said, No, you don't need to—I can take it. When it was all over, he said he'd never do that again.

During the storm Gearhart had decided to watch from his doorway. He wanted to witness the intensity of the storm; plus, he wanted to see if he could match its force. His wife had other ideas. She huddled in a closet. Afterward, when he told Gaillard about it, Gearhart said, It almost put me down, but it didn't. He had held onto that doorframe and stood through the tornado. It beat him with debris so that he had splinters all over his body and welts that would turn into bruises, but he stood through the whole thing.

During the cleanup Gaillard bumped into another neighbor, the schoolteacher Mr. Wyckoff. The Wyckoff family had lived across the street from the high school and beside Mrs. Simons, the piano teacher and doctor's widow. When the tornado blew apart the Wyckoff's house, it also took Rickey, their four-year-old son.

Wyckoff told Gaillard that after the tornado, with the rain still pounding, he went out searching for his son. He panicked and prayed that he might find him alive. The father called and cried and stumbled over debris. Suddenly Mrs. Simons appeared dressed in white. She pointed toward her backyard. She said: Don't go there. There's an old cistern there, and you'll fall in.

Mrs. Simons had already died in the storm, but Wyckoff saw her, and she saved his life. Only later the next day did rescuers find Wyckoff's son's body blocks away.

11   The Long Process of Working Through

BOBBY ATKINSON WAS GRATEFUL TO BE IN THE HOSPITAL—THESE doctors and nurses had saved his life, after all. But he felt cooped up and bored. He had no TV in his room and none in any lounge, and with his arms in casts, he had trouble turning pages to read what few magazines and westerns interested him. Sometimes he snuck down the back stairwell to the basement, where he spent time with the janitor. Sometimes he just sat on the bench by the back entrance. He wanted to move around and get outside for a hike. He missed his new ten-speed, the open-air rush of going fast.

And at night, alone in his room, Bobby let himself wonder deeper into what else he missed—his room and home and friends. His mother and two brothers, now gone. And his dad struggling in another hospital a mile or so away.

Why him? Bobby sometimes wondered. Why was he spared? Why did that tornado strike his house and town and kill so many people? But then again, why *not* him? God didn't randomly make such violent storms. That was just how the world somehow worked, right?

The mail for the City of Udall kept arriving in overflowing bags, and Mayor Toots Rowe and John Arbuckle, the city clerk, tried to keep up with opening the envelopes and responding if they could. People from all over the country sent letters and donations.

122

Three packages arrived simply addressed to "The Mayor." Inside one, Toots found a cowboy hat and immediately recognized it. Ben Rudd, the man Gaillard had found sitting in his yard after the tornado and who died a few minutes later, always wore it, and sure enough, his name was on a tag inside. The sender of the cowboy hat included a note saying he had found it in his yard in El Dorado, forty-five miles northeast of Udall. He wondered if the mayor might be able to give it back to Ben Rudd. Toots wished he could. The best he could do was give it to one of Ben's relatives.

Another item sent to Toots from El Dorado was the tattered and muddied remains of a Udall High School diploma from 1943. He couldn't read three of the signatures in the bottom left, but the main name centered in large, fancy font was Gaillard K. Thompson. Toots let out a laugh and looked forward to returning the diploma to his neighbor and best friend.

The third package Toots opened contained pictures and a letter from a woman who also lived many miles away to the northeast. In a field near her house, she wrote, she had found a muddy, damaged camera with a roll of film inside. She had had the film developed and included in the package the negatives and pictures. Could you find out who these belong to and give it to them? she finished her letter.

Toots examined the small stack of pictures. Most were of a bedroom, a young girl's probably, that looked newly decorated. Then he came to a photo of a tall man with a big smile, and Toots immediately recognized him—it was George Karnes, the manager of the Udall Co-op Elevator and fellow city councilman. There were other pictures, of George's wife, Wreatha, and son, Gerald. Karnes's daughter, Maxine, age eleven, must've taken these before the storm. Somehow the film had survived inside the damaged camera.

By now Toots had befriended many of the newspaper reporters in the region. He asked them to put out a call for any relatives of the Karnes family. Soon he was contacted by kinfolk living in Oklahoma, and Toots mailed them the photographs, a small memento of an entire family now gone.

Aileen Holtje, the bride-to-be, and Roy Wittenborn, her fiancé, debated whether to go ahead with their wedding. Before the storm, they had set the date, sent out all the invitations, and finalized the ceremony details. But now, with so many people dead or injured or homeless, they weren't sure it would be appropriate to wed so soon. Their families, however, said it'd be all right, so eleven days after the tornado, on June 5, 1955, their original wedding date, their families and friends gathered at the Trinity Lutheran Church in Winfield. Aileen's sister, Normajean, was maid of honor, and her other sister, LaRue, was bridesmaid, while Roy's brother was best man. Aileen wore a strand of pearls Roy had given her, and she carried a cascade of red roses and a white orchid. Afterward they honeymooned in Missouri at Lake Taneycomo, before settling in a house they built in Arkansas City.

Two weeks after the storm, Toots met with the high school and grade school principals, Ernest Woods and W. R. Creech. Woods and his wife had both been hospitalized after the storm. In fact, they had had to leave the hospital for a few hours the previous week to bury their six-year-old son, Michael, who died in the tornado. How do you offer consoling words when you know they are so inadequate? Toots hoped the new work of rebuilding would help.

The mayor wanted to see if these men, along with the Udall School Board, were committed to overseeing new construction. The principals both said yes. They didn't yet know if there would be enough money from the Civil Defense and insurance payout to cover the costs of rebuild-ing, but the board voted to proceed. They decided to call the architect in Wichita who had designed the previous schools; they could use those plans once again. This time, though, they made one addition—a storm cellar underneath the high school, large enough to accommodate all stu-dents, teachers, and staff for both schools. It also would have access both inside and out, so that it could be open to anyone in the community who needed shelter.

To finance their new house, Gaillard and Betty Jo Thompson took out a loan with the Small Business Association for $10,000. The SBA offered a special lower interest rate of 3 percent for storm victims, and most everyone who rebuilt in Udall had to borrow money.

That $10,000 was all the Thompsons would spend on the structure. Before their lot was cleared, Gaillard had already hired a builder named Charlie English out of Mulvane, Kansas. Many of the Udall families hired English and his crew. Before she agreed to move back, Betty Jo made sure the new house would have a cave, a shelter for the next storm. Gaillard agreed. English had never built a storm cave, but he did for them.

While the Thompson family lived in Gaillard's boss's summerhouse near Rock through June and July, Gaillard kept working to pay the bills. Every evening after work, he drove the seven or so miles to check on the builders' progress. They worked quickly, but Gaillard wished they could finish even sooner.

Three weeks after the tornado, the *Wichita Eagle* reported that the "most annoying problems" for Udallians were "tourists and flies." Every weekend thousands of tourists packed the roads, stopping in the middle of streets, blocking traffic, just to take pictures and buy postcards. The flies didn't wait for the weekends. They, too, came by the thousands, and no one was sure why.

Among the Udall residents, a friendly competition had developed to see who could be first to return to live in the town full-time. It looked like Lora and Lester Grant would win. Their house by the railroad tracks, where the wedding shower party and others had found shelter the night of the storm, had to be demolished because it was so damaged. But the Grants had a rental house a few blocks away that they were in the process of repairing. That's where they hoped to be living soon, and from there they could build anew where they had previously lived. But Lora Grant confided that she couldn't sleep at night. "It's my nerves, I guess," she said. "I wake up . . . and can't get back to sleep. I'm worse now than at first." Still, she wanted to return.

Others hoping to return soon were the Footes, whose house was destroyed and whose daughter was still in the hospital after having her leg amputated. Mr. Foote worked for Boeing in Wichita, and on weekends, twenty to thirty of his fellow employees volunteered to build his family's new house. The walls were up and roof almost completed in just a few weeks.

Several other families were also getting help from fellow workers to rebuild, sometimes fixing up garages that were still standing so that the families could live there while they built new homes.

Before he left Udall after his three-week check-in, the *Wichita Eagle* reporter talked with two other individuals. One was Tracy Hilderbrand, the local banker, who reported that he'd had to hire two new employees because he'd been so busy. With so many insurance payments coming in, deposits in the bank had almost doubled since the storm, closing in on $1 million.

The other person interviewed was Mrs. Grey, from Dewey, Oklahoma. She had set up a canopy near the new City Building and was selling postcards to the tourists. She and her husband and son lived in a trailer outfitted with photographic equipment. They had come to Udall shortly after the tornado, taken pictures, and reproduced them into postcards. "This is our twentieth storm," Mrs. Grey said. "Last Sunday we sold 2,500 postcards, at 10 cents apiece."

Meanwhile, the death toll from the tornado still rose. The newspaper reported on the death of Zack West, a farmer who had retired to Udall. On the night of the tornado, along with several injuries, he had been exposed to the elements for so long that he also contracted pneumonia, killing him several weeks later, at the age of seventy-one.

Across the street from Gaillard and Betty Jo Thompson's, the frame walls of Toots and Lola's house were going up quickly. While their old house had been a bungalow with a wide porch, the new house was a ranch, also with a wide porch. And the new one, like the old, had a storm cellar. This time, though, the Rowes asked the builder to construct a storage room over the cellar and to connect it to the house. If a storm came up, the family could move to the shelter without going outside.

Toots and his daughter Pat visited their house site almost every day that summer. They'd get up early and drive the ten or so miles from their temporary house to Udall. There they'd walk around the newly poured foundation or slip through the pale-yellow stud walls or peer through new windows. They'd talk about what furniture they wanted to buy, what color to paint the walls. The children got to choose the colors for their bedrooms, Pat picking pink, along with a pale gray bedroom set. Then after checking on the builders, Toots would take his daughter the half-mile to Uncle Ira and Aunt Emma's farm, where Pat helped her aunt with the many farm and kitchen chores, including feeding a huge crew of men at harvesttime.

Toots returned to his temporary mayoral office and began again the long process of working through all the necessary applications to rebuild his town. He usually worked into the evening, returning to the Stelbar ranch house for supper with his family, and then, if the long summer evening was still hot, he would light his cigarette and watch his kids splash and swim in the big stock tank.

12 Something to Hold Onto

THE NURSES AT ST. MARY'S HOSPITAL PITIED BOBBY. THEY BROUGHT him comic books, which he struggled to read because it took so much effort to turn a page with both arms still in casts. And they snuck candy bars, which they had to unwrap and feed to him, one bite at a time. Bobby loved the irony, a nurse feeding him something so unhealthy, but he loved the sweet kindness even more.

One night one of the nurses, Betty Coffey, came into his room with an odd grin. Another nurse stood outside the door, looking up and down the hallway while pretending to read a chart. Betty acted like she was checking Bobby's blood pressure. She glanced toward the door. Then in a low voice, she asked, Bobby, do you want to go for a ride?

What? Bobby thought he'd misheard her.

A ride. Do you want to go for a ride in my car? They had talked about cars before, and Bobby knew she had a brand-new Ford convertible.

With the top down?

Of course, she said.

Bobby only had his bathrobe and slippers, the robe not made to go over his casted arms. His mangled leg and back still hurt immensely, but the nurses helped Bobby work his way down the back stairs, the women on both sides as Bobby hopped on one leg. They situated him sideways in the car's back seat, his leg propped up on the cushion.

And then Betty drove Bobby up and down Winfield's Main Street. The summer night slipped under his casts, cooled all the sweaty skin he couldn't reach. He forgot about the hospital, the pain, the loss. Bobby couldn't stop smiling. He wanted to holler but didn't want to get the nurses into trouble. The one in the front passenger seat turned so she could watch him, and Betty drove but also kept checking on him in her rearview mirror. They both laughed at his immense grin, their long hair blowing in their eyes. That summer night air, it tasted absolutely delicious.

In early July the Red Cross finished processing relief applications and began distributing money. These funds went mainly to families who didn't have adequate insurance to cover what they had lost. In all the Red Cross gave out $341,000 to 221 families in Udall and served over sixty-five thousand meals to anyone there—survivors, rescuers, rebuilders, and others. With this new money now dispersed, more hammers and saws sounded across the town.

Throughout this time the Red Cross played an instrumental part in recovery and rebuilding, but the relief organization's relationship with Udall citizens was not always an easy one. Its leaders could be difficult to work with and strident about following rules. If, for example, a family had built their own house before the tornado, the Red Cross would buy the materials to build a new one but not supply any money for labor. They figured the family had done it earlier and could do it again. It seemed like the Red Cross didn't want to disrupt the social order of how life had been before May 25, 1955. So, if a Udall family of three originally lived in a sixteen-by-twenty-foot home, even though the family needed more rooms, Red Cross only funded the reconstruction of what was originally there, another very small house.

Mayor Rowe heard from his neighbors of their struggles. Earlier the Mennonites had approached him with offers to volunteer, so he contacted them with specific names of families who had failed to meet the Red Cross's standards and yet still needed help. The Mennonite leaders called for more men from their congregations, and again they came.

Believing that a well-organized group would leave a greater testimony, they usually had one man who served as foreman–organizer–family liaison. His presence gave the family and work coherence, as carloads of men traveled from throughout the region, bringing hammers and saws and setting to work.

For one family the Mennonites rebuilt the home completely, from foundation to interior decorations. They took on similar projects for other families, including even rebuilding a grade A dairy barn and silo. In all the Mennonites helped four families in Udall, plus several more in Blackwell and Cheyenne, Oklahoma, two towns also devasted by the same storm.

One other need the Mennonites learned about concerned the great swath of debris scattered by the tornado. To the north and east beyond the Udall town limits, field after field was covered with boards and nails and sheets of tin roofing—all of what used to be Udall. Before any farmer could even begin to work his fields, he had to clear this debris. The Mennonites offered to help. One day four hundred volunteers gathered at the edge of town. Once assembled and organized, they spread out to form a line of men two miles long, all facing northeast. Then, slowly, these men worked their way forward, gathering the waste. They piled it at field edges, working together to move the heavier pieces. By the end of the day, they had walked over eight miles, the four hundred of them cleaning debris from sixteen square miles.

With the help of relatives from Pretty Prairie, Douglas, and Wichita, Beth Morgan's parents put a new roof on their house and replaced the windows. And most important to Beth, they built a storm cellar in the backyard. Beth watched them dig and lay up block and brought tools when asked. By the end of July, as soon as the power company rebuilt the lines and connected their house, the family moved back, one of the first in Udall. They still had a great deal of work to do, especially cleaning every crack and crevice that the tornado had blown full of dirt, but the Morgan family was back where they belonged. They were home, all alive and now, again, all under their own roof.

But they did not feel alone. The Morgans soon became part of what felt like a carnival freakshow, especially on weekends. People from all over the region continued to flock to Udall just to look. Sometimes at the edge of town, the line of cars was over two miles long as the strangers waited their turn to drop a dollar or two into the volunteers' outstretched buckets. And then they drove the streets, up and down, back and forth, bumper to bumper, pointing, wide-eyed and open-mouthed. If the visitors forgot their cameras, they could buy souvenir postcards that showed the massive devastation. And if they wanted to take home more souvenirs, some tried to steal from the lost and found table. One newspaper headline read, "Vultures Landed," and reported that on "July 12, 1955, Mayor Earl Rowe put restrictions on visiting in the relief room of the Udall community building. Sightseers had been caught pilfering articles salvaged after the May tornado; most of the items were personal belongings of stricken families."

In all of this, Beth Morgan felt like a monkey in a zoo. She'd be outside cleaning up the house, and all these cars just kept poking along, full of watchers. If she could, she hid in her room or hiked the mile west to her best friend's, Allene's, house. No one came out there. But often she had to stay working there in the yard while the cars full of cameras slowly rolled by.

The storm left a great hole in Beth's confidence. She became more fearful and often had nightmares. After waking from a bad dream, she hurried across the hall to slip into her parents' bed. Even though she was sixteen, they didn't refuse her.

A week or so after they moved back, Beth's parents wanted to drive north to the small town of Ransom. Her dad wanted to check out a new lawnmower that could run by remote control. He thought he might be able to sell several of them. It would be an overnight trip, and her parents insisted that Beth go along. For days she had refused. She didn't want to leave the storm cave. Her parents persisted, saying they'd only travel when the weather was clear. So, when the weatherman gave a clear forecast, all three took the journey, and all the way there and back, Beth kept looking at the sky, making sure no monster clouds were forming on the horizon.

By mid-July Toots Rowe could see his small town heading in the right direction—buildings were going up, insurance money coming in, and the paperwork seemed to be under control. From May 26 through July 1, his boss at Stelbar had paid his salary. Mr. Shawver had also given the Rowes a place to live and guaranteed his job would be waiting for as long as he needed. Toots felt it was time, so on the evening of July 20, he returned to his full-time job on the oil rig. His crew greeted him with their usual banter, which he quickly returned. And then they set to work.

The next day, after some sleep, Earl returned to the City Building to check in. He still had mayoral work to do, just now on a part-time schedule.

Even though Bobby Atkinson and his father still lay injured in separate hospitals, their family grocery store was being rebuilt. Bobby's grandfather and uncle and friends navigated the paperwork of permits, bought materials, and set to laying brick and hammering nails. A photograph on the front page of the *Wichita Sunday Beacon* from July 24, 1955, showed the new construction of First Street. Atkinson's Grocery had a new roof, and the front was completely rebricked, with two spaces on either side of the entry open and awaiting the large plate glass windows. What his grandfather and uncle could salvage from the old store, they did, plus Calvert's department store in Winfield gave the Atkinson's several shelving units, and other stores donated display cases. By late July the Atkinson clan had moved the display cases into the rebuilt store. They expected to reopen soon.

Across the street from Atkinson's Grocery, Mom and Pop's Coffee Shop had already opened in the shell of what had survived. All the construction meant construction workers, and they had to eat, so Mr. and Mrs. Whitehead, the owners of the diner, rebuilt what they could quickly and kept busy cooking and serving.

Next door to Atkinson's Grocery, Kennedy's Hardware Store also had a new brick front and openings for large windows. And it, too, contained many items salvaged from the old store after the storm. Lawrence Kennedy threw himself into his work. He had lost his house, his store building, and two children to the tornado, and he had a cast on his broken arm. Yet Kennedy reopened his hardware business two days after the storm.

With so many new houses under construction, as fast as he could buy lumber, it was sold. And he also built many of the small, new homes, working hard to bring back his hometown. When a *Wichita Sunday Beacon* reporter visited Udall, he wrote, "Everywhere . . . the skyline is broken by raw frame works of new homes going up." One of the new structures pictured in the paper was Gaillard and Betty Jo Thompson's. It even had a tree in the corner of the lot that had survived enough to leaf out.

John Arbuckle, the city clerk, reported that twenty-five families had already returned, some living in trailers as they rebuilt. In the two months since the tornado, Arbuckle had issued forty-six building permits, with more new ones being applied for daily.

Yet six survivors still remained in the hospitals, including Bobby and his father. And around the town, signs of the twister remained—barkless trees, brick walls with holes, broken sidewalks. And the new leaves of corn. When the grain elevator blew down, the seed it stored spread across the town. On the bare ground where houses once stood, green corn sprouted and grew, planted by the tornado.

The minister of the Hicks Chapel Methodist Church called Toots one evening and invited him and his daughter Patricia to a picnic. The next Sunday evening was one of those beautiful summer evenings when the heat had waned and light poured through the trees. Father and daughter drove out into the country toward Dexter to find the small church and the grassy lot full of cars. Food weighed down the tables—platters of fried chicken and fresh corn on the cob, bowls of potato salad from newly dug potatoes, dishes of homegrown tomatoes and deviled eggs. A separate table held cakes and pies, beside which sat several freezers of homemade ice cream.

After the feast, they sang hymns, then the minister asked Toots to talk. The mayor told them about the storm, how he and his family had been lucky to survive; he mentioned many of the dead and the destruction of so many homes and businesses; and he talked about the rebuilding of Udall, of how some families had already returned. The congregation took up a collection for their neighbors to the northwest, the plates overflowing.

Then a woman called for Pat to come to the front. Pat didn't expect this; she had only come along to keep her dad company. What was this attention about? In her teenage awkwardness, she pressed down her skirt and moved to the front of the congregation, where the woman smiled and gave her a carefully wrapped gift. Go ahead and open it, the woman said. Pat pulled back the paper and cardboard. Inside she found a new Brownie Camera, just like the one she had lost. Pat burst into tears at the kindness of these strangers. They had read the comments she'd told a reporter what seemed like years ago about missing her most-prized Brownie. And here was another—something small in so much lost yet something to hold onto.

Fig. 1. The Udall Water Tower before the tornado. The house to the right of the tower belonged to Henry and Sadie Storey, who both died in the storm. Udall Community Historical Society Museum.

Fig. 2. Men and dog search the rubble. In the foreground, what appears to be a mangled baby stroller. The *Mennonite*, July 28, 1964, 465. Mennonite Church USA Archives, Udall, Kansas, NARA 283889.tif, Wikimedia Commons.

GRADE SCHOOL.

Fig. 3. The grade school was a shambles after the tornado. It and the high school were rebuilt with large underground shelters. Kenneth Spencer Research Library, University of Kansas.

32. LOOKING N E FROM GRADE SCHOOL.

Fig. 4. Looking northeast from the grade school, with a bulldozer clearing debris (*on right*) and downtown and railroad cars in the distance. Udall Community Historical Society Museum.

Fig. 5. Men from the Mennonite Disaster Service came by the hundreds to help with search and rescue and then with cleanup and rebuilding. Downtown and the Seaman house are in the background. Mennonite Library and Archives, Bethel College, North Newton, KS. #2005-0107.

Fig. 6. The remains of Udall's Water Tower. It fell directly west into the street, hitting no houses. Udall Community Historical Society Museum.

Fig. 7. Truck frame in a tree. The driver's body was reportedly found far away. In the background, the ruined high school and part of the remains of the town piled for burning. Udall Community Historical Society Museum.

WRECKAGE OF CONGREGATIONAL CHURCH

Fig. 8. Wreckage of the Congregational church and pastor's home. Cowley County Museum and Historical Society.

Fig. 9. Udall Volunteer Fire Department truck. It was restored and returned to service. Udall Community Historical Society Museum.

Fig. 10. Udall's downtown, the day after, looking south, showing the temporary Red Cross and Salvation Army headquarters and the archway where many had found shelter. Joyce and Bill Shook; Greg Proctor.

Fig. 11. Udall's downtown on May 26, 1955, looking north. The shell of Atkinson's Grocery (far left). The National Guard sent many soldiers to assist in the search, rescue, and cleanup. Joyce and Bill Shook; Greg Proctor.

Fig. 12. Udall's downtown on May 26, 1955, looking northwest. Behind the bare tree in the center are the remains of the Community Building, where a wedding shower had taken place and where fourteen people survived under all the rubble. Joyce and Bill Shook; Greg Proctor.

Fig. 13. Rear view of the wreckage of Udall's Community Building and Kennedy's Hardware Store, where sacks of cement remained unmoved by tornado. Joyce and Bill Shook; Greg Proctor.

Fig. 14. The tornado passed over parked railroad cars. Cars on the north were blown off the tracks to the southwest, and cars on the south were blown to the northeast. Cars in the middle, where the center of the tornado passed over and where railroad workers slept, stayed on the tracks. No men were injured. Udall Community Historical Society Museum.

Fig. 15. The Seaman home, a few days after the tornado, twisted off its foundation yet still standing. Udall Community Historical Society Museum.

Fig. 16. Aerial view of downtown Udall the day after the tornado. In the center a bulldozer clears the wreckage where the Community Building once stood and where the temporary City Building would be built. Kenneth Spencer Research Library, University of Kansas.

Fig. 17. Linemen restoring phone and electricity lines north of town the day after the storm. People from all over the region formed long lines of traffic to see the destruction. Joyce and Bill Shook; Greg Proctor.

Fig. 18. Pat Hurd, Udall telephone company owner and tornado survivor, took a break from repairing lines to talk with reporters a day or two after. Used with permission by Randy Hoffman and Abby Beard of Wheat State Technologies, formerly Wheat State Telephone.

Fig. 19. After the tornado, truckloads of donated clothing were sorted and given out in a nearby barn and college gymnasium. Cowley County Museum and Historical Society.

Fig. 20. One of many funerals held shortly after the tornado. Udall Community Historical Society Museum.

Fig. 21. Two weeks after the tornado, the town was cleared of rubble; the remains of the high school and debris pile in distance. Udall Community Historical Society Museum.

Fig. 22. Months later, firemen burn the Udall debris pile. At right they spray a garage to keep it from igniting. Udall Community Historical Society Museum.

AFTERMATH OF THE TORNADO.   73

Fig. 23. Rubble burns near the new high school gymnasium in early August 1955 as workers pause from rebuilding the bleachers. Udall Community Historical Society Museum.

Fig. 24. Udall, circa 1956. Gearhart's gas station at left; Clark Grocery's new building in center, with Wheat State Telephone's beside it; and the temporary City Hall at right, where the Community Building had stood and where the rebuilt one now stands. Udall Community Historical Society Museum.

13 The Smoke of What Used to Be

BOBBY ATKINSON WAS READY TO GET OUT. AND THE ST. MARY'S HOS-pital staff probably had had enough of the bored teenage boy in the top-floor room. Often, after his leg was healed enough for the cast to come off, he climbed out of bed without assistance—which he wasn't supposed to do; he fidgeted away the long hours of no TV and few visitors, but even his fidgets were constrained by the casts still on both arms. When no one was looking, he unwound a clothes hanger to slide into his casts to scratch those unreachable itches, then he hid the wire for later use under his mattress. Whatever books and magazines came his way bored him. Sometimes he played cards with the janitor in the basement. Often he sat on the bench outside by the back door, the closest he could get to freedom. He was ready to go.

After two months the doctors thought him well enough to be released earlier than planned. Since Bobby had no home to go to, he went to live with his father's parents, Grandma and Grandpa Atkinson. But they, too, had lost their home in the tornado; they were renting a farmhouse a few miles west of Udall. Bobby would live with them in different houses for the next three years, until he graduated from high school.

The night of his release, Bobby walked out of the hospital on his own—his leg had fully healed, but he still had those white plaster casts on both arms and bandages wound around his head. He wanted to see his father, so his grandparents drove across town to the other hospital in Winfield to visit Bob Atkinson Sr.

When Bob arrived at Newton Memorial the night of May 25, one orderly described him as "human hash." Another admitted him into the hospital as a two hundred–pound unidentified male. He was among the last to be found, and thus, by the time he arrived at the hospital, all beds were occupied, and cots and pallets on the floor lined the corridors. On the second floor, though, in a sun porch at the end of the hall, the nurses found him a spot, where he had to wait several hours for the operating room to open.

No one expected him to live. In a hospital overflowing with tornado victims, Atkinson's injuries were among the worst. Doctors considered amputating his left leg, it was so mangled. The tornado had pummeled his head and torn off his scalp. His eyes were swollen shut, one possibly permanently blind. Like his son, Atkinson had also had a board driven into his chest cavity. Before being found that night, he had pulled it out himself. And like his son, Bob Sr. had thousands of rocks and splinters rammed into his body.

His condition was so bad that doctors assigned a special nurse to stay by Atkinson's side all night and to check his vital signs every fifteen minutes. He was unconscious, though he rolled and tossed in his bed. The doctors feared his throat would swell shut, so they intubated him. Anyone outside his door could hear his labored breathing through this metal tube. He survived the night, surprising everyone.

Bob kept surviving the next day and night and the next, still in a coma, sometimes rolling in delirium. On the third day he leapt out of bed. He believed he was back in his home with the tornado coming. His leg couldn't support him, so he fell hard to the floor, waking to pain and confusion. The nurse helped him back in bed, where again he slipped into a coma.

After five days Atkinson regained consciousness. His first question was about his family. Someone—his parents or a doctor or nurse—told him the truth: his wife and two youngest sons were gone. The boys were found dead the night of the storm, probably from drowning. Nina lasted a few days in a Wichita hospital. All three had just been buried. His oldest son, Bobby, was still alive in another hospital. For that Bob Sr. was grateful.

That night an orderly visited Atkinson to find him awake.

"Have you tried counting sheep?" the orderly asked.

Bob paused, his mouth and face swollen, making it difficult to talk. "No," he said, "I haven't been counting sheep; I've been counting my blessings instead. I've lost a lot, but I still have a few left."

His faith was deep, his disposition calm and bright. A few days after the tornado, another storm blew in, filling the Kansas sky with lightning and wind. Many patients panicked, clamoring downstairs for shelter in the basement. Not Bob. An orderly found him sitting in his sunroom, the window open. No lights, just the flicker of his cigarette and the lightning.

A few weeks into his stay, a hospital volunteer who had helped him on the night of the tornado came back to visit. Bob sat in his room by the open window looking out, enjoying the view, his eyes healed. The volunteer asked if, when his eyes were swollen shut, had he thought he might have to live the rest of his life in darkness.

Bob said his faith had never wavered, despite blindness and loss and cancer. He told her about how before the storm, he and his wife had worried about how she would take care of the boys, especially the two youngest. The couple believed the doctors' predictions, that the cancer would shorten his life, that he probably wouldn't live another year. The thought of leaving his wife with so much responsibility had deeply troubled him. But now, he realized, the Lord had taken care of that. And Bob Atkinson was not bitter at all.

So, when, two months after the tornado, his son Bobby came hobbling into his room, an immense joy and sadness filled them both. They tried to hug, but Bobby's casts got in the way. And Bob Sr.'s mouth and face were still swollen from the storm injuries and the cancer, so he could hardly talk. They just held hands and cried and realized they didn't need to talk, not yet.

One evening Beth's dad, Cecil Morgan, came home from a city council meeting with what he thought was good news. He and other council members had debated for weeks about the water tower. They knew they needed a new one, especially as finished houses hooked back up to the water system. So, in one of their many meetings, they decided to move the location of the new water tower out of the middle of two streets and over to the town park. This would make the streets safer and the tower maintenance easier.

The news disappointed Beth and her friends. Before, when any high schooler wanted to "cruise," the route had definition—you started on one end of town by the railroad tracks, drove down what everyone called Main Street, even though the signs read First, looped around that water tower, and headed back to the tracks. After every ball game and on every Friday night, this was the ritual for generations—honk your horn and drive fast around the tower. Now that the water tower wasn't there anymore, how would they know when to turn around? Beth knew this was a minor issue after so much had happened, but it was just one more change in her town that she hated to accept.

Toots Rowe liked to make things happen, especially when a group of people worked together for the good of everyone. That's why he enjoyed his job on the oil rig, where his crew labored alongside one another to build and drill and pump, much of this work at the edge of a little danger—a gasket could fail, a pipe could bust, a weld could break—and who knew what might happen then.

Plus, Toots enjoyed being in charge, where he could size up a problem and figure out how to proceed. He knew the men who worked for him, their talents and weaknesses, and Toots knew how to keep them motivated with good words and a lot of teasing and pranks.

So, naturally, Toots was drawn to the Udall Volunteer Fire Department, a squad he helped lead for many years as they put out house or barn or brush fires. A few months after the tornado, in early August, it fell to the UVFD and the Civil Defense to burn the debris pile.

For weeks volunteers had worked cleaning up, first on the streets, then each lot. The cranes filled dump trucks, lifting bucket by bucket the larger pieces—the bricks, the walls, the trees—followed by other volunteers doing the slow, handwork of picking up the smaller pieces. They filled who knows how many dump trucks, which hauled the remains of this town the few short blocks to the high school football field. There the debris pile grew and grew, haul trucks dumping, while another crane stacked and bulldozers pushed it all together. The demolished cars, roughly one hundred in number, lined the side of the field, to eventually be hauled away. The final debris pile was so big it could be seen from any part of town as well as miles out into the country. It dwarfed the long one-story remains of the high school that was being renovated. One newspaper described the debris pile as resembling "a mountainous grave" and went on to estimate that it was "two blocks square and 25 feet high." Another newspaper reported that "55,000 yards of storm debris" would be "buried at the cost of $24,500, paid for by civil defense."

Toots and the fire department had to wait for the ideal weather— little to no wind and rain predicted the next day. The pile lay directly to the west of the school and town—so when they burned, the winds had to be coming from the east. Otherwise, sparks might fall on what little remained of Udall and start a larger fire.

On August 3 Toots and the other volunteers circled the huge pile. Every hundred feet or so, they made small stacks of paper, kindling, and dried wood. On top of a few of these, they also added an old car tire—something that would burn hot and long. Then they sprayed oil as high up onto the stack as possible. The *Winfield Courier* called the huge stack "the funeral pyre of 'Old Udall'" and noted that "eighty barrels of oil were poured on the remains."

When all was ready, men circled the huge pyre with torches, and when they finished, small columns of smoke wavered into the blue sky. Soon the starter fires grew and joined, the small plumes merging into a massive, rising cloud. It didn't swirl. It didn't spin. But in some ways it looked like a tornado—gray, tall, and foreboding. The column billowed up in a huge cloud, black and thick and visible for miles.

The flames and heat grew, and the firefighters moved back to the edge of the field. The UVFD hadn't yet replaced its trucks, so other towns' fire departments volunteered to help. They had little to do but spray water on the roofs of nearby buildings and put out any grass fires. Mostly, they just watched. There goes my house, someone probably joked. Yeah, that was my roof over there, someone else said. They knew the vehicles that had lined the field—cars that had carried them on first dates. And in that fiery mound, they knew the rooms, they knew the tables and chairs and beds that had filled them, they knew the lives that had carried on as normal as sunrise and sunset. The ignited memories rose to drift off and disappear.

One of the first things Bobby wanted to do after he came home from the hospital was go for a ride. His grandparents hesitated, yet they knew they couldn't shield their grandson—he had already suffered too much. So the three of them climbed into the car, Bobby riding in the back seat to stretch out his bad leg.

They drove the few miles to Udall, and halfway there the tornado's pathway became starkly visible—few trees stood, and those that did were debarked and leafless. And the town's skyline had changed. The water tower was gone. Bobby knew this, remembered climbing over its fallen remains to find help that wet night so long ago, but still it surprised him. And the bareness of it all, that surprised him too. Some shells of downtown buildings stood, plus Stella Kennedy's house and few others in the northwest corner, like Beth Morgan's. The rest was cleaned up and hauled off, lot after lot, flat and bare as a table. The town was different, he realized, and would forever be different, and Bobby also understood that he, too, had changed, that he, too, would be forever different.

At the west edge of Udall, they saw the smoldering debris pile, the wind blowing ash over their car. Then, nearby, they stopped at the cemetery. Bobby pulled himself out of the back seat and limped the few yards to the three graves. A hard wind blew out of the west, scattering up dust from the bare dirt of the three plots. Some grass had started growing on the slight mounds. His grandfather told him that the gravestones would be coming in a few weeks; the monument maker had been overwhelmed by so many sudden orders. Bobby took in the three rectangles, two of them smaller than the third. He remembered the last time he said good night to his mother and the heavy breaths coming from his sleeping brothers. But he didn't cry. He had done that in the hospital.

His grandmother guided Bobby back to the car, then his grandfather drove up and down the streets, steering around construction crews. Bobby was surprised to see several houses already had their roofs built. But the houses he had grown up knowing—Gaillard Thompson's brick one-story, Mrs. Simons' wide-porched Victorian—all the ones he delivered papers to, were gone. And all the six or seven houses his family had lived in over the years, they, too, were gone. They passed what was left of the high school and again saw the rubble heap. His grandfather told him that soon earthmovers would dig and fill a pit with what hadn't burned. He pointed to the far edge of the field and told Bobby about the row of storm-demolished cars, now all hauled away. Bobby imagined his father's Chevy, remembered its shelter from the hailstorm.

When they turned onto Second Street, they came to the Atkinson family's lot. That house had been the first one his family had owned; now like so much else, it existed only in memory. He and his grandparents said nothing and slowly drove on.

They came to his grandparents' new house, a block and a half west, the stud walls just raised, the rafters framing slots of blue sky. During the storm Bobby's grandparents, Hugh and Sylvia Atkinson, had taken shelter in their basement. The tornado ripped everything off the foundation and threw debris onto them in their shelter. They had cuts and bruises but, luckily, nothing bad.

Granddad Atkinson and Uncle Dick had been working every day to rebuild the house, one of the first to go up in the whole town. In a month or so, when they had finished and moved in, they planned to restore the Atkinson's Grocery building a few blocks away. The tornado had ripped off the store's roof and most of the top floor, so Bobby's granddad told him they'd firm up what was left and then build a new roof, one story lower. Bobby wished he could help.

Beth Morgan looked forward to being a senior. All her life her mother had been a teacher, so Beth learned to like school, knew it as a place to put up bulletin boards or record grades or laugh with friends.

During the summer of 1955, the school board located an old two-story barracks in Planeview, a town several miles away, near Wichita. It came in two sections on two tractor trailers, and once situated on the old school grounds, the barracks became Udall's temporary school for grades one through eight. Through that summer Beth wondered if she'd spend this last, special year going to classes in a barracks or, worse, getting bused to some other school. As the heat of June and July poured down, the new high school slowly rose. In late August students dressed in their Sunday best to register for classes in one of the school's finished classrooms. The *Wichita Eagle* sent a photographer to capture the event. One photo showed Aileen Holtje, now Mrs. Roy Wittenborn, talking with elementary students about their upcoming classes. Another captured Aileen registering Barbara Ann Braddy, a six-year-old using crutches; doctors had had to amputate her wounded foot after the tornado. Another photograph showed high school students registering for classes. Bobby Atkinson stood tall as he waited in line. The caption noted he had lost his two brothers and mother in the tornado. The photo didn't reveal his scars.

By early September the barracks had been fully moved and reassembled for the elementary students, and most of the new high school was finished, so schools opened.

The tornado had destroyed the south and west sides of the high school, mainly the gymnasium and classes around it. It left other rooms, like the school office, mostly intact, except for blown-out windows. As a result, some days Beth had English in one wing; other days she and her classmates would have it in what had been the office, as the new school was rebuilt around them. The hammering and sawing, the shouting and jackhammering, competed with the teachers, who often had to yell to be heard. Through the construction upheaval, no one complained. They had a school, and that was enough.

They also had the biggest pile of debris to ever cover a football field, or so it seemed. After the first big fire, now every few days, the bulldozers pushed the remaining rubble together, and men once again lit the fires. The smoke plumed dark and high. Sometimes it drifted into the school, hazing the hallways, slipping under doors. This smoke had been their neighbors' houses, their churches and stores, their own homes; they breathed in their history.

The class sizes in the school were small. Beth's class of 1956 had eight students, Allene's class of 1957 had twenty-two, Bobby's class of 1958 also had eight. There were approximately 75 to 85 students total in grades 9 through 12. All these students, plus all the teachers and staff, everyone, carried that tornado with them. When they went to the cafeteria, they remembered the school cook and her son, Hazel Standridge and Truman Turner, who had died in the storm. When they saw the high school principal and his wife, who coached the girls' sports teams, they remembered Michael Woods, their dead six-year-old son. Everyone had lost classmates or friends, siblings or parents. Each survivor knew someone who had died.

Gradually, as the year progressed, more rooms became finished and ready for use, and school life settled a little more. The school still put on its annual play, and in the spring, the seniors took their annual trip. And the juniors and seniors still had their prom.

Some days after school, Beth and her friends gathered at her house. Often, while they played records or did homework, they'd just stare down a hall or wander into the kitchen or living room. They'd be quiet or even cry. Her house comforted them because it looked like it had before the tornado. It looked like home.

After she wed in June, Aileen Holtje Wittenborn had planned to teach in a different school to be closer to her new home and her husband's work. But because of the storm, she decided to teach at Udall one more year. It would help her first, second, and third graders feel more secure, something the first weeks of school confirmed. Her children were unsettled and often cried. It didn't help that when storm clouds rose to the west, mothers rushed to the school to retrieve their children. And it didn't help that most of the students were physically unsettled as well; they had to live with friends or relatives out in the country while new homes were being built in town.

The barracks used for the elementary students had no air conditioning or insulation. At the start of the school year, it was hot; during the winter, everyone wore long johns and winter coats. And no playground equipment yet existed to replace the old, so the children made do, playing baseball or tag, hopscotch or jacks.

Aileen and Cleo Tschopp, the other elementary teacher, shared the first floor of the barracks, one room on each end with a lavatory in the middle. No door closed between the two rooms; it was all just an open space. So it was noisy, very noisy, and also very crowded and very hot in the fall, with no room for a fan. The two joined rooms only had one exit; if the students in one class had recess, they always had to travel through the other class to get outside. The teachers had only a few supplies, which included tiny blackboards that wobbled on flimsy stands.

Even as they could see their flattened town out the windows and watch the rebuilding, they didn't talk about the tornado. It might appear in some of the children's artwork or play, but the devastating loss was not discussed. Instead, the teachers made a great effort to resume a normal schedule. They believed it helped everyone to move on.

14 Trying to Find Normal

ALMOST THREE MONTHS AFTER THE STORM, AND A MONTH AFTER BOBBY came home, his father was released from the hospital to live with Bobby and his grandparents. It had taken Bob Sr. longer to recover from his tornado injuries because of his cancer. Eventually, the doctors said they could do little more, so home he came in a wheelchair he didn't like. At first his leg, covered in a cast, weighed too much for his busted-up knee to carry, and crutches hurt his arms, but soon he was able to hobble from room to room in his parents' house. He could barely write and barely walk, but after a while, he regained enough strength to drive his mother's car. He propped his leg to ease the pain and then drove the few miles to Udall; often he visited his wife's and sons' graves. Then he'd drive the half-mile to the family's grocery store, to watch it being rebuilt. He couldn't do much, but he answered questions, oversaw the construction, and slowly signed his signature to bills. Bobby helped where he could, but school had started, and that took most of his time.

One evening, shortly after Bob Sr. came home from the hospital, a few Mennonite men knocked on the Atkinson front door. They wore their plain clothes, black pants and blue or white shirts, and oddly, the men who refused to carry guns now carried three, or parts of three, along with something else.

These men had cleaned up debris in Udall, searching for anything they could save. Now they presented to Bobby and his father what they had uncovered at the Atkinson lot.

The Atkinsons turned the guns in their hands, inspecting them with surprise.

Look at what that storm did to this, Bobby said, as he held his single-shot .22, the one he liked to take out in the fields to shoot rabbits and squirrels. Its barrel curved so that it had a bow in it, like it was made to shoot around a tree.

How in the world? Bob Sr. said. He held his double-barrel 12-gauge shotgun, the one he used for hunting quail and pheasants, but it no longer had a stock. The wooden part was broken off and gone, and one of the barrels had a dent, like someone with a metal punch had spent hours pounding on it.

The third gun was a new .410 shotgun. This had been Gary's birthday present last October, the thing he had desired for a long time. Bob Sr. held it and remembered Nina putting aside a little of their income, saving up to give this special gift to Gary on his twelfth birthday. Gary had been a good shot, and the three Atkinsons had gone out into the fields around town often that winter, bringing home game for the family table. Now the shotgun no longer had the firing pin—the tornado had sucked it right out. And even if it still had that pin, it no longer had an owner who polished its wood until it mirrored his young face.

The Mennonite men held one more item. The guns had been in the same closet with Bob Sr.'s dress slacks. And the last item they found was not any of these slacks but the pocket of one that the storm had ripped out. That pocket held Bob Sr.'s billfold, a few bills and pictures, his army discharge papers, and his driver's license, all water stained but intact.

The Atkinsons thanked the Mennonites and watched them drive away. Afterward Bobby wondered about the quart jar of alcohol that had stood on their mantel, the one that held his father's finger cut off in the oil fields, Gary's big toe, greasy from when the bicycle sprocket cut it off, and Bobby's adenoids, big as a child's fists. Could they have survived the tornado? He knew they hadn't, but Bobby had to laugh at the thought of someone finding these odd family mementos.

Gaillard and Betty Jo Thompson's first house had previously been a horse stable. Gaillard liked to tell this to strangers, just as he liked to tell them about he and Betty Jo meeting on a blanket as infants. Back in the 1940s,

Gaillard and his dad moved this first house on a big truck, driving the stable fifteen miles from the small town of Derby, where it had stood. The stable had been long and narrow but solid, until the storm came.

All through the summer of 1955, Gaillard worked in the oil fields during the day, then drove to their new home in Udall to check on construction. The couple had decided to expand the original house size, so the new house was wider and longer, including a living room, another bedroom, and their own storm shelter. When Betty Jo visited the house site that summer, she always checked on the progress of their cave. She and Gaillard made sure the builder connected the cave to the house through a new back porch, so they'd never have to run through the rain to find shelter again.

The Thompsons' and Rowes' houses both went up quickly, some of the first to be completed. In late August, Gaillard and his family moved into their new home. On September 1 the Rowes moved into theirs.

The railroad tracks had also been cleared and repaired shortly after the storm, so the train was running again when Gaillard and Betty Jo moved into their new house. That first night, Gaillard set out his workclothes for the next day, wound his clock, and set the alarm. He was exhausted from hauling furniture, so he easily drifted off to sleep. A few hours later, in the middle of the night, the freight train came through. Just a block away from the Thompson's, the railroad crossing threw down its arm and began its *ding-ding* alarm.

Gaillard sat straight up, panicked and heart booming in his chest. He was back in the storm, the tornado bearing down. He had to get his family. They had to get to safety. Then he realized the booming was constant, more of a vibration. Then he heard Betty Jo's steady breaths. He felt her warm body beside him. Slowly, he realized that she, who always ran to the storm cellar first, was still asleep; that there was no other rumble besides the boxcars bumping down the tracks; that there was no storm.

For months afterward, the *ding-ding* alarm woke Gaillard. Sometimes he even raced to get the kids to the cave.

Patricia Rowe, like most of her peers, was ready for school—ready to try to find some normalcy, to be back with friends as she entered eighth grade. But she knew even before she walked into her classroom that it wouldn't be a normal year, that it never could be. Where, for example, was Gary Atkinson, Pat's classmate for seven years? She knew, but she didn't want to.

The teachers, staff, and students tried to carry on, tried to build routine back into their daily lives, even though a view out the classroom window showed how unfamiliar it all was.

Pat's eighth grade class met on the second floor of the barracks, and Pat's teacher, Mrs. Morgan, Beth's mother, also taught the seventh graders across the hall. Often she taught both classes by standing in the middle of the hall.

One of Pat's classmates, Ray Holmes, Allene's brother, had his desk against the outside wall. He had an elevated window view of the construction in town, and since the barracks building was old, he had a crack where the wall and floor met, a little slot into the uninsulated wall chamber. In it Ray ditched whatever papers he didn't want to take home to show his parents—his very own secret trash can. Plus, he thought, this'll add a little insulation to keep us warm. The school had no cafeteria, so everyone brought sack lunches. Ray sometimes didn't finish his sandwich, but that didn't matter; he just threw it down his private dump chute, where he could hear it land ten feet below. By spring all the discarded food scraps began to stink. He pitied the first grader who had to sit directly below him and directly beside the stench.

Pat Rowe played basketball for the school team, and after classes she and other players of both the boys and girls teams rode a bus to Belle Plaine, ten miles away, where they practiced in another school's gym. All year they had to be the visiting team, always playing their games on the opponent's court, never in their home gym. That space didn't exist yet, but slowly, as the school year progressed, out their classroom window they watched the gym and new school building rising next door.

Over the next months, Bobby Atkinson's grandfather took him to Dr. Grosjean's office in Winfield twice a week. There Ruth Comstock, the nurse, changed the dressings on his head and back, and the doctor checked his wounds. Besides all the major injuries—the broken arms and hand, the punctured lung and broken ribs, the stitched flesh all over his back and head—Bobby had dozens of smaller wounds, where the tornado's wind had driven rocks and splinters into his flesh. For years afterward, debris would work its way to the skin's surface, a pebble popping out behind his ear like some magic trick.

Dr. Grosjean had an instrument that looked like a pair of needle-nose pliers with a hook on the end, and he used this tool all over Bobby's body. He'd find the swollen infection and dig around until the splinter emerged, Bobby stoically grimacing and not saying a word. But on Bobby's knee, one piece of wood eluded the doctor. He knew something was buried there, the wound seeping and infected, but he couldn't get the debris out. The old doctor had a temper, and Bobby's knee usually made it flair.

One night Bobby and a few of his high school buddies, Dale Braddy and Dick Rutter, drove west to Belle Plaine. They wanted to visit this one particular field on this one particular farm at the edge of town. All summer they'd been watching the field's crop, calculating ripeness, and they figured it was time. They slowed the car to a stop on the shoulder of the road near some trees, cut off the headlights, and sat, watching and listening. The farmhouse was dark, hopefully everyone inside asleep. The field lay behind the house, so the boys planned to skirt the woods and keep to the backside of the barns.

The three teens slipped out of the car and into the field, the cicadas so loud the boys couldn't whisper. The moonlight on Bobby's head bandage and arms glowed, the casts like white flags, an easy target. He hoped the farmer stayed asleep.

Bobby's leg still pained him, so he hobbled to keep up. He was glad he had come along—watermelons covered the field, moonlight casting an odd shadow beside each melon. The boys went about thumping with their thumbs, trying to find the ripest ones. One of them laughed too loudly, and that set the farmer's dog to barking. So Dale and Dick pulled a melon up under each arm and started running. Bobby hauled up the biggest one he found, held it between his two casts, and started hobbling along as fast as he could.

The house lights came on, then the porch light. Dale and Dick were almost to the car, Bobby only halfway there. The screen door slammed, and Bobby looked back to see the farmer's silhouette. He held something long. Then the farmer fired his shotgun into the air. The boom jolted Bobby, so he tried to run faster—he heard the car start, saw the open door. His friends yelled: Come on, Bobby! Hurry! Bobby dropped his watermelon onto the floor of the car and dove onto the back seat. The car spun out and fishtailed down the road, the watermelons rolling side to side, the boys hooting and pounding the car roof.

Back in Udall, they found a quiet spot and devoured the fruits of their juicy, ripe thievery.

The next morning Bobby woke and swung his legs over the side of the bed. When he bent his knee, he heard a *phht* sound, and the pain suddenly eased. After over two months of constant piercing jolts, he knew—that watermelon run had worked his splinter upward to the surface of his skin, and it popped out. He limped to the other side of the room, to where the piece of wood had fallen. The splinter was about three inches long and as big around as a pencil. He couldn't wait to show it to Doc Grosjean.

On his next visit, Bobby climbed onto the examination table. He pointed to his knee, then held out his hand, the piece of wood in his palm.

I got it out.

The doctor held the splinter up to his thick-framed glasses, which always slid down his nose.

There's no way you could get that out!

Bobby shrugged and waited. Dr. Grosjean pulled out his special needle-nose pliers and sat down on his stool. He prodded Bobby's knee and no longer felt the hard lump. I'll declare, he said. How'd you do that?

Bobby told him about just waking up and swinging his leg over the bed and the splinter flying clear across the room. He said nothing about the watermelon run.

15 Marching On

ACROSS THE ALLEY BEHIND BETH MORGAN'S HOUSE, WORKERS BEGAN building the new Congregational church. It was her family's church, where everyone had been baptized, married, or buried. It was also the Rowe's church, where Lola served as pianist and where every child had the same Sunday school teacher, Minnie Satterthwaite, Lola's sister-in-law, Pat Rowe's aunt.

Every day Beth Morgan watched the workers. Instead of building on the old foundation, they dug and built the block walls for a huge basement. After this a crane set cement beams across the span. When the builders finished, both church and new parsonage had storm shelters. Beth always felt safe if she could run to church when another storm came.

A few blocks away, the Methodists were also rebuilding. Right after the storm, they met in a schoolhouse a few miles away, out in the country, then at the high school gym once it became available. Slowly, they rebuilt the original church structure. Unlike the Congregational church, though, and because of expenses, they didn't immediately build a shelter or basement, but they included one later, when they added a Fellowship Hall.

Sightseers, though fewer, still came on weekends, and Beth still tried to hide. Sometimes strangers caught her on the street to ask, Are you going to build back? Beth nodded and kept walking. Most Udallians did rebuild because they, like Beth, believed that once you lived under the Udall water tower, you could never leave for good. Udall was home. You came back. The tornado survivors still had a piece of land—it still had water and septic, and soon it would have electricity and gas. Sure, a tornado might strike again, but one might strike anywhere, so they decided to rebuild where they had lived. For some, especially the elderly, the Red Cross built small one-bedroom houses. These small homes didn't have the grandeur of their previous two-story homes with wraparound porches and gingerbread trim, but each one had a roof, and they were thankful for that.

The open prairie, the wide sky, the smell of dirt—Bobby Atkinson had missed so much while he was cramped up in that hospital. He tried to take in what he could, spending afternoons hiking the streams or visiting the farmers he used to help.

Two of those farmers, Harold "Shorty" and Rex Minson, father and son, worked the 160-acre quarter section the Atkinson family owned, just northeast of Udall. Some days Bobby hiked out to stand at the field's edge and watch Rex plow on his old John Deere D.

Or try to plow.

The field was one of the first the tornado touched, right after destroying Udall, so as the storm faded in energy, it dropped its cargo all over that land—railroad spikes and car fenders, shards of glass and sheets of metal roofing, and lots of splintered boards full of nails. The tornado also carried and dropped tons of topsoil that buried and hid this debris. The first time the Minson men started plowing, they soon had a flat rear tire. It was a good field, though, and Rex wanted to plant it, so he came up with a new method of working the soil. He tied a rope to the steering wheel, put the tractor in its creeper gear, lowered the plow, gunned the gas, let out the clutch, then he hopped off. In this lowest gear, the tractor moved slowly enough that Rex could walk along beside it. He turned the steering wheel with the rope while he picked up trash. He had to walk every round. On the backside of the acreage, he disappeared over a small rise. Bobby listened to the John Deere strain, charting its progress. By the time Rex returned, he had trash piled all over the tractor—parts of doors, flaps of tin roofing. He stopped to throw the debris off to the side, then started all over.

Rex and Shorty had hired a teenager from Derby to help, only to discover the kid didn't like to work. Plus, he about killed himself coming around a turn too fast, almost tipping over the two-and-a-half-ton tractor. Shorty was ready to run him off. One day he saw Bobby and asked, You ready to get on the tractor?

The cast on Bobby's left arm had come off a week or so earlier, but the cast on his right arm still ran from shoulder to palm. Bobby grinned and said, Sure. He wanted to work, loved to feel that engine pulling.

But I don't think I can pull that plow, he said, pointing to the cast. He'd plowed before with two good arms, one to steer and the other to reach around and grab the rope to trip the plow. But that was a long reach he knew he couldn't make now.

Well, Shorty said. We'll fix that. He dug through his truck's toolbox, found a handsaw, and told Bobby to brace his arm against the tailgate. Shorty gripped the cast in his left hand and gingerly cut the plaster right below the elbow, working the saw in a circle around the forearm without cutting any of Bobby's flesh. Then Shorty made a second cut up the length of Bobby's bicep. The white dust swirled around them, and chunks of plaster coated their feet. Shorty slid his big fingers under the edges, pried, and broke the cast off.

There, he said, as he threw the cast onto the debris pile.

Dirt caked Bobby's upper arm, months' worth of it, thick and dark. And the stench was so bad that Bobby had to turn away.

Now you can work, Shorty said.

And Bobby did—driving the tractor over the rolling hills he loved, pulling the plow, stopping to pick up debris. His right hand could never grip well, but the work was worth what little pain he still felt.

Shortly after the Wichita Builders Association finished the new City Building, Toots Rowe and John Arbuckle, city mayor and city clerk, set up office. They had asked the builders to construct a counter to divide the space. The larger area became the relief room, filled with tables and chairs for anyone who needed a break from cleaning up or rebuilding. This space also was used for council and other meetings. Then, behind the counter, Rowe and Arbuckle worked on salvaged tables. Few Udall city forms or records from before May 25 had survived the tornado, so they created what they needed as best they could.

Because of a spine injury from an accident years earlier, Arbuckle had no use of his fingers. To type, he held a special stick in his mouth to press each key. For years this is how he had typed up the city council meeting minutes, and now it was how he created and approved each house building permit.

At his desk Toots liked to be organized. He had neat stacks of documents and forms to decipher, fill out, and mail. The insurance claims came first—for the grade school and high school, the water tower, the old City Building and Community Building, the utilities and streetlights, and the fire department building and trucks. Ironically, the day before the tornado, a new two-bay fire hall had just been completed and occupied. And then destroyed.

Toots worried about the money. He didn't want to have to ask the council to raise taxes, and he didn't want to burden his fellow Udallians with more costs after so much loss. So, when the insurance adjusters visited to assess the damage, Toots walked with them to make sure they saw nothing remained and that they'd fulfill the entire amount of the claims.

The Civil Defense Service, backed by the telegram from President Eisenhower's promise of $250,000, seemed like a sure source of needed money as well. Toots had met with two CDS officials the night after the tornado, and he had filled out all the paperwork, yet the funds were slow in coming. Many of the builders were constructing houses on faith, believing Toots and the CDS officials that the money would come, yet for months Toots had nothing to give them. Then, finally, in early August, the government money arrived, and though it meant still more paperwork, Toots and John Arbuckle were happy to distribute it.

A reporter from Wichita asked Mayor Rowe about the "deluge of paperwork," and Toots smiled and said that sure, there were lots of forms, "but the $325,000 given for rebuilding city utilities and schools was an outright gift. We do not have to repay it in any form. Our tax load will not change for that." He was thankful that the Civil Defense Service funds

MARCHING ON

had a minimal amount of red tape. "As soon as each city construction job is completed, it is paid for," Toots said. And he added, "Everything we've applied for from Civil Defense in the way of utilities and schools has been passed." Then he listed all the amounts: for the new high school, CDS gave $94,000, and $241,000 came from insurance; for the grade school, CDS gave $83,150, and $60,000 came from insurance; for utilities, CDS paid $144,850, with insurance covering $10,000 on streetlights, $4,000 on the water tower, and $900 on the city building. Insurance also covered the fire truck.

The electric system was finally completed and in full operation on October 1, the same day the new fifty thousand–gallon water tower opened its valves to take in and distribute water. The other major job completed in October included the removal of the debris pile at the football field. After it burned in August, a company was hired with Civil Defense money to save what scrap metal it could to haul off for recycling. With nothing else left to salvage, excavators dug a large pit and bulldozed all that didn't burn.

"The town has a great future," Toots said. "Reconstruction is going on all the time." He told the reporter about expansion, how recently the council had added forty acres to the city limits and how another developer "has 80 acres plotted south of town—for a 30-acre lake and 103 building sites." When a new home was finished, it sold, he noted. Before the storm, the city had "183 electric meters." Now it had well over two-thirds of that. "I hope our town grows to about 1,000 population. I hope it gets that large so we can get a doctor, a dentist, and a drugstore here. We need those badly."

Then Toots recalled the doubt of many right after the storm, including government officials, who thought that rebuilding the whole town would be impossible. "I told them give us the [money for utilities and schools], and the people would return."

"And," he added, "they did."

In summers before the tornado, Bobby Atkinson's family used to go to the movies shown on the large, flapping sheet hung on the side of a building in the middle of town. Sometimes his parents dropped the three boys off with a grandparent and headed to a show in Oxford or Mulvane. His father especially loved movies, so after the storm, when his dad could get out, Bobby drove the two of them to Winfield to take in a show. They sat up in the balcony, where Bob Sr. could stretch out his bad leg and rest it on the banister. Bobby did the same. They watched *Oklahoma!* or westerns like *The Man from Laramie*, the picture show framed by their feet.

In early September, Bobby went back to school with the rest of his classmates, or what was left of their school. He walked through the halls amid the piles of new blocks and lumber, the sounds of pounding hammers making the teachers yell. Sometimes he turned to the seat behind him, where his best friends used to sit, only to remember that Wilmer Butcher was gone, and so was Truman Turner. Wilmer was short enough to slide under tackles on the football team, and Truman played linebacker and could hit hard. He also liked to eat an onion, raw and whole, like everyone else ate an apple. Bobby's class was small to begin with—only eleven students. And after the tornado killed two and one moved away, there were now only eight.

Bobby looked forward to sports, tried to, anyway. Baseball was his favorite, though they never had a decent diamond to play on, just a converted cow pasture. He had a good arm, accurate and strong, even with all the tornado had done to it, so as the star pitcher, he pitched most games. He played basketball too, first-string forward, but he never felt like he could play that sport as well as baseball or football. During football season he started as quarterback. The coaches only allowed Bobby into the game after taping sponge rubber onto his back. With the deaths and injuries, Bobby knew the team was a sad-looking bunch. But at least they could play.

That first year all the sports teams had to practice and play at other schools' gyms and fields. Then the next year, and for years after, before every game, the football players spread out across the field and started walking back and forth, slowly, searching. They knew from experience bits of debris worked up through the ground, nails and scrap iron, shards of glass and slivers of metal and pieces of boards. They dug around to pull out what poked up and then hauled it to a trash pile at the far corner of the field. Like the splinters that worked out of Bobby's and Allene's knees, the debris kept working up out of the skin of the earth.

At every game, in all three sports, Bobby knew he could find Toots Rowe in the bleachers, cheering him on. Toots and Bobby's father, Bob Sr., had played basketball together in the 1930s on a championship-winning Udall High School team. And now, as Bobby struggled with so much loss, Toots and another family friend, Leonard Defore, took Bobby on as a godson. They checked on him often, took him fishing, let him ride along as they worked. They did what they could, but Bobby still often felt overwhelmingly alone.

Bobby was already tall for his age, but now as he walked the school halls, the other students seemed even smaller, like little bitty kids. What did they know about death? He had made straight A's as a freshman; as a sophomore, he struggled to earn C's.

Always he sat near a window; always, Bobby watched the weather. If the wind picked up and blew the dirt around the school, he got agitated. If the wind brought in storm clouds, he had to get out. He just stood from his seat and walked down the rows of his classmates, out of the classroom and down the hall, pushing open the exit door and standing in the alcove. If it was dry, the dust blew hard into his face. If it was raining, he watched and listened. His teachers never said anything. They understood.

Beth Morgan played clarinet for the high school band. Her best friend, Allene Holmes, played snare drums. Bobby Atkinson played trombone. Pat Rowe also played clarinet and was a twirler, hoping some year she might become drum major.

The tornado, though, had destroyed all their uniforms and most of the instruments, including Bobby's trombone. Right after the storm, Cunningham Music Store of Winfield sent a check to Mr. Lanning, the band director, to buy instruments, which he quickly did. Other schools donated what they could spare, and a company in Wisconsin sent over $1,000 worth of new instruments as well. When it came time to begin band practice that fall, Bobby had a new horn.

But every time he looked back to the row behind him, he knew he'd never see his younger brother Gary beating on his drum. Gary had just started playing—he would've joined the band in a year. That loss just didn't go away. And it wasn't just Bobby—many band members had lost family and friends. And yet here they were. Here were their instruments. Here was this impulse to make music. So they did.

Back in the spring right before the tornado, Mr. Lanning had committed the band to march at the annual Kansas State Fair held in mid-September in Hutchinson, eighty miles away. Now the state fair was only weeks away. Though they had new instruments, the band still had no uniforms. After the tornado, people found coats without sleeves and other parts of uniforms spread across the county, none of them complete. At practice one day, Mr. Lanning gave the students two options. We can cancel, he said, or we can all wear what we have that is the same. He paused, watching their young faces. What if everyone wore blue jeans and white shirts? he asked. What do you think of that? Mr. Lanning knew they would have to agree, they would have to be willing to stand out, to be different, not as fancy as all the other bands there. The Udall band members looked at each other for a moment, then they all said yes. Even the poorest among them had decent jeans they wore to school and a white shirt. So, that's what they planned to do.

When they climbed off the bus at Hutchinson, the Udall students tried not to notice the other bands, with their bright uniforms and feather-plumed helmets. But they were everywhere and impossible to ignore. Beth and Allene stuck together; so did the others. Bobby assembled his trombone, Beth her clarinet; Allene slid the snare drum strap over her shoulder. Pat, one of the youngest, tried to keep her chin up. She and the other twirlers wore blue jean skirts, instead of jeans. On their white shirts, everyone wore a pinned-on tag that said Udall High School Band.

In front of the band, Pat helped two members of the color guard unfurl their homemade banner, a big sheet with their name. The lone tuba also had a "Udall" sheet clipped over the mouth of his horn. Then they practiced—their notes, their rat-a-tats, their twirls. Mr. Lanning walked up to everyone, reassuring them and tuning the wind instruments by ear. He smiled, nodded when the player adjusted his instrument to the right pitch, and moved to the next. Mr. Lanning was young, not much older than the seniors, and he was proud. They were nervous, all of them, including him, but they had practiced, and they were ready.

Other bands marched past, bright banners naming their hometowns: Wichita, Topeka, Wellington. Like a river, their colors flooded down Hutchinson's Main Street toward the stadium, a steady stream of orange and blue, gold and red. The Udall teens watched until finally it was their turn. Mr. Lanning gave the signal, the drum major gave the order, and Allene and the other drummers beat out their opening call rhythm. The Udall band stepped out on the long march. A few miles later, at the stadium entrance, the drum major again blew her whistle, and they all began to play their Udall High School song.

Out front, right after the banner, Pat twirled in time with the song, all the twirlers following the routine they had practiced for weeks. Beth stepped off in the front row with the other woodwinds. In the middle Bobby gripped his trombone's slide and played. At the rear Allene marched beside the bass drum, her wrists moving her sticks in that steady beat on her snare. They all tried to stay focused on the song, on the others playing beside them, and Bobby worried about hitting the person in front with this slide. But he didn't. And while they played, they kept their heads forward as Mr. Lanning had taught, focused ahead. Though they also snuck looks out of the corners of their eyes.

To their left the other bands that had marched before them now stood at attention in the field observing. To the right, in the stands, the large crowd watched and listened and clapped politely as they had for all the others. When the small Udall High School band approached the midway, the announcer called out their name, and suddenly something changed—the crowd realized who these oddly dressed teenagers were, and the people understood. It was as if the band was saying, We might not have fancy uniforms, and we've lost some players, but this is us—we're here, and we're here to play. The crowd all stood. They clapped and yelled, cheering on the band, their resolve to march, despite having lost so much. Beth, Bobby, Allene, Pat, and the others felt buoyed by this river of good cheer.

Afterward the local paper ran an article titled "Band of the Year." "More than 100 school bands have been in Hutchinson the past five days," it started. "This one was largest. That one played the finest. A third had the most dazzling uniforms," the writer continued. "There is no question, however, as to which band touched the greatest number of hearts." Then he described: "It was a small band and its musicians were less than the average age. . . . This band had no uniforms. Those in it, both boys and girls alike, were dressed simply in white shirts and blue jeans. Some of the jeans were well worn, but all of them were scrupulously clean. This band didn't even have a scarlet banner, blazoned with gold. There was only a red cloth, stretched across the mouth of the big horn, on which was lettered in white a sing word: Udall."

One man in the crowd that day witnessed this small band's determination. He went home to his Elks Club and told the group the story. They decided to send Mr. Lanning a check. This man petitioned all the Elks Clubs across the state to contribute money so the band could buy new uniforms. Soon the checks started arriving in the Udall High School mailbox, small amounts and large. Mr. Lanning deposited them in the school account, and when he realized the scope, he told the students they were getting new uniforms—forty-one of them, costing over $2,000.

Before the end of the school year, the new uniforms arrived—gray slacks and red jackets trimmed in white with a white belt, stiff shoulder pads, and white plumes flowing from their red hats. The twirlers' uniforms were white trimmed in red, and they wore white boots. Everyone was ecstatic as they tried on jackets, stiff and new smelling. Some of the band members bobbed their heads to make the plumes move, and the boys in the drumming line snapped their belts.

The next month they wore their new uniforms for the first time at their spring concert. The next fall they marched again into the Kansas State Fair, the sun making the red jackets even brighter, the wind dancing with each feather plume.

16 Everybody Deserves a Picture

WINTER 1956–MAY 1957

SEVEN TO TWELVE MONTHS AFTER

BOB ATKINSON SR. WENT FROM A MAN WHO HAD SURVIVED FOUR years of cancer to a man who had survived four years of cancer and a tornado. He had lost his wife, his youngest two sons, and his grocery store, his source of income, but he still had Bobby, and he still had other family to help. What energy he could muster he focused on his oldest son and on rebuilding their store.

The tornado had ripped off the upper floor of the store, so Bob Sr. bought materials, and his father and brother rebuilt the store's roof, making it a one-story building instead of two. They replaced the front windows and rebuilt and painted the interior walls. A clothing store in Winfield gave them shelving and display cases. And every day when Bobby returned home from school, he, too, picked up a hammer or paintbrush.

But Bob Sr. couldn't do these things. Once he had partially recovered from his tornado injuries, the doctors resumed giving him radiation to try to stop the cancer in his sinuses. So much poison targeted the side of his face that the whiskers stopped growing. It didn't work. The cancer seemed to accelerate, as if the tornado had given it more energy. The doctors tried heavier doses that just burned him even more. He traveled to the Mayo Clinic in Minnesota, and the doctors there told him that they'd have to remove his nose and one eye. It would be a delicate operation with no guarantee of success. Bob Sr. said no thanks. Through all of this, somehow—around Bobby, at least—he kept his good-spirited nature.

If Bob Sr. could get the store back and operating and then sell it, he'd give that money to Bobby, a gift to help him along, a nest egg for the future. By Thanksgiving, Bob Sr.'s father and brother had the building completed, the shelving installed, and the canned goods all purchased. They opened on December 1 and put the business up for sale at the same time. A month later they sold it, and Bob Sr. was relieved.

By Christmas he could no longer drive. He couldn't work in the grocery store. He couldn't really do anything.

Before the cancer and the radiation, Bob Sr. had beautiful penmanship. He took his time, curving the *A* of *Atkinson* in an elegant manner. When he finally signed over the deed to the store in January 1956, he couldn't read his own signature.

He died January 20, 1956. Two days later Bobby turned sixteen.

When his father died, Bobby knew it was just him now. No brothers, no mother, no father, just him. And he realized there were two ways he could go. He chose to focus only on the one. He knew he had to go forward.

For months Mennonite women packed lunches and sent their men off to Udall. They heard the stories of the immense destruction caused by the tornado, and they witnessed the purpose the men had found in being able to swing a hammer to rebuild a home for someone in need. So the women wanted to participate. They set to raising money, gathering materials, and assembling what they called linen, or towel, kits. Each bundle included a toothbrush, toothpaste, soap, and washcloth, all wrapped in a towel and pinned together with a safety pin. With money donated from the town of Hebron, Nebraska, which had suffered a tornado a few years earlier, the Mennonites also purchased 225 blankets, enough to give every family at least one.

The women wanted to deliver these kits in person, so they waited until December, when most families had resettled in their new homes. One cold day they came to the Morgan's house, the door newly painted. Beth Morgan watched out the window as these strangers stood on the porch. Beth's mother greeted them kindly, unsure of their purpose. Can I help you? she asked.

Oh no, we're here to give you something. They asked how many people lived in the Morgan house, then they pulled from their box three kits.

Mrs. Morgan tried to refuse. We still have all of this from before the tornado. I don't want to be rude, but we don't need this.

The Mennonites ignored her. She repeated her gentle rebuke. The strangers just handed her a blanket and a kit for each member of the family. It doesn't matter who lost more or less, one woman said. Everyone receives a kit. We want to make sure you do too.

In all the Mennonite women gave out over 2,000 kits to tornado survivors in Kansas and Oklahoma. In Udall they visited with 197 families and distributed 541 kits. But they also noted that even by December, some families had not returned to Udall yet, and some never would.

As more and more people moved back to Udall and as winter turned to spring, Mayor Rowe, Marshal Keely, and other town leaders decided they could do more to avoid another disaster. Some gathered materials, while others chipped in money to buy items, such as heavy telephone poles, windows, and roofing tin. On the far side of the high school football field, they anchored four poles deep in the earth. On top of them, twenty feet high, they built a platform and a small, ten-foot-square hut. It had windows on all sides and a walk-around. Now they had a watchtower, which allowed them to better see what might be coming.

Marshal Wayne Keely was in charge. Anyone, women or men, over the age of fourteen could take a shift, and shifts of two people lasted two to four hours. When the Weather Bureau issued a storm warning, Keely had volunteers in the tower constantly, through the night and day.

Before anyone could volunteer, though, they had to take a short class on weather and planes because the tower served as a lookout not only for storms but also for suspicious aircraft. With the Cold War heating up, the Udall citizens wanted to help with Civil Defense, so they learned to identify planes. Every time one flew over, the observers recorded in a log—time, direction traveling, and type of plane.

Along with Keely and Toots, many people took shifts in what they called "the Tornado Tower," including Gaillard and Betty Jo Thompson, Clara

Lacey, Jerrold Hoffman, and Beth Morgan Evans's husband, Clifford. Over 120 people signed up, and they ranged in age from fourteen to eighty. All of them had other responsibilities, tending children or working a late shift, but they made time to stand watch and help.

All through her high school years, Pat Rowe, Toots and Lola's eldest, often volunteered with her best friend. They'd sit and gossip and look through binoculars at their homes, but they also listened for aircraft and learned to know the different types of clouds. As Jerrold Hoffman said, though, "When it got a little stormy, it took guts to stay up there!"

To make it truly effective, the watchtower had a direct line to City Hall and the marshal's offices. If an observer noticed suspicious planes or clouds, they pressed the alarm. Likewise, weather spotters spread out across the countryside in their cars, using radios to communicate with others.

During that first year after the tornado, an alarm for severe storms went up five different times from the watchtower. Five times the warning siren pierced the surrounding countryside, and five times everyone left the comfort of their homes to seek shelter in their storm caves. Each time block captains prowled their neighborhoods to make sure lights came on in every house. If no one in a house woke up from the siren, the block captain banged on the door until the lights came on. Also, with every alarm, emergency calls went out to surrounding towns, police officers and firemen asking their nearby colleagues to be on standby. As one newspaper put it, "If at all humanly possible, there will be no communications blackout again for Udall before word of an impending disaster is spread." Each time after the siren stopped, people emerged from their cellars thankful that another tornado hadn't descended.

Beth Morgan's class tried to have as normal a senior year as possible, despite the tornado. They ventured to the Lake of the Ozarks for their senior trip, the four boys in one car, the four girls in another, both driven by chaperones. There in Missouri, they sang and swam and tried cigar smoking for the first time, which made the boys sick but not the girls.

Back in Udall, the carpenters had completed the gymnasium in time for

EVERYBODY DESERVES A PICTURE

the students to have their class play, junior-senior prom, and graduation. At the beginning of the prom, as was the tradition, a junior class member formally welcomed the seniors with a short speech, and a senior gave the response. Her classmates chose Beth to make this formal thank-you speech, which she nervously did. As was also prom tradition, the juniors hosted the seniors, decorating the gym with crepe paper flowers and playing records for the dance. Junior class parents prepared the food. No catering, no live music, and no dates. Instead, everyone danced together, happy to have finished high school and a little sad too.

Graduation made Beth even more nervous. She was valedictorian, which meant she had to give the graduation speech. This time the audience included more than her classmates and a few parents and teachers. This time it included additional faculty and families and adults from the community. Her mother helped her write the speech, and on graduation day, Beth spoke about the turbulent year they had endured and the gratitude they felt to all who had helped them. Then the eight members of the class of 1956 walked across the new stage to receive their diplomas.

On the one-year anniversary of the storm, Udall held a memorial service to honor the dead and recognize how far they had come in such a short time. The new Community Building had been rebuilt in only four months, all with donated labor. The new Congregational church and parsonage were also completed. And builders had just finished the new phone company building, so all four structures had dedication ceremonies. The phone headquarters included a plaque honoring Mary Taylor, the switchboard operator who had died there while on duty.

At the intersection of the two main streets, 150 or so people gathered. Mayor Rowe wanted a simple affair that included several minutes of silent prayer. And he wanted it in the street, in the middle of the business district, because, as he told a reporter, "It's the center of everything here—that night and now."

Toots gave a brief speech. "Only the courage, faith, and determination of you people," he said, "has made it so we can meet here today to show our respect to our loved ones and our neighbors that we lost." Despite this loss, the mayor expressed his town's gratitude to God for sparing so many and to the neighboring communities that came to their aid. The town, he said, is also grateful "to friends throughout the world, thousands of miles away," who rallied in their support. "Udall is not even a dot on the map of the United States, but we couldn't lose our courage here when we learned that people 6,000 to 7,000 miles away from us were praying for us. We are rebuilding on the faith of God and prayers," he said. "This is our home. We said we'd rebuild it—and that's what we've done." Ministers led the gatherers in prayer, the names of those who died in the tornado were read, and the ceremony ended.

Also a year after the tornado, newspaper reporters returned to Udall to recount the tragedy and report on how the town had rebuilt. One paper featured a photograph of the town's new City Building under construction. The reporter interviewed John Arbuckle, city clerk, who said fifteen businesses had returned or been started, and the new high school was finished. New houses almost all had storm cellars, and the "storm warning center," a tower at the edge of the football field, was "operated around-the-clock." Arbuckle estimated the current population was 385, well below what it had been before the storm. But the residents now had a storm siren to blare any warnings. This "whistle" featured prominently in the photo.

Another newspaper reporter spent more time in town, especially with the Rowes. While Toots was still out working on the oil rig and their son, Gary, was playing outside, the reporter talked with Lola. He told her the newspaper wanted to give the woman's perspective of the tornado. She took a long look out the window that faced the vacant lot, the space that had been her aunt Emmie Foulk's home, where she had died in the tornado. Lola deflected the reporter's question, saying: "I guess there is no 'woman's angle.' Everybody was wonderful. Why even the kids pitched in." She talked about how many people had come to help right after the storm, relatives and strangers like the Mennonites. She told the reporter about Toots's boss giving him time off so that he could "build back a town." And Lola also mentioned how many people were rebuilding, including many of the older citizens, like the Gearharts, in their late seventies, yet going into debt to rebuild their home and garage. Or Lola's own parents, the Satterthwaites, aged eighty and seventy-five, who decided to move from their farm outside of town and retire to Udall. They invested $30,000 to build their new house, along with three rental houses "to encourage teachers and new people" to move to Udall.

Lola and Earl had started rebuilding their own house just twelve days after the tornado, using insurance money and savings. But, Lola told the reporter, some families "just couldn't come back. . . . They'd lost everything but their own lives—and it's hard to go on alone . . . with just memories." She noted that "ten complete families were wiped out"; their vacant lots remained empty as relatives settled the estates.

When the reporter asked if she had ever thought about leaving, building somewhere else, Lola didn't hesitate: "Land, no! I was born and raised here, and Earl's lived here since he was a baby—no place else would be home." She added, "Most folks felt the same," so that now the town had "nearly as big a population as before."

Gary had come in from playing, his father following him. When they heard the conversation, Gary chimed in, "We've got more kids in grade school this year than last." Toots boasted that at the high school "despite the loss through death we have one student more than last year."

Lola told the reporter about how the high school students had had to register for classes the previous August, even though they had no school, and that everyone just had to carry forth. "There are so many tales of courage and hope and help," Lola said. "The story has never really been told. . . . But maybe it can never be."

Before he left, the reporter asked for a tour of their new house and if he could take some photos for his piece. Lola said she didn't mind, but "I don't want people to think I want to be having my picture taken. Everybody here should have his picture taken. . . . We were just lucky—that's all—we and our kids were lucky. We're alive."

In May 1957 Allene Holmes and her class went on their senior trip. They had worked all four years raising money, collecting scrap iron and selling soda and candy at football games.

But first, they had to convince their classmate Marilyn Foote to go along with them. During the tornado the terrific winds had driven a board through her right leg with such force that the doctors could not save it. Foote knew before anyone told her that her leg would have to be removed, and that long night after the storm, the doctors amputated it above the knee. Two years later, she still stumbled often and hadn't yet mastered walking well with her prosthesis. She didn't think she could manage the amount of walking required for the trip, but she didn't want to make her classmates push her wheelchair everywhere.

She also needed help getting dressed. She wore a special sock under the prosthetic with a strap around her waist to help hold it on. Allene and others said they'd help, so Marilyn's mother taught them how to pull on and adjust the sock and strap. On the trip they planned to take turns helping Marilyn dress and pushing her wheelchair from place to place.

Early one morning the Udall High School seniors piled into their charter bus, with Marilyn hopping up the steps along with everyone else. They claimed seats and stowed suitcases and leaned on pillows, too excited to even pretend to sleep. First stop: the Indianapolis Speedway, where the boys wished they could drive around the huge oval track. Then they headed east to Washington DC, where they met their senator, toured the White House, and walked the Mall. Allene was amazed by the Wright brothers' airplane hanging there above her in the Smithsonian. After three full days in DC, they headed to New York City.

In the city they again had a full itinerary, which included visiting the Statue of Liberty, the Empire State Building, and Coney Island. On their last day, they had to make a choice—either venture to Yankee Stadium to see a baseball game or go to Macy's. Allene Holmes's boyfriend, Roy Kistler, wanted her to go with him to watch the Yankees play the Kansas City Athletics. Allene chose the upscale shopping experience instead. It was their first fight.

At Macy's, Allene rode an escalator for the first time. But Marilyn couldn't ride the moving steps, so Allene also rode the elevator. Up they went, a group of girls with little money on a shopping spree. Their wide eyes and giggles betrayed their pretend sophistication.

Back on the bus, Allene didn't tell Roy about the escalator. He only told her the Yankees won and that she had missed seeing Micky Mantle and Yogi Berra play. The Udall Yearbook King and Queen forgave each other and settled in for a nap. Seven months later, Allene and Roy would marry, and they would stay married for over sixty years. But now, on that bus the seniors headed to Niagara Falls, where they stood at the edge and felt the mist of the falls blow over them. Then they headed west to make the twelve hundred–mile journey home in time for graduation.

17 Remembering

TWO YEARS AFTER THE TORNADO, THE ONLY BUILDING STILL UNDER construction in Udall was the city hall, which also would house the police and fire stations. The rest of the town had been rebuilt. On First Street a new bank sat next to a remodeled Mom and Pop's Coffee Shop, where coffee still cost a nickel and where Beth and Allene sometimes gathered with friends. Across the street, the new Community Building, with its "1956" cornerstone, already had been used for gatherings. The Post Office had moved into a new building, and the shiny, red-roofed water tower sat in the town park. Three new churches lined the streets between all the green lawns dotted with young trees next to new homes.

At the high school, Bobby played basketball in a new gym and walked down shiny new hallways. Next door, the elementary school also had just been completed, taking longer to finish than the high school. Enrollment had held steady for the primary students compared to pre-tornado times, and for the high school, the number of students had increased from 60 in 1955 to 73 in 1957, in part because new families were moving in. The town had expanded into the surrounding fields, and developers had built thirty new homes, each with its own storm cellar.

But not everyone had rebuilt; vacant lots with only grass and sometimes the remains of a block foundation were scattered throughout the town. These lots were like the thick skin of scars, healed but visible.

The brick walls of the new city hall slowly went up. Volunteers from sixteen different labor unions worked on the building, using materials donated from several different suppliers. When finished, the UVFD would move its two trucks—one new, one a refurbished tornado survivor—out of a nearby shed. The building would also give both the city marshal and Toots, the mayor, their own offices. Each office would have a window for keeping an eye on the weather.

By 1958 Toots Rowe and the city council members who had served during and after the storm had stepped down from their offices. Toots and his colleagues had used their positions to lead as well as to promote their town. They had two new schools, they proclaimed, together valued at well over a half-million dollars. They had new water and septic facilities and "one of the most modern telephone systems in the United States." Four new churches dotted the town's map, along with the new Community Building for gatherings and the new City Building for the library, fire and police stations, and the mayor's and clerk's offices. And the homes that lined the streets, they, too, were mostly new.

Ellis Sherrard took over as mayor, and he and the council continued the practice of promotion by adopting a new slogan: "Udall, America's Safest City." To tell the world, they erected billboards at the edges of town, talked to as many journalists as would listen, and invited the public to an open house.

One of the key points in their claim of safety was the fact that if a nuclear bomb or another tornado threatened, Udall had more than enough space for everyone to shelter. As one city official would say years later, "We can put everybody in town underground." Both schools had extensive shelters that could house over five hundred people, and they were opened to the public when storms threatened. At least two of the churches also had storm caves, and approximately 70 percent of the 168 individual homes had their own storm cellars.

Articles promoting Udall also always mentioned the extensive warning system the town had in place, the watchtower and storm spotters, the sirens (now two) and the extensive communications networks—if something bad was about to happen, Udall was ready. Even *Popular Mechanics* ran a piece on Udall's preparedness. This national magazine ended its short article by saying: "Udall has 22 volunteer firemen, 8 auxiliary policemen, 30 people trained in first aid, 75 trained in mass feeding and four have radiological training to run a fixed monitoring station. The line of succession for the office of mayor has been set. Udall is prepared."

And three years after the storm, Udall was growing. Its population was back above six hundred, slightly higher than 1955. Mayor Sherrard claimed that all these individuals were saving money by choosing to live in Udall. Along with the town's low tax rates, it had low insurance rates because companies recognized its extensive safety measures.

Now Udall just needed even more people and businesses. In his proclamation Mayor Sherrard made it clear that the town was ready to expand. A new subdivision was in the works for mobile homes along with a potential shopping center. The citizens wanted new businesses, Sherrard said, including "manufacturing, retail clothing stores, recreation—such as bowling alleys, supermarkets, a doctor, [and] a dentist." He invited everyone to come to Udall to see how safe and modern the town really was.

Once the city council adopted the "Safest City" slogan, Sherrard sent a challenge to the National Safety Council "offering to defend [Udall's] claims against any other city in the nation." An official from the Safety Council planned to attend the community's open house. This open house, Sherrard hoped, would also "impress upon all persons that safety is both a public and private responsibility." He ended by saying, "In this way, we may help to repay our government for its assistance to us in our hour of need."

The five-year anniversary of the tornado was an even bigger affair. As part of the annual meeting of the Kansas Civil Defense directors, an all-day program in the Community Building focused primarily on Cold War defense, including a speech about how "strength . . . is the only answer to the Communist threat," demonstrations of rescue equipment, and tours of the Udall Elementary School storm shelter. Models of five types of shelters were also on display in the school gymnasium, and guests watched

Operation Cue, a movie, in color, of a nuclear test bomb in Nevada, its detonation and resulting damage. Toots Rowe served on a panel discussion about the Udall tornado, which also included the screening of footage taken the day after the storm.

Late in the afternoon, guests boarded three school busses for tours around the town, guided by tornado survivors. The high point of the event was a supper prepared by women of the Methodist church and a speech by a Civil Defense director. Before the speech, Mayor Sherrard read a telegraph he had just received from President Eisenhower. It stated: "Honorable Ellis Sherrard, Mayor of Udall: As a fellow Kansan I join you and the people of Udall in solemn commemoration of the disaster which destroyed your city five years ago. That disaster however did not destroy the spirit of the people. They recovered from their losses, rebuilt their community, and organized to prevent a recurrence of any such catastrophe. Congratulations and best wishes to each one. Dwight D. Eisenhower." Supper ended a half-hour before sunset so that the day could conclude with a memorial service led by four Udall pastors.

The 1965 ten-year storm anniversary was noteworthy in several ways. The first was the inauguration of a new warning system invented by the new mayor, Jerrold Hoffman. Hoffman, a survivor of the 1955 tornado, explained to a local reporter that most people in the area now had storm caves but they still needed a better warning system. He worked for the Udall telephone company and created a series of circuits and switches that could send three sharp warning signals through everyone's phone within a five-mile area. Roughly a thousand people could be warned within fifteen seconds.

At some point around this time, the watchtower built at the edge of town fell out of use. People grew tired of spending hours looking at prairie and clouds, and more likely, they found that weather spotters in cars with CB radios could do just as good a job with fewer people. Plus, the National Weather Service had improved, so that warnings were more accurate and timelier. The watchtower became the "Eagle's Nest" for the Udall High football team, where they announced and filmed games.

One other way the tenth anniversary was noteworthy, ironically, was for its lack of noteworthiness. Only pastors, town leaders, and families and friends of those who died attended a memorial service for those killed by the tornado, making it a much smaller event than the five-year anniversary. They gathered at the Udall Cemetery, not the Community Building, and they gathered on Memorial Day, the thirty-first of May, not on the tornado's anniversary, the twenty-fifth. Gone was any promotional salesmanship of the town. The local paper ran a photograph of the cemetery, and the photo's caption was the only mention of the service.

This smaller, more private memorial preceded many years of the same. The Udall community might have honored and remembered its tornado dead, but no mention of large, more public events filled the newspapers for many years.

Why might people keep marking a tragedy's anniversary? Or why might they stop? For Udall, the tornado was a defining moment in the town's life, and yet it was also painful to remember. Udall mayor Gary Tiller said in 1976: "We try not to think about [the tornado] . . . because it's so unpleasant. But it's still pretty vivid in many people's minds." Organizing any event takes a great deal of work. Many people must give their time and energy to make it happen. Add to this the continual tug between that which made a people, their history, and that which they want to make, their future. As newer generations grew to call Udall home, the history became something that defined their parents', grandparents', or strangers' lives, not necessarily their own. And yet, as the *Wichita Eagle* stated in 2015, "No recognition of where Udall is today—and where it wants to go from here—can be complete without an understanding of the nightmare it endured." Even new residents now living in Udall must understand the town's history in order to fully appreciate the place they call home.

In 1995 the *Wichita Eagle* devoted a great deal of space to the fortieth anniversary of the Udall tornado. Reporters interviewed several survivors, including Clara Lacey, Wayne Keely, and Bud Sweet, and their stories became the main feature of the coverage. A diagram titled "Making a Killer Tornado" described how a tornado forms. Another article told the story of one of the rescuers, Jerry Bonner, who rushed with friends from a nearby college to help. A photograph taken that night showed him carrying the body of a dead boy; that photo became the tornado's "most enduring image." Forty years later, Bonner told the reporter that he remembered "exactly how that boy felt as I carried him. . . . There was no question that he was dead. He was just totally limp. I remember . . . I was wanting to put him down ever so gently, and particularly to somehow cradle his head as I put him down." Bonner became haunted by the experience and the weight of that nameless child. He dropped out of college for a few years before realizing he wanted to become a teacher and to help others. Bonner still wondered who the boy was, and no one really knows. Near his story, the *Wichita Eagle* ran a list of the dead, implying the boy was one of those listed, but no one knew which one.

Another article in the *Eagle*'s special feature was a short piece about the upcoming anniversary event. The reporters sensed the shift in the town's attitude. They wrote, "After years of grappling uneasily with the tornado and its aftermath, Udall has begun to accept, and even embrace, its place in history as Kansas' 'tornado town.'" They announced that the small city would mark the fortieth anniversary "with a community celebration called Fun-nel Days." Funnel cakes would be for sale, along with "mugs, buttons, ball caps, and T-shirts bearing the town logo—a tornado funnel bearing down on homes, barns, trees, and power lines." The tornado had evolved from a dark event to something a visitor could eat or drink from or wear.

The town still gathered for a solemn memorial service, this time held in the park. The organizers asked former mayor Jerrold Hoffman to serve as master of ceremonies. He recognized city leaders from 1955, most of them, including Toots Rowe, now deceased. Toots and Lola Rowe's daughters, Pat and Jan, offered reflections on their experiences from the first memorial service in 1956. Hoffman also read the names of all the mayors since 1955, including his own, having served in that capacity for ten years. The Udall Community Historical Society was recognized, and rightly so, for over the past year, it had created the Udall Museum as well as a new memorial for the storm victims. Jerry Bonner, the college student who had helped with the rescue and whose photograph carrying a child's dead body was transmitted all over the world, also spoke.

The organizers held this 1995 memorial on the city park's lawn in order to unveil a large granite slab. On the upright stone, engravers had chiseled all the names of the Udall tornado's dead. Gaillard Thompson, now seventy-one years old, took on the task of confirming the list, double-checking records and obituaries. The final tally came to seventy-seven, excluding the five King children, who lived a few miles away in Oxford. After another hymn and prayer, the service ended with the remaining tornado survivors standing for a photograph around the memorial stone.

Gone from the town's observance of the storm's fiftieth anniversary, in 2005, was any mention of the town's logo or "Fun-nel Days," as there had been ten years earlier. Instead, newspaper reporters focused on newly released U.S. Air Force photographs of the tornado's aftermath, which, to Jerrold Hoffman, made Udall look like Hiroshima. After seeing them for the first time, Hoffman said quietly: "This has left me . . . shaken. . . . I kept looking for things I could recognize, but . . . there's nothing there that says 'This is Udall.'"

The *Wichita Eagle* interviewed survivors and provided a summary of the storm and several photographs, including a contemporary one of Udall in 2005. In addition, reporters focused on "the legacy of Kansas' deadliest tornado," specifically in terms of how it had saved lives since. After 1955, across the nation, the National Weather Service created annual training classes for storm spotters and redoubled its efforts to improve communication between the weather service, media outlets, police departments, and the public. The weather predicting technology had also greatly improved in fifty years. In 1999 these changes allowed forecasters to better predict and warn the public about an F4 tornado that touched down on May 3 in Haysville, just twenty-three miles from Udall. With a twenty-minute warning, only six people died in that storm, compared to no warning and seventy-seven deaths in Udall in 1955. And yet, even today, with earlier warnings, tornadoes still inflict great damage and death.

The Udall memorial program in 2005 featured tours of the museum and two guest speakers: one, from the National Weather Service, shed new light on how the 1955 tornado had changed the Weather Service; the second speaker, a retired popular weatherman from a Wichita TV station, talked about his experiences reporting on the 1955 tornado, which was one of his first assignments. As fitting, the program ended with prayers, taps, and a lowering of the flag.

Beth Morgan Evans was one of the organizers of the sixtieth anniversary memorial, in 2015. The committee also had new, younger members, descendants of tornado survivors, who helped create a new display in the Udall Museum. Instead of just a list of the names of the dead, each person now had an image, a photograph framed and accompanied by the person's obituary:

—Aunt Emmie Foulk in her large, round glasses gives a shy smile;

—Ora and Mary Clodfelter, dressed in their Sunday best, have huge grins as they cut their fiftieth wedding anniversary cake;

—And Stanley Atkinson gives his tough-cowboy scowl, bottom lip out, as he holds his cap gun pistol aimed at the camera. Patches on his knees, cuffs rolled up, he squints in the sun and sits on a wooden porch floor. Big holsters hang from each side of his belt. Beside him, his birthday cake with four candles.

All these photographs hung on a long wall above items found after the tornado, like a basketball from the high school, a stick driven through a tree branch, and an elderly victim's Swedish Psalms.

To find photographs for some of the victims, organizers had to search for descendants, not an easy task sixty years removed. But they did have luck connecting to kin of several victims who just happened to be visiting Udall the day of the storm or whose surviving family had moved away afterward. Where no photograph could be found, organizers used a black profile silhouette. Looking at this long wall, one begins to feel the immensity of the loss and the specifics of tragedy. Eleven of the adults killed in the tornado died with eighteen of their children or grand- or great-grandchildren.

The 2015 memorial service took place in the Community Building. Some of the victims' relatives who had sent photographs for the memorial wall attended the service for the first time, reconnecting with the community after six decades. The seating capacity for the Community Building is two hundred, but over five hundred attended. So many people showed up that the town had to borrow chairs from the Methodist church. The fire chief kept telling Beth Morgan Evans, Now don't you count—don't you count how many are here! They both knew they were over the limit, but they carried on with a standing room–only, very packed room.

The gatherers sang hymns and listened to local leaders. The Udall mayor, Steve Brown, had earlier told the *Wichita Eagle* about the significance of the tornado, saying, "Even after 60 years, you just can't say it's not relevant anymore . . . [because] the whole signature of the town was changed, the landscape." He added: "We have to remain mindful of that moment in history. . . . I think any time you lose sight of an historical event, you lose sight of your roots, of what's come before you." He repeated these ideas at the memorial.

Bobby Atkinson's granddaughter followed the mayor's speech by reading "The Night Udall Died," an essay she had written and performed for her high school forensics class; she had won several awards performing it in regional competitions. Bobby Atkinson himself then took the stage, where in his gentle voice he read the names of everyone killed in the tornado, including his mother and brothers. After prayer and another hymn, everyone stayed for food and fellowship. Beth was overwhelmed by the outpouring of support. The night before, she had dreamed that only fifty people would show up, if that. And to have over five hundred—she couldn't quite believe it.

18 The People Moving Forward

EARL TOOTS ROWE SERVED AS MAYOR FOR FOUR MORE YEARS AFTER the storm. He decided Udall was then well on the road to recovery, so he didn't run for office again. He continued on as fire chief of the volunteer fire department for over thirty years. Toots kept working for Stelbar Oil until 1964, when he became a superintendent for Slawson Oil, overseeing oil production for the entire state of Kansas for the next twenty years. Toots also farmed during this time, mainly wheat and mainly on his farm north of Udall. For a few years, he owned and operated a Udall gas station. Though he always worked hard, he enjoyed his life, especially with his family, making sure they went on summer vacations, and he enjoyed serving as a deacon in the Udall Congregational Church.

Toots also loved sports. He played on a championship basketball team during his time at Udall High, and as an adult, he attended every Udall game, at home or away. Once the basketball team had to play a game far away from Udall. They traveled through snow, sleet, and extreme cold, and in the opposing school's gymnasium, they expected to find their side of the bleachers empty. Instead, when they took the floor, they looked up, and there was Toots, their biggest fan. Even when he had no family member playing, he attended.

In January 1984, while cheering on his granddaughter at a basketball game, he had a massive heart attack and died. He was sixty-six years old. A year or so later, a new scoreboard was installed in the Udall gym with money from Toots's memorial fund. When the scoreboard lights up, at the bottom it reads, "In memory of Earl 'Toots' Rowe, 1917–1984."

LOLA SATTERTHWAITE ROWE, like her husband, Toots, lived her whole life in or near Udall. She loved music and was an accomplished pianist, giving lessons and serving as the Udall Congregational Church's pianist for over fifty years. She also loved to cook, grow flowers, and quilt, spending much of her time with the church's quilting bee. After Toots died, she continued to live in their home, built right after the storm, and often, like before, she enjoyed time on the porch in the evening, visiting with family and friends. She and Toots had been married forty-five years, and she lived on for almost twenty more years after his death. She died in 2003 and is buried beside Toots in the Udall Cemetery.

Toots and Lola Rowe's oldest child, PAT ROWE KRAUS, graduated from Udall High in 1960 and earned a degree from the American Business College in Wichita. She and her husband, Neal, lived in Florida for a few years before settling back in Udall. Pat worked first as assistant clerk for the city, and then, after seven years, she became the Udall middle school–high school secretary, a position she held for thirty-six years, before retiring in 2011. Neal died in 1995, after working in the oil business for many years. Pat still lives in Udall.

GARY ROWE, Toots and Lola's second child, graduated from Udall High, Cowley County Community College, and Wichita State University, with a degree in education. For eight years he taught physical education and driver's ed as well as coached, serving his alma mater, Udall High, for six of those eight years. Then he followed his father into the oil business. He worked for many different companies for fifty years before retiring to start his own. Gary still lives in the region, and he still has the scar on his neck from when the tornado pierced it with a wire.

Toots and Lola Rowe's youngest child, JAN ROWE CLASEN, like her brother, also graduated from Udall High and Wichita State University, with a degree in education. She married her high school sweetheart and settled in Udall to raise a family and occasionally substitute teach. For a while she also served as assistant postmaster at the local post office. She died of cancer in 1999 at the age of forty-nine.

GAILLARD KEITH THOMPSON continued to work in the oil fields, retiring as superintendent after forty-two years. During this time he served in the volunteer fire department and on the Udall city council for several terms and held many different roles in the Udall United Methodist Church. Gaillard relished his retirement, during which he kept growing a bountiful garden and fished wherever he could, including fly-fishing trips to the Colorado mountains with his wife, Betty Jo. He took up woodworking, building several beautiful pieces of furniture—end tables for Betty Jo, rocking horses for grandchildren, an oak cabinet for the Methodist church. Out of a walnut tree that grew on his grandfather's farm, Gaillard made a grandfather clock for his brother. An avid reader, he often read four or five books a week. He especially loved westerns. In his last years Gaillard found he had a talent for making pies, which became frequently requested for any community or family event. He died at age ninety-four in 2019.

BETTY JO SEAMAN THOMPSON graduated from Udall High and lived her whole life in the town. Before marrying Gaillard, she worked, during World War II, as a riveter for an airplane factory in Wichita. After the war she worked as the treasurer of Udall, a job she held for over forty years. She enjoyed quilting, traveling, and fly-fishing. Betty Jo and Gaillard were married for sixty-six years. She died in 2011 at the age of eighty-six.

The Thompsons' two children, Sawny and Clinton, still live in the region, along with Gaillard and Betty Jo's many grandchildren and great-grandchildren.

AILEEN HOLTJE WITTENBORN taught for thirty-nine years, all in Cowley County schools. She started teaching in one-room schools in the Udall area, then spent eight years in the primary grades in Udall Elementary School; this is when the tornado struck. The remaining twenty-one years, Aileen taught elementary students in Arkansas City.

She and Roy had two sons and lived in the house they built in 1957, not far from Arkansas City. Roy kept working for the newspaper the *Arkansas City Traveler*. For forty-one years he ran the shop as production manager, making sure the equipment worked and the newspaper was printed on time. Roy also was an accomplished carpenter, making all the cabinets in their home as well as grandfather clocks with his two sons. Both sons still live in the area, and one runs the farm where the Holtje sisters grew up; the farm has been in the family since 1934.

Roy Wittenborn passed away on June 5, 2015, at the age of eighty-nine. He died on his and Aileen's sixtieth wedding anniversary.

As a high school student, NORMAJEAN HOLTJE sometimes visited her older sister's classroom to help teach the elementary students. She decided that teaching was *not* for her, mainly because she didn't want to grade papers every night. So, in college, Normajean studied business, and during her sophomore year, she found a part-time job as a bookkeeper for a clothing store. After two weeks she realized how bored she was doing this work, so she changed her mind and became a teacher. She began teaching in 1951 at Olive Rural School near Udall, a one-room school, where she taught grades one through seven. She taught at Olive School for nine years, followed by six years of teaching reading in a number of schools in Cowley County. She then taught in the Title I Reading and Math program in Arkansas City for thirty years. She retired after having taught for forty-five years.

Aileen and Normajean's youngest sister, LARUE HOLTJE, like her siblings, also graduated from Udall High, and went on to college to become a teacher. She taught kindergarten in Arkansas City for ten years, and during this time she and Normajean shared an apartment. LaRue also enjoyed playing the violin. She died in 1968 at age thirty-two from a rare blood disease. During the 1955 storm, a piece of debris from the tornado hit LaRue on the shoulder and left a shallow cut. She didn't go to the doctor for any treatment, but after her death, her sisters wondered if that cut allowed some germ to enter her body and eventually cause her death.

On one of my last visits with the Holtje sisters, Normajean told me about her grandniece, Aileen's granddaughter, Janelle, who survived the Joplin, Missouri tornado. All her life the young woman had heard about the Holtje wedding shower and the Udall tornado of 1955. Then almost exactly fifty-six years later, May 22, 2011, she, too, felt the great power and fright of such a storm. She was in college, living in an apartment complex, and she wanted to make lasagna for supper, so she drove to the nearby grocery store. On the way she saw the threatening weather. She had grown up in the Midwest, though, so she was accustomed to big storms.

Then, at 5:17 p.m., the warning sirens started. The cashiers in the checkout line talked among themselves, wondering if they should lock down their registers. Janelle hadn't heard the siren and didn't know what they were talking about. She checked out at five eighteen (she still has the receipt). Outside the store she heard the siren and rushed the mile and a half back to her apartment. She and the others in her complex huddled in a bathroom on the first floor. They felt the pressure change and heard the great roar. Part of their apartment's roof blew off. Two blocks away, the tornado destroyed everything, including the apartment Janelle had lived in the year before. Dillons Grocery store, where she had just been, also was leveled. When the storm roar faded and the sirens stopped, Janelle and her friends walked out to a different world. They were unharmed, but in the thirty-eight minutes the tornado had passed through the city, it killed 158 people.

When Aileen and Normajean saw pictures and heard the young woman's account, it all brought back memories of the Udall tornado. They were extremely thankful for Janelle's safety.

Aileen still lives in the house she and Roy built in 1957, and she still occasionally pulls out the waffle iron and mixer they salvaged from the Community Building the day after the wedding shower and tornado. Both appliances still work. On one of my visits, she opened a drawer to show me the linen tablecloth that also survived. She and Normajean held it up so we could see its many warm colors. It had wide stripes of orange, yellow, brown, blue, and green, accented by smaller stripes of red, white, and gray, a many-colored plaid. The tornado had ripped small holes along one side and in two corners, but it still was soft, and Aileen still used it.

BETH MORGAN EVANS graduated from Udall High in 1956, and a few weeks later, she and her family moved, first to Topeka, where her father worked on the new turnpike and where he taught Beth how to drive on the new road. Then the family moved to Wichita, where her mother got a new teaching job and Beth enrolled at Wichita University (eventually

Wichita State University). For two years she studied education, and in the summer of 1958, she and her mother took courses in library science together.

During this time Beth also fell in love. She had driven down to Udall for a basketball game, cheering on her friends and making fun of the team from Wichita. They picked on one fellow in particular, jeering at his skinny legs. After the game players and fans gathered in the local drugstore to sit around a table and drink sodas. When it came time to leave, the skinny-legged fellow, named Clifford Evans, walked Beth to her car and asked for her number.

They dated for a while in Wichita, where Clifford worked maintaining towering elevators for a grain company. Beth only had twenty more credit hours to finish her degree, but she decided to leave Wichita University and start a family. She and Clifford married in the fall of 1958 and had the first of their three children the next year.

Beth wanted to return to Udall, so she and Clifford moved back in 1960. They bought her family's old home, the house Beth had grown up in, the house that had survived the tornado. After a few years Clifford started working as the maintenance man for the two Udall schools, fixing broken fans, keeping the boilers running, and mending whatever needed attention.

By 1962 the young couple had three children. When thunderclouds blew up, Beth kept her family close to their storm cave. Sometimes Clifford would be away at work or on duty at the watchtower, so Beth worried about which of the three infants to grab in case of a tornado. Often she and her children slept in the cellar.

In 1963 Beth started working as a part-time clerk for the Udall Post Office. Then, in 1977, the postmaster retired, and she took that position. A similar postmaster job that paid a little more opened in a nearby town, Oxford, so in 1991 she started working there until she retired in January 1999. She loved the busy Christmas season—people were in good moods, telling her about the presents they were mailing to distant relatives or the cards they had received from faraway places. So Beth had to have one more Christmas before she retired.

She and Clifford continued to live in Udall as their children grew up, moved away, and started new families. Clifford even served as mayor of Udall in 1981, during the town's centennial. He died in 2018. They were married for almost sixty years. Beth still lives within sight of the Udall Water Tower.

ALLENE HOLMES KISTLER and her friend Beth Morgan Evans like to joke that even though Allene is older, Beth graduated from high school a year ahead because her mother had started her in first grade a year earlier than normal. So, when the two friends talk about their ages, Beth often says that Allene is twelve days older, then Allene adds, "And twelve days wiser."

During the summer of 1955, after the tornado, Roy Kistler helped his brother Frank with his gas station at the edge of town, pumping gas and fixing cars. One day Allene and her dad stopped for gas in their truck. Her dad always liked to buy a pop for himself and whoever rode along, so he sent Allene in for soda. That's when she and Roy first met.

Roy lived out in the country with his parents and attended Winfield schools. But he liked Udall—his job working with his brother, the people who came in, and a certain young woman—so he decided to transfer to Udall High at the beginning of his junior year. There he played football and baseball with Bobby Atkinson. Roy was a running back and a catcher, so during practices and games, Bobby handed him the football or threw strikes into Roy's catcher's mitt.

Allene and Roy graduated from Udall High in 1957 and married in January 1958. Roy enlisted in the army, so the newly married couple lived for a while in New Mexico. One day their car died, and they had no money to buy another, so Roy called Tracy Hildebrand, the Udall banker who had survived the tornado and helped the town rebuild. Roy told him where he was and why, then asked for a loan to buy another car. Tracy Hildebrand didn't really know Roy because he had only moved to town a few years earlier. Hildebrand asked Roy who his brother was and who his father-in-law was, and after Roy told him, the banker said, Yes, you can have a loan. Go find a car and give me a call, and the next time one of your family is in town, have them sign the papers. As Allene said years later, "Now that is a banker."

Eventually, Allene and Roy came back to Udall to settle and raise their four children, and Roy returned to work as a mechanic at the Kistler Service Station. Retired now, Allene and Roy still live near enough to Udall that when the leaves are not on the trees, they can see the water tower five miles away. They've been married for over sixty years.

In 2016 the Udall High School had a $6 million upgrade, including a new auditorium. Allene and Roy's eldest son was construction superintendent for the project, so he asked his mother where the burn pile from 1955 had been. Allene checked a photograph at the Udall Community Historical Museum, and looking at it, they thought the new auditorium should not be affected. When the excavators started digging, though, they found layers and layers of debris, what had been left over and buried after the big fire. The auditorium foundation couldn't be poured until after they dug and hauled away this debris and brought in an extra four feet of fill dirt. All that debris filling so many trucks served as a reminder to a new generation of what their parents and grandparents had gone through so many decades earlier.

BOBBY ATKINSON graduated from Udall High in 1958. That year he made good grades, like he had his freshman year, before the storm. But those were three long years for him. He was very glad to get out of high school.

And that was all the schooling he desired. Instead, Bob pursued his love of fixing things, especially by welding, which he learned from a friend who worked as a welder in the oil fields. Mostly, though, Bob taught himself the trade, even building a generator for his welder out of an old airplane engine. For several years Bob worked third shift at Boeing, where he perfected his craft and even worked on the Saturn rocket that went to the moon.

During this time Bob also started working on his own, building his shop in 1967 and also building a road boring machine. He traveled the state auguring beneath highways. Bob retired after several decades, and now one of his sons and a grandson run the business.

Back in 1960, Bob Atkinson received his draft notice. The army wanted him to help fight the Cold War. He was to report for duty at Kansas City.

Early one hot morning, he drove the 50 miles to Newton to board a train to take him another 180 miles into the city. He found the processing center near the depot, and immediately, an officer told him to strip to his underwear and get in line for his physical exam. Two other draftees were in line ahead of him, their backs glistening with sweat like his. At the front of the line, a doctor sat at a desk. The doctor asked the first man his name and if he had any scars, tattoos, or other identifying marks. The young man pointed to some small scars on his hands and another on his arm. The doctor made notes on his chart. He never looked up. In a gruff voice, he told the young man to move to another table, where another doctor took his vitals.

The first doctor called for the next draftee and asked his question. This time the recruit pointed to a scar on his knee. Again, the doctor wrote notes and never looked up.

"Next," the doctor called, and Bob stepped forward.

"Do you have any scars, tattoos, or other identifying marks?"

"I've got some scars," Bob said.

"Well, where are they?"

"On my arms, my leg, and my back."

"Where's the worst one?" The doctor still hadn't looked up. His pen wavered above the form.

"On my back," Bob said.

The doctor raised his head and glared. "Turn around," he said.

Bob showed him his back.

"Get the hell out of this line," the doctor said, then called for the next recruit.

Bobby stepped aside, but he didn't know where to go or what to do. He just stood there until two other doctors walked up. One had his chart, and he said, "Walk out there and back."

So Bob walked to the far end of the room and came back.

"How can you even walk?" one of the new doctors asked.

"I can walk as good as anybody," Bob said.

"You can't carry a pack with that back the way it is."

"I can carry a pack as good as anybody."

The doctor read aloud from Bob's chart: "Punctured lung, punctured kidneys, five broken ribs, pinned bones in your hand, a metal plate in the back of your head."

He put the chart down. "Son, put your clothes on and go back down to the depot and drink a beer, 'cause we don't want you."

And that was the end of Bob's military career.

It was also almost the end of his working career. The next day Bob went to the Boeing factory in Wichita to apply for a job. The personnel department, though, saw that 4F from the army and wouldn't hire him. They were afraid he wouldn't be able to do the work. Bob went home and called a family friend who worked in management at Boeing. The friend called the personnel department, and Bob got hired. He worked there for over five years.

The only long-term health effects Bob has had from his tornado injuries involve his right hand, where his knuckles were mashed. He doesn't have a good grip, so sometimes a hammer might fly out of his hand if he's not careful. Otherwise, as he said in an interview, "I can get up in the morning and I don't hurt."

At the start of Bobby's junior year, in 1956, a new freshman moved to Udall. Like Bobby, Carole Mamoth was an orphan, having lost her parents when she was eight years old. Before coming to Udall, she had already lived in nineteen foster homes and orphanages. Two of her siblings came with her; they hoped they could settle for good with their new foster parents.

Bobby noticed her—how could he not when she joined the band and played the big bass drum—but it took another year or two before he worked up the courage to ask her out. For their first date, he took her to the theater to see Elvis Presley in *King Creole*.

Carole graduated from Udall in 1960, and her foster parents enrolled her in college in Oklahoma, so Bob drove those long roads to see her. She wanted to marry, but Bobby wasn't so sure. He didn't want to put anyone through what he had gone through or what Carole had, losing both parents and being separated from her siblings by the foster care system. What if they had children and then he or Carole died? Bob didn't want anyone else to experience that pain. But Carole convinced him love was worth the risk, and finally, in 1962, they married.

All their lives, though, they both felt a hole. When they had kids, four boys, those boys had no grandparents—a whole generation of love and knowledge and help all gone. Bob never knew what it was like to have in-laws, nor did Carole. And most of Bob's grandparents had died by this time, so the only grandparent that their four boys had was Grandma Atkinson, who was their great-grandmother. She was Bobby's grandmother, but she was also Grandma to all of them.

At the end of one interview, Bob said the only things left of his parents and their store—all he could pass on to his children—were a few pencils with the inscription ATKINSON'S GROCERY. He could give his love and all the stories he could remember but nothing else.

Bobby Atkinson's class of 1958 had a senior trip similar to the previous Udall classes. They traveled to Washington DC, Gettysburg, New York City, and Niagara Falls. Because they only had eight students, they went with another school's senior class, which also was small.

One highlight from that trip seems emblematic of Bobby Atkinson and his life. On the very first day at their very first rest stop, in eastern Kansas, the bus driver realized their charter bus had no reverse. No matter how he tried, the gear shift wouldn't go into reverse. He stood at the front of the bus before all the students and sponsors sitting in their seats and apologized. The reverse has gone out, he said. Do you want to go back and get another bus? The seniors all said No, let's keep going on. One of the boys yelled, We'll get out and push. You just let us know. And so the bus driver put it in gear, and they journeyed on. In all those next days of going through busy cities, they only had to push the bus once.

Just like Bobby realized the first time he saw his hometown after the tornado, there was only one way to go, and that was forward.

Epilogue

SOON AFTER THE TORNADO, MAYOR TOOTS ROWE BECAME THE MAIN teller of the Udall story. Somehow—instinctively—he knew it was his job to create this narrative. He had to tell the world about the horrible loss, to put words to the pain. And he had to tell Wayne Keely: *To hell you're leaving. I'm rebuilding, and you're still going to be my neighbor.*

What stories are we creating now to carry us forward through the great upheaval called the climate crisis? One version, the easy one, is to say we're all doomed and to give up. In contrast, any story of hope requires so much more work than that. And this work, based in compassion and justice and focused on what's good in the moment, might save us. When the doomsayers' predictions overwhelm, we can still, like Toots, pick up a hammer and start to rebuild. Intentions, actions, and persistence matter.

Toots persisted through immense loss as well as months of cleanup, paperwork, and sweat. His obstinate tenacity shaped the Udall that now exists. Persistence—like new stories—is something we all can own. This determination, this desire for a better world, is in each of us, not just in Toots and a select few.

The Kansas state motto, "Ad astra per aspera," translates to "To the stars, through difficulties." One native son restated it, "To the stars by hard ways . . . and kindly note the 'hard ways.'"

Those difficulties, those hard ways, are predicted to only get harder over the coming decades. As one study indicated, "The world has witnessed a

191

tenfold increase in the number of natural disasters." In 1960, for example, only 39 natural disasters occurred; in 2019 that number had jumped to 396.

In Kansas the climate crisis might not cause more supercell thunderstorms that spawn tornadoes but, instead, more droughts. In 2015 the National Aeronautics and Space Administration published research under the headline "NASA Study Finds Carbon Emissions Could Dramatically Increase Risk of U.S. Megadroughts." Bad droughts, like the Dust Bowl of the 1930s, last roughly a decade. Megadroughts, by contrast, last over thirty years. This NASA study predicts that if we continue to pump out mega-doses of greenhouse gases, there's an "80 percent likelihood of a decades-long megadrought in the Southwest and Central Plains between the years 2050 and 2099." These places as we know them—the Midwest, the Southwest, along with all of Mexico and Central America—will dry up. The grasses will die, the moisture will evaporate, and the soil will become dust that fills the air.

As I write this, in October 2022, not dust but rain fills the air as the remnants of Hurricane Ian sit over my home in Virginia. Five inches of rain are predicted here, compared to some places in Florida, where the same storm dropped over twenty-four inches of rain. This past July I experienced a different storm in the mountains of Kentucky, where nine inches of rain fell in one night. The stream that flowed through where I was staying, named Troublesome Creek, went from its normal six-inch depth to over twenty feet deep. Daily the news fills with new disasters, while the people affected by the less recent ones get forgotten in their years-long recovery.

Through this all, the Udall story becomes more and more relevant. Will we, for example, give of ourselves, like the Mennonites, the railroad workers, and so many others to the labor of rescuing and rebuilding? Like Beth Morgan Evans and most of the town of Udall today, will we be more prepared for the next storm with a shelter close by that can withstand a tornado or hurricane, a fire or flood? There will be orphans like Bobby Atkinson, along with widows and widowers; will we take them in? We need strong communities, and we will need stronger, generous communities to help others when they struggle. To lift our spirits and help us remember, we'll need high school marching bands and musicians and artists of all sorts to help us create and celebrate these new stories. And we will need each other.

There are two central questions we all must face. The first concerns love. Will we act out of love, giving it freely, or we will do the opposite and live in fear? The Udall tornado revealed so many people acting out of love and kindness: scores of strangers searching for survivors or giving rides to hospitals; the wedding-shower survivors finding welcomed warmth in the remains of the Grant's house, where Lora Grant opened her linen closet and told them to take whatever they needed to dry off; Toots yelling for his son, finding him, wounded and covered by debris; and then Gaillard chopping open a hole so Toots and his family could find shelter in the cave.

For contrast, take the example of how one would-be rescuer treated Bobby Atkinson. With his concussions and broken arms, mangled leg and punctured lung, Bobby spent that long night alone in the shelter of his parents' windowless car. Consciousness came and went as he waited for help. Then someone finally shined his light on Bobby, talked with him, saw he wasn't who he was looking for, and moved on. Even if this man thought Bobby was just hours from death, he still could've carried him to help or sent someone else back. But he didn't.

Bobby recognized him. Bobby has lived his whole life knowing who he was. Once Bobby told me the man was probably so focused on finding his kin that he just moved on.

And Bobby has moved on too; somehow, he's found a way to love and forgive the other.

The second question the Udall tornado asks is this: What stories will we create to carry us forward? After the tornado, one of the most photographed oddities was the truck in the tree. This massive mangle of wood and metal stood over twenty feet tall, dwarfing everyone who came to look at it.

Any photograph, especially such a dramatic one, implies a story, a string of events, the before and the after. But the narrative isn't known for this image, not clearly anyway.

The before part of the story supposedly consists of a man driving at night on a country road southwest of Udall. Maybe he's coming home from a date; maybe he's had to work late. Maybe he's listening to a base-ball game on the radio. The rain sheets his windshield, his wipers not working fast enough. Soon hail bounces off his hood, pounds the pickup's roof, drowning out the radio. Then the funnel sweeps him up and kills him, deconstructing his truck and leaving the frame pierced by the tree.

Supposedly, someone found the man's body one or two miles away, but I've never been able to confirm this, and I don't know that his name appears on the list of the dead. If he existed, who was he?

Another version of this before-story might be that the truck was parked at someone's farm, unoccupied, and the storm just did its work on the vehicle—no person inside, no one lifted into the cloud, no driver dying. But nobody knows now, and I could find no written sources to confirm or deny.

The after part of this story we don't really know either.

Sometimes the photographs of the truck in the tree include people, National Guardsmen in ponchos or firemen wearing heavy boots. In these pictures the men look up, the question on their faces saying, How did such a thing as a truck frame get stripped, twisted, hurled, and speared onto this tree?

My favorite of these photos is of two volunteer firemen, one in a white jumpsuit with AUGUSTA FIRE DEPARTMENT on the back, both in helmets. The question in their postures and faces seems to be not, How did this happen? but, How are we going to get this tangle down?

They might've asked a crane operator to save the tree by gingerly picking the frame loose, but that puzzle of metal and wood looks too convoluted to undo. Instead, workers might've taken a chainsaw to the tree and cut it down, thus saving the tree's roots so it could resprout and grow again. But that looks risky for whoever would operate the saw underneath so much weight. A third option is someone bulldozed the whole mass of metal and wood onto the ground, the bulldozer struggling against the roots, the tree not wanting to give, the dozer operator afraid some metal might boomerang back onto him, the machine straining against the load until it all toppled. Then someone with a crane lifted the remains of the truck and tree onto a dump truck that hauled it to the rubble pile not far away. This last choice, the most logical, would've killed the tree.

Yet there's another way this story might have ended.

I wonder if anyone in the cleanup crew suggested just leaving the truck in the tree. Make it a memorial, a reminder. Let it be. Most trees that still stood after the storm had few limbs and little bark; the tornado stripped each elm or cottonwood to bareness. But unlike these others, even another one in the same photograph, the tree with the truck still had its bark, so it could've still been alive to sprout new limbs and leaves. Maybe, for years after, tornado survivors and tourists could have touched it and felt its resilience and strength.

Like those men, we too are looking at the results of disaster and wondering how we are going to get through this climate crisis. Toots is yelling at us, *To hell you're leaving*, and he's right, because we have no other planet to call home. Toots is challenging us to tell better stories, like he did his friend, to say, we'll get through this if we stick together. Any part of the rest of this story, any path through the climate crisis will not be easy because the upheaval will be—and already is—great. Yet we have to learn that these two larger questions—about love and stories—are really one. Any narrative that carries us through to thriving, justice-filled, vibrant communities must be a story of love strong enough to say, *To hell you're leaving. I'm rebuilding, and you are still going to be my neighbor.*

APPENDIX

THOSE KILLED BY THE MAY 25, 1955, TORNADO:

Allison, Yuton Pierson, 22

Atkins, Jenny Mae, 69

Atkins, William H., 46

Atkinson, Gary Dean, 12

Atkinson, Nina A., 36

Atkinson, Stanley Joe, 4

Bailey, Nona C., 80

Beall, Malinda "Linnie" Caroline, 69

Binkey, Mary, 86

Boyd, Florence Lawson, 55

Boyd, Patricia Kaye, 9

Braddy, Richard "Dickie," 11

Butcher, Nolan Wilmer, 45

Butcher, Oran Paul, 6

Butcher, Wilmer Edward, 15

Carlson, Anna Karlson, 72

Clay, Clara Belle D., 61

Clodfelter, Mary E., 76

Clodfelter, Ora S., 79

Costlow, Clara Marie, 18

Costlow, Robert Leroy, 20 months

Council, David F., 26

Foulk, Emma R. Shaffer, 79

Hart, Ida May, 72

Harvey, Anna S., 59

Horn, Mary Florence, 6

Iry, Minnie M., 85

Jeffries, Frances, 28

Jeffries, Kathryn, 5

Karnes, George L., 37

Karnes, Gerald Kent, 9

Karnes, Maxine Faye, 11

Karnes, Wreatha V., 30

Kastle, John K., 79

Kennedy, Billy Ray, 6

Kennedy, Harvey Ray, 4

Kennedy, Lea Ann, 8

Kennedy, Lester Lee, 5

Kennedy, Stella B., 73

Kinkey, Mary, 80

Lane, Drusilla W., 81

Lawson, Alpha J., 24

LeForce, Sarah P., 86

Mangrum, Ila LaVone, 25

Mangrum, Michael Ray, 4

Mangrum, Sylvia Ann, 6 months

Miller, Augusta, 85

Nash, Ada Inez, 52

Nash, Leroy Nowell, 50

Nash, Loren Milton, 53

Paddock, Jennie, 77

Reeves, James A., 76

Reeves, Mary E., 72

Rudd, Benjamin F., 85

Sargent, Lutie, 80

Satterthwaite, Joseph J., 80

Selbe, Richard L., 69

Serrot, John F., 74

Sherman, Arthur C., 60

Sherman, Opal F., 57

Simons, Mary Ellen F., 68

Standridge, Donnie Glen, 4

Standridge, Hazel J., 33

Stone, Harold "Dick," 63

Stone, Mary Jane, 60

Storey, Henry F., 67

Storey, Sadie S., 62

Taylor, James Edward "Eddie," 39

Taylor, Mary Ellen, 62

Turner, Clinton Wayne, 9

Turner, Truman, 16

Walker, Loucinda L., 79

Ward, Gertie M., 84

West, Zachariah "Zack" T., 71

Williams, Gertie E., 75

Woods, Michael "Mike," 6

Wyckoff, Rickey Joe, 4

APPENDIX

THE FIVE CHILDREN KILLED AT OXFORD, KANSAS,
NEAR UDALL, BY THE SAME STORM:

King, Barbara A., 11 months
King, Billie Wayne, 5
King, Nancy Faye, 12
King, Ronnie Wade, 6
King, Victor "Vickie" Alan, 3

ACKNOWLEDGMENTS

THIS BOOK TOOK OVER TWELVE YEARS TO COMPLETE, WHICH MEANS *many* people helped. To any I miss here, my apologies.

First, great gratitude to the people of Udall, especially the survivors who shared their stories. Before our first interviews, in 2011, I had just finished a novel, so I was primed to make this book about the Udall tornado also a work of fiction. But as I listened to these tremendous stories and experienced the generosity of so many survivors, I realized that writing this book as nonfiction would best honor these people. I hope this book does that.

Specifically, in Udall, thanks to Pat Rowe Kraus, Gary Rowe, and Sheryl Propst; Bob and Carole Atkinson; Beth Morgan Evans, Allene Holmes Kistler, and Ray Holmes; Aileen Holtje Wittenborn, Normajean Holtje, and Janelle Wittenborn; Gaillard Thompson and Sawny Thompson Klaaseen; Clara and Ray Lacey; Gene Beard and Cheryl McDermeit; Jerrold Hoffman, Fred Satterthwaite, and Larry Dale; Jewell Lacey, Barbara Seaman, Diana Seaman-Klein, Linda Morton, and all the quilters; and Carlton Smail, Lulita Hopkins, and Matt Dennis.

For my weather-related questions, the fine folks at the National Weather Service showed great patience and kindness. These individuals include Donald Burgess, Dick Elder, Kenneth Cook, Chance Hayes, Suzanne Fortin, and Jim Caruso.

For all things Mennonite, I'm particularly grateful to Beth Bontrager, who queried the Mennonite community for me as well as rounded up archival material. Others in this community who helped, some sharing their memories of working in Udall right after the tornado, include Marion Bontrager, Ralph Claassen, Virgil Claassen, Frank Peachey, Jason Kauffman, Dick Rempel, Howard Hershberger, Martha Hershberger, John Thiesen, and Paul Unruh.

Libraries and librarians make the world such a better place. Those who tried to answer my questions include Mary Nelson and Jessica Cerri, Wichita State University; Kate Flower, Massachusetts College of Liberal Arts; Daniel Barbiero, National Academy of Sciences; Cynthia Franco, Southern Methodist University; Jan Zauha, Montana State University; Susan K. Forbes, Kansas Historical Society; and Ken Warner and Robert Tucker, Wichita Public Library. The Winfield Public Library also proved invaluable.

Other individuals who helped include Gary Greenburg, Wichita State University; Sarah Werner, Stephanie Humphries, and Lou Tharp, Cowley County Historical Society; Jami Frazier Tracy, Wichita–Sedgwick County Historical Museum; Phyllis Hamilton and Kathy Hamilton.

Augusta University and Radford University offered financial support to this project, for which I'm grateful. At AU Melissa Johnson provided immense research assistance and good cheer. Also at AU, I'm grateful for support from Rhonda Armstrong, Anna Harris-Parker, Seretha Williams, Simon Grant, Spencer Wise, Blaire Zeiders, Guirdex Masse, Christina Heckman, Lee Anna Maynard, Liana Babayan, Giada Biasetti, Christopher Botero, Todd Hoffman, Jared Hegwood, and many other faculty, staff, and students. At Radford University my thanks to Rosemary Guruswamy, Bud Bennett, Rick Van Noy, Tim Poland, April Asbury, Parks Lanier, Ruth Derrick, Matt Dunleavy, and Ricky Cox, answerer of all questions mechanical. Also at RU, Grace Edwards and Theresa Burriss have been steadfast friends—thanks to you both.

Early readers or listeners of this project include Craig Nova and my fellow University of North Carolina–Greensboro MFA students; and colleagues and students at Converse College's MFA program, especially Rick

Mulkey, Robert Olmstead, Cinelle Barnes, and Jonathan Burgess. Friends who have supported this work include Holly Goddard Jones, Michael Bowen, Juli Berwald, Susan Gregg Gilmore, Robin Black, Darnell Arnoult, Robert Gipe, Kevin O'Donnell, David Joy, Abigail DeWitt, Pam Hanson, and Pam Campbell.

For help with photographs, Carlton Smail deserves a second shout-out—many of these would not be in this book without his kindness. Others who helped with the photographs include Greg Proctor; Jason Kauffman, John Theisen, Lori Wise, and Kat Brennen for the Mennonite photos; Lisa Keys at the Kansas Historical Society; at the Spencer Research Library, University of Kansas, Kathy Lafferty; Stephanie A. Humphries, and Lou and Bill Tharp, Cowley County Museum and Historical Society; and Randy Hoffman and Abby Beard at Wheat State Technologies.

My agent, Gail Hochman, is one of great faith and tenacity. Thank you.

For their kind words and generosity, my thanks to Holly Bailey, David Bristow, Joyce Dyer, David Joy, and David Laskin.

At the University of Nebraska Press, many thanks to Bridget Barry for her clear vision and patience and to all the other staff and independent workers who help make beautiful books. This includes Emily Casillas, Abigail Kwambamba, Tish Fobben, Rosemary Sekora, Ann Baker, Elizabeth Gratch, and Erin Greb.

My family has provided invaluable love and support—thank you, Glenn and Susan Minick and Carl and Jerry Dowdey. Cora Mettling opened doors with such grace and answered too many questions—thank you for such kindness. Kathryn Minick and Karen Mettling, birders and researchers extraordinaire, thanks to you both for participating in and recording all of these interviews, for slogging through hours of reading microfilm, for good food, and for good birding.

And always, my thanks to Sarah.

BIBLIOGRAPHIC ESSAY

THE BOOK'S EPIGRAPH, BY WENDY S. WALTERS, COMES FROM AMY Wright, *Paper Concert: A Conversation in the Round* (Louisville: Sarabande Books, 2021).

1. What Used to Be

The heart of this book belongs to the many Udall tornado survivors who shared their lives and stories with me, usually over many visits. These interviews, phone conversations, and correspondences took place from 2011 to 2022. I am deeply indebted to them for their immense generosity and trust.

Throughout this whole book, unless otherwise noted, information about specific individuals and their families came from the following:

The Atkinsons: Bob Atkinson

The Holtjes: Aileen Holtje Wittenborn and Normajean Holtje

The Holmes: Allene Holmes Kistler

The Morgans: Beth Morgan Evans

The Rowes: Pat Rowe Kraus

The Thompsons: Gaillard K. Thompson

Bob Atkinson also provided all information regarding Gary's paper route. The idea of a "tour of the town" using this paper route came from

David McCullough's *The Johnstown Flood* (New York: Simon & Schuster, 1968), in which he uses a parade to do the same.

Details and stories about the town used in this chapter also came from conversations with these Udall survivors: Beth Morgan Evans, Jerrold Hoffman, Ray Holmes, Clara Lacey, and Jewell Lacey.

I found the *Winfield Daily Courier* editions from 1955 in the Winfield Public Library, Winfield, Kansas.

The Wichita Office of the National Oceanic and Atmospheric Administration (NOAA) has a web page devoted to the 1955 Udall tornado. All Severe Weather Warnings and Storm Reports came from this page, unless otherwise noted ("Info on the Udall Kansas Tornado," National Weather Service, weather.gov/ict/udall). The Severe Weather Warnings are the original texts, with typographical errors, as sent from the National Weather Service office in Wichita. The first two warning areas did not include Udall. The Storm Reports were filed several days after the storm.

The detail about Toots moving his car into the garage right before the storm came from an interview with Toots in a *Wichita Beacon* article published in 1965, on the tornado's ten-year anniversary. Information about Mrs. Simons, the piano teacher, came from interviews with Normajean Holtje, Pat Rowe Kraus, Cora Mettling, and Aileen Holtje Wittenborn, who all took lessons from her and adored her.

Information regarding the wedding shower and Community Building came from interviews with Beth Morgan Evans, Normajean Holtje, Allene Holmes Kistler, Gaillard K. Thompson, and Aileen Holtje Wittenborn. Also, in 1956, on the storm's one-year anniversary, the *Winfield Daily Courier* published an article by Cleo Tschopp in which she recounted her experiences at the wedding shower that night.

The Udall Community Historical Society Museum has a wealth of information and resources, including a wall displaying obituaries and photographs of individuals killed in the tornado. Descriptions of the dead, like that of Nina Atkinson, came from this display.

Unlike the first two Severe Weather Warnings, SWW #3 from NOAA Weather Station, Wichita, came from retired meteorologist Donald Burgess's personal archives.

2. The Weight of It

All information in this chapter came from the interviews cited earlier and the Cleo Tschopp article.

3. What the Lightning Revealed

Severe Weather Warning #4 from NOAA Weather Station, Wichita, also came from retired meteorologist Donald Burgess's personal archives.

This line is a direct quotation from Cleo Tschopp's 1956 account: it felt "as if someone had poured a bucket of water in my face, and I gasped for breath."

4. Hit by Emptiness

Officer Lester Thompson's account of coming to Udall immediately after the tornado was found in two sources: Robert V. Hamilton, Ross M. Taylor, and George E. Rice Jr., *A Social Psychological Interpretation of the Udall, KS Tornado* (Wichita: University of Wichita Press, 1955); and Ernest Havemann, "Tornado Struck," a clipping of what looks like an article published sometime in 1956, found in the Udall Community Historical Society Museum (additional bibliographic information was not available).

Other information about the initial cries for help also came from interviews found in Hamilton, Taylor, and Rice, *Social Psychological Interpretation*. These three authors were professors at the University of Wichita in 1955, and they wanted "to study human reaction to disaster caused by tornadoes." They had just applied for a grant from the National Academy of Sciences to do so. When the tornado struck, they received an emergency grant to allow them to interview and record many people—survivors, rescuers, disaster relief providers, physicians, and others. In all they interviewed 111 individuals and "recorded approximately 42 hours of verbatim responses." Sadly, none of these recordings or transcripts can be found.

The Storm Report for Udall came from both the Wichita Office of NOAA's web page devoted to the 1955 Udall tornado ("Info on the Udall Kansas Tornado") and from retired meteorologist Donald Burgess's personal archives.

5. Something Shifted Inside

Details regarding the search and rescue efforts immediately after the tornado came from several articles in the *Wichita Beacon*, the *Wichita Eagle*, and the *Winfield Daily Courier* as well as Hamilton, Taylor, and Rice, *Social Psychological Interpretation*.

Fred Satterthwaite told me of his and his wife's experiences in an interview in 2011. Likewise, Gene Beard told me of his experiences in 2018. Ernest Santos was as an air force man from McConnell Air Force base helping with the rescue efforts after the 1955 tornado. He shared his experiences in the comments section of a 1995 *Wichita Eagle* article.

6. Bigness of Heart

Information about area hospitals came from the *Winfield Daily Courier*. Toots Rowe's reactions the day after the tornado came from the *Wichita Eagle*. Information about the search and rescue, as well as cleanup, including specifics about the Weather Bureau and John Arbuckle, came from the *Wichita Beacon*, the *Wichita Eagle*, and the *Winfield Daily Courier*. Also, material about the history of tornado forecasting was found in the May 23, 2016, *New York Times* article "Tornado Sirens, an Old Technology, Still Play a Vital Role" by Christopher Mele.

Wayne Keely was interviewed by Toots and Lola Rowe's granddaughter, Kristi Clasen, on March 2, 1985, as well as for the *Wichita Eagle* on the tornado's fortieth anniversary. Kristi Clasen also interviewed her grandmother, Lola Rowe, at the same time. A copy of her report is available in the Udall Community Historical Society Museum.

7. People Will Return

The *Wichita Eagle* provided information about the undertakers.

The *New York Times* quoted both Toots Rowe and Gaillard Thompson. Other information about the cleanup, the oddities left after the tornado, and Rowe's determination to rebuild came from the *Wichita Beacon*, the *Wichita Eagle*, and the *Winfield Daily Courier*.

In addition to playing host and introducing me to so many tornado survivors, Cora Mettling also shared her wedding ring story.

8. Overwhelmed

Information about the Udall City Council came from the *Wichita Eagle*, the *Winfield Daily Courier*, Gaillard Thompson, and the Udall City Council Minutes. Other parts of this chapter, like on the clothing donations, the Lannings, and Governor Hall's visit, also came from the *Winfield Daily Courier*. All three papers (two from Wichita plus one from Winfield) covered the tourists' traffic jams and the rebuilding, especially of the temporary city hall. Hamilton, Taylor, and Rice, *Social Psychological Interpretation*, provided extensive material about the rebuilding and the festive nature after the first days. The *Wichita Eagle* included Eisenhower's telegram, and the *Winfield Daily Courier* covered the severe storm that threatened the area two days after the Udall tornado.

9. So Many Dead

Material for this chapter again came from the three main newspapers in the area at the time: the *Wichita Beacon*, the *Wichita Eagle*, and the *Winfield Daily Courier*.

I interviewed Clara and Ray Lacey in 2011 and 2018 and Jerrold Hoffman in 2011 and 2016. Both Clara and Jerrold, as well as Beth Morgan Evans, were also featured in the 1995 *Wichita Eagle* tornado anniversary article.

Information about the King family came from the *Wichita Eagle*; the *Winfield Daily Courier*; and Hamilton, Taylor, and Ross, *Social Psychological Interpretation*.

10. Distributing Kindness

Beth Bontrager opened the door to the Mennonite Disaster Services, including histories of this organization and personal archives of leaders at the time of the Udall tornado. For example, the "Who are all these people?" anecdote came from a personal correspondence of Elmer Ediger, June 1, 1955. The *Wichita Eagle* also had information about the Mennonites' work.

11. The Long Process of Working Through

Gaillard Thompson's high school diploma is on display at the Udall Community Historical Society Museum.

Material for this chapter again came from the three main newspapers in the area at the time: the *Wichita Beacon*, the *Wichita Eagle*, and the *Winfield Daily Courier*.

12. Something to Hold Onto

Material in this chapter on the Mennonites' work in Udall came from personal archives of leaders at the time, and other information for this chapter came from the three main regional newspapers: the *Wichita Beacon*, the *Wichita Eagle*, and the *Winfield Daily Courier*.

13. The Smoke of What Used to Be

Bob Atkinson Sr.'s experience of the storm came from Dale J. Hatch, "A Hero among Heroes," a personal account of Hatch's work in the hospital after the tornado. This article is available at the Udall Community Historical Society Museum. Bobby Atkinson also provided information about his father.

Information about the cleanup effort and debris pile came from the three regional newspapers.

14. Trying to Find Normal

Ray Holmes shared his schooling stories with me in a 2018 interview.

15. Marching On

Information about the United Methodist Church rebuilding came from Cora Mettling in conversations over several years.

The three main regional newspapers—the *Wichita Beacon*, the *Wichita Eagle*, and the *Winfield Daily Courier*—provided material on the rebuilding efforts and costs as well as the marching band. In addition, newspaper clippings in the Udall Community Historical Society Museum added to this chapter, including an article titled "Band of the Year" from the *Hutchinson (KS) News Herald*. Also in the museum are several letters from band teacher Norman Lanning's files that document the many contributions from all over the region.

16. Everybody Deserves a Picture

Information on the Mennonite women's work in Udall came from personal archives of Mennonite leaders at the time.

In 2011 and 2016 Jerrold Hoffman told me about his and others' experiences with the "Tornado Tower." The three regional newspapers at the time also had information about the watchtower.

17. Remembering

In addition to the three regional newspapers' coverage of the anniversary commemorations, other media outlets with information used in this chapter include several unattributed newspaper clippings in the Udall Community Historical Society Museum; the *Kansas City Times*, May 26, 1956; the *Denver Post*, July 20, 1978; Robert Pearman, "Udall, Kansas—City on the Alert," *Popular Mechanics*, 1962; the *Arkansas City Daily Traveler*, April 19, 1965; and Lisa Teachman, "Then & Now: After Udall," KSN.com, May 23, 2018.

The museum also has a copy of President Eisenhower's 1960 telegram and programs for the Fortieth and Fiftieth Anniversary Memorial Ceremonies.

18. The People Moving Forward

In addition to the main interviewees, Gary Rowe and Sawny Thompson Klaaseen, as well as Janelle Wittenborn, contributed to this chapter.

Epilogue

Joanna Macy, *Active Hope: How to Face the Mess We're in without Going Crazy* (Novato CA: New World Library, 2012), shaped my thinking on hope based on compassion, intention, and presence as well as persistence and good work. The comment about the Kansas state motto comes from William Allen White in *What Kansas Means to Me*, edited by Thomas Averill (Lawrence: University Press of Kansas, 1991). The increase in natural disasters was found on the Vision of Humanity website ("Increase in Natural Disasters on a Global Scale by Ten Times," Institute for Economics & Peace. Ecological Threat Register 2020: Understanding Ecological Threats,

Resilience and Peace, Sydney, September 2020, http://visionofhumanity
.org/reports.) The information about megadroughts comes from "NASA
Study: Carbon Emissions Could Increase Risk of U.S. Megadroughts," NASA
website, February 12, 2015, https://www.nasa.gov/press/2015/february
/nasa-study-finds-carbon-emissions-could-dramatically-increase-risk
-of-us.

Appendix

I originally found the list of those killed by the May 25, 1955, tornado on
the NOAA "List of Fatalities from the Udall Tornado," National Weather
Service, accessed May 1, 2020, https://www.weather.gov/ict/udall_dead;
"Info on the Udall Kansas Tornado." However, a much more accurate list,
compiled by Carlton Smail, is found at the Find a Grave website: "1955
Udall Tornado Victims: A Virtual Cemetery," accessed May 20, 2022,
https://www.findagrave.com/virtual-cemetery/369277.

CPSIA information can be obtained
at www.ICGtesting.com
Printed in the USA
LVHW040859040323
740803LV00003B/3